Classics In
Child Development

FACTORS DETERMINING
INTELLECTUAL
ATTAINMENT

ARNO PRESS

A New York Times Company

New York — 1975

Reprint Edition 1975 by Arno Press Inc.

Copyright © 1975 by Arno Press Inc.

"Studies of Identical Twins Reared Apart" was
   reprinted by permission of the American
   Psychological Association.
"A Final Follow-Up Study of One Hundred Adopted
   Children" and "Consistency and Variability in
   the Growth of Intelligence..." were reprinted
   by permission of The Journal Press.

Classics in Child Development
ISBN for complete set: 0-405-06450-0
See last pages of this volume for titles.

Manufactured in the United States of America

Library of Congress Cataloging in Publication Data

Main entry under title:

Factors determining intellectual attainment.

   (Classics in child development)
   Reprint of Studies of identical twins reared apart,
 by B. S. Burks, and A. Roe, first published 1949 in
Psychological monographs, Washington; of A final follow-
up study of one hundred adopted children, by M. S.
Skodak and H. M. Skeels, first published 1949 in v. 75
of Journal of genetic psychology, Provincetown, Mass.;
of Consistency and variability in the growth of
intelligence from birth to eighteen years, by N. Bayley,
first published 1949 in v. 75 of Journal of genetic
psychology, Provincetown, Mass.; and of Environmental
influences on mental development, by H. E. Jones,
first published 1946 in Manual of child psychology, New
York.
   1. Intellect--Addresses, essays, lectures.
2. Nature and nurture--Addresses, essays, lectures.
3. Child study--Addresses, essays, lectures. I. Arno
Press. II. Series.
BF431.F25 1975   153.9'2   74-21406
ISBN 0-405-06458-6

CONTENTS

Studies of Identical Twins Reared Apart

By

BARBARA S. BURKS AND ANNE ROE

With Foreword and Introduction by
LEWIS M. TERMAN

7142

Volume 63
Number 5

Whole No. 300
1949

Psychological Monographs:
General and Applied

Combining the *Applied Psychology Monographs* and the *Archives of Psychology*
with the *Psychological Monographs*

HERBERT S. CONRAD, *Editor*

Studies of Identical Twins
Reared Apart

By

BARBARA S. BURKS AND ANNE ROE

With Foreword and Introduction by
LEWIS M. TERMAN

Accepted for publication, December 7, 1948

Published by
THE AMERICAN PSYCHOLOGICAL ASSOCIATION
1515 MASSACHUSETTS AVE., N.W., WASHINGTON 5, D.C.

Barbara S. Burks

FOREWORD

THE TRAGIC death of Barbara Stoddard Burks on May 25, 1943, at the early age of 40 years, was a truly serious loss not only to psychology but also to biology, sociology, and education. Her record for creative productivity, which has rarely been equalled by one of her years either in quantity or quality, was made possible by an extraordinary combination of intellect, energy, and scientific enthusiasm.

Barbara graduated from Stanford in 1924 with Phi Beta Kappa honors and "with great distinction." She was my research assistant from 1924 to 1929 and my research associate in 1929-30. Her Ph.D. dissertation was completed in 1927, but because of her extensive collaboration with me on other research and writing she did not receive her degree until 1929. Her later academic career was as follows: school psychologist in Pasadena, 1931-32; research associate in child welfare at the University of California, 1932-34; General Education Board Fellow, 1934-36; research associate at the Carnegie Institution, 1936-43. For two years preceding her death she was also associate in psychology at Columbia University.

Barbara's minor field of study for the doctorate was mathematics, with emphasis on statistical procedures applicable to bio-social problems. As a graduate student she also found time to master, as few psychologists ever do, the fundamental principles of genetics. Her interests were primarily oriented toward the nature and nurture factors that determine human development, rather than toward any one discipline as such; she was willing to equip herself in whatever border-zone fields would contribute to this end.

The early flowering of Barbara's genius is indicated by the fact that she had planned the main outlines of her life work on nature and nurture by the age of 20 years and had completed her famous study of California foster children soon after her 24th birthday, notwithstanding the extensive assistance she was giving me at the time in a follow-up of my gifted group and in the preparation of the 1928 *Yearbook* of the National Society for the Study of Education. Nor is it any disparagement of her later work to say that this study deserves to be ranked among the best of her entire career, indeed among the dozen or so most important contributions in the history of nature-nurture research from Galton to the present.

Although Barbara's later researches covered a wide range of topics, the nature-nurture problem remained her strongest interest. For some time before her death she had been engaged in a second study of foster children in the state of New York. This research was financed by the Carnegie Corporation and was being carried out under the auspices of the Social Science Research Council. While engaged in this study she discovered several pairs of identical twins who had been reared apart, and only a month before her death she was awarded a Guggenheim Fellowship to enable her to complete her study of these and such other pairs of separated identical twins as she might be able to locate.

Prior to the award of this fellowship Barbara had published a detailed analysis of the personality characterisitcs of one identical-twin pair. This analysis was a masterpiece of finesse in ferreting out minor as well as major differences in personality and in behavior and it indicates the type of work she planned to do with

iii

ten or a dozen other pairs during the term of her Guggenheim Fellowship. Before her death she had collected a considerable amount of data on four additional pairs and it is this material which has been brought together and summarized by Dr. Anne Roe in the present monograph.

The monograph has been prepared under the auspices of a Committee on the Barbara Burks Memorial Fund, to which contributions were made by 62 friends of Barbara's or organizations of which she was a member. Ruth S. Tolman was chairman of the committee and its other members were Gordon Allport, Katherine Brehme, Robert Cook, Kurt Lewin, Theodore Newcomb, Lewis M. Terman, and Robert S. Woodworth.

The material left by Barbara consisted almost entirely of raw data and notes which were in several respects incomplete and sometimes difficult to decipher. Needless to say, the summarizing of another's material is inevitably a difficult task, and the sponsoring committee feels greatly indebted to Dr. Roe for her willingness to take time out from her own researches to salvage what could be salvaged of the data Barbara had collected.

Dr. Roe was the unanimous choice of the committee for the undertaking both because of her professional competence and because she had worked for a time with Barbara and was familiar with the project. Barbara's sister, Frances Burks Newman, who worked with her in the study of some of the twin pairs, has reviewed the manuscript and enriched it appreciably by many valuable suggestions. The monograph owes much to the editorial work of Dr. Tolman, chairman of the sponsoring committee.

In view of the incompleteness of the record at the time of Barbara's death, it was not to be expected that this summary and interpretation could be anything like as conclusive as one would wish. Dr. Roe has made the most of the material that was available, but the outcome is far short of what Barbara would have accomplished if she had lived to complete the study. Nevertheless, because of the great scarcity of scientific data on identical twins reared apart, it has seemed to our committee desirable to make the records available to other workers in this important field of research.

LEWIS M. TERMAN

TABLE OF CONTENTS

CHAPTER I

INTRODUCTION

Lewis M. Terman

NEARLY three-quarters of a century have passed since Galton (4) initiated the scientific study of twins as a method of assessing the relative contributions of nature and nurture to human development. The influence of this pioneer study is attested by the hundreds of twin researches that have been published, in many languages, since Galton's tentative conclusions were first made known. The great majority of these researches have dealt with the relative degree of similarity in monozygotic and dizygotic twins. The results of such studies, if taken at their face value, indicate that twins of monozygotic origin are far more alike not only in physique, but also in their abilities and temperament, than are dizygotics. The precise significance of this finding for nature-nurture theory has been questioned, however, on the ground that environment is likely to be more nearly the same for identical than for fraternal twins, and on the ground that it is difficult to establish with certainty the zygosity of a twin pair.

The first of these problems can be met by the study of identical twins reared apart. If two such twins are separated in early childhood and are subjected to unlike physical and mental environments, then in all probability marked differences between them in later years would have to be accredited to the differing environments in which they were placed. We have to say "in all probability," rather than "certainly," because of two other possibilities: (1) it is possible for one twin of an identical pair to suffer a birth injury which the other escapes; (2) it sometimes happens that the two embryos from a single egg are unequally nourished or that the normal development of one is interfered with by its position in utero with relation to the other (12, 13). It is not always easy to rule out the developmental influence of these factors.

More serious is the problem of establishing zygosity. Many of the early investigators, including Galton, assumed that if twins resemble one another so closely as to be hardly distinguishable in general appearance they must be identicals. Usually they are, but the converse of this rule does not hold. That is, there are identical twins sufficiently unlike physically that they are easily distinguished from each other but whose one-egg origin can be established with practical certainty by the combined evidence from various kinds of physical data, including fingerprints, pigmentation, dental occlusion, hair diameter, hair distribution, cephalic index, and mirror-image effects. Close resemblances in height, weight, and similar physical measurements have some value as corroborative evidence but are never crucial when considered alone. Mirror-imaging in hair whorl, palm patterns, dentition, or handedness is strong evidence of monozygosity, but its absence is no proof of dizygosity. It was formerly believed that certain diagnosis was possible by examination of the fetal membranes, but it is now known that this method is by no means infallible (7, 10, 14). Whether identical twins have separate chorions or separate placentae may depend upon

1

how early the cleavage occurs in embryonic development (11, p. 34).

When diagnoses are made by practiced experts using all the accepted lines of physical evidence, zygosity can be determined with a high degree of certainty in something like 97 or 98 per cent of twin pairs (2). The less practiced observer, of course, is more likely to make a wrong classification. The twins Johnny and Jimmy, selected by McGraw (8) as identicals and subjected by her to a long course of differential physical training, were widely publicized as proof of the potency of environmental factors. Later, however, it was established that these twins were not identicals but fraternals. The data on which a diagnosis of zygosity has been made always call for most careful scrutiny.

There is another circumstance which makes the study of identical twins reared apart less crucial than one could wish. Even if the monozygosity of the twin pairs has been satisfactorily established, and if the effects of birth injury and inequalities of prenatal environment have also been ruled out, the resemblance shown by a given separated pair might be due to the similarity of their environments. The ideal experiment would be to separate a large number of identical pairs in early infancy and to rear the two members of each pair in *radically different* environments. Because of the practical difficulties of carrying out a controlled experiment of this kind, it is necessary to locate identical twins who for one reason or another have been separated in early life and kept apart. Unfortunately, the number of such cases is extremely small in this country. The ten-year study by Newman, Freeman, and Holzinger (11) brought to light only 19 pairs. Perhaps this number would have yielded fairly conclusive results if the two members of every pair had been subjected to widely differing environments. This was true, however, for only four or five pairs out of the 19. Apart from these few cases, resemblance between the identical twins reared apart was about as close as the authors had found for 50 pairs of identical twins reared together. It thus appears that environmental differences have to be fairly large to produce much effect upon trait differences, though the amount of effect varies from trait to trait, being greater for school achievement and personality traits than for physical traits (11).

Another approach to the problem is by the method of co-twin control in learning experiments. This involves the selection of young identical-twin pairs, the subjection of one twin to a period of intensive training which the other is not given, and later follow-up to check the permanency of training effects. The method was first suggested by Gesell and has been used by him and his co-workers in a number of interesting studies to test the permanency of training in such activities as talking, stair climbing, and other motor skills (5, 6, 15). The ill-fated experiment by McGraw, previously mentioned, was an attempt to apply this technique to training in athletic stunts. Theoretically, the method has great possibilities; the chief limitation to its usefulness is the practical difficulty of arranging for long periods of training during which the untrained twin must be deprived of opportunity to benefit from the training given the other. Because of this difficulty, the training periods have usually been relatively brief and the training-effects quite ephemeral. How permanent the effects would be with longer and more intensive training remains to be determined.

It is clear, even from this all too brief

discussion, that data on separated twins are often difficult to interpret and that they provide a less definitive test of nature and nurture influences than some investigators have expected (9). Nevertheless, the method is important. Especially valuable are such highly detailed qualitative comparisons as those made by Dr. Burks on a single pair (1). If similarly detailed studies could be made of 20 or 30 pairs the results might be more significant than the usual kinds of measurements applied to a much larger population.

The following case reports, of four pairs of identical twins who were reared apart, are summaries and analyses of data collected by Barbara Burks and found in her files after her death. There are often cryptic notations which were obviously intended to remind her of incidents or opinions which she would have remembered in analyzing the data. The impossibility of deciphering these and lack of personal acquaintance with any of the subjects necessarily rob this published record of that warm, personal touch which Barbara Burks was so richly able to give the raw clinical data, and make judgment of many points of clinical interest impracticable. The aim has been therefore only to arrange and organize the data so that they will be available for other investigators in this field. Everything which was definite in the records has been included.

An attempt has been made as far as the data permit to follow the plan used by Dr. Burks in her study of the first pair of twins, Adelaide and Beatrice. The names used are fictitious and have been assigned in accordance with the scheme used in the report of A and B, so that the initials of the names follow alphabetically.[1]

Further study might profitably be made of Adelaide and Beatrice, of Clara and Doris, of Earl and Frank, and of James and Keith. The other pair cannot be studied again because Helen, one of the members of the pair, died shortly after Dr. Burks' interviews were made.

---

[1] See Reference 1.

CHAPTER II

TWINS CLARA AND DORIS

THE TWIN girls Clara and Doris were born in 1902, among the youngest of 14 children, including three sets of twins. Five were living at the time of the study, the rest having died either at the orphanage in which most of them were placed, or at other institutions. In a summary of the family history in the neuropsychiatric hospital record of Doris, it is stated: "Our patient is one of 14 children and in this sibling generation are numerous instances of unstable, peculiar, maladjusted individuals."

Their own father is reported to have been an illiterate logger of German descent, heavily alcoholic, and a promiscuous rover. He was a Methodist in religion. Their own mother was English and is reputed to have been a dancer. It seems apparent that all of the children were neglected; it is said that these twins were left in a buggy all day while their mother took in washing. (In such a case, she must have been making some attempt to look after her family.) Doris says that the State removed the children from their own parents on the complaints of the neighbors, but Clara's story is that the mother, becoming discouraged when the father left, burned down the house, and put the children in an institution because she could not support them.

In any case, they did not remain long with their own parents, but were placed in an orphanage before they were two years old. Shortly afterward Clara was taken from the orphanage by foster parents, who adopted her the following year. Doris was adopted a year later by the family with whom she lived during her second placement. When they were about 30, the two sisters saw each other

for the first time since infancy, and they kept in close touch with each other from that time on.

EVIDENCE FOR MONOZYGOTIC ORIGIN OF THE TWINS

Comparison of Clara and Doris with respect to a selection of physical traits in standard use as criteria for one-egg origin of twins indicates that they are monozygotic. They appear to be at least as similar on these traits as did the twins Adelaide and Beatrice, whose "classification as monozygotic seemed well established" by Dr. Burks' analysis.[2] The evidence is summarized in Table 1.

ENVIRONMENTAL SURROUNDINGS AND HISTORY

Community. Clara was brought up in an urban comunity of moderate size, but Doris, after a few years in smaller communities, was taken to a large Eastern city where she grew up.

The foster homes. Clara was brought up as an only child. Her foster father had a notion store, with residence on the floor above. When Clara was about 11, he became a minor county official. He liked building things and Clara spent much time with him, sharing his work at home. Her foster mother was a little older than the father, a little melancholy, and her chief interest was her garden. She also sewed and cooked skillfully but let Clara help her in the kitchen only on special occasions. Clara "used to watch her," though, and "picked up things," so that when her mother went to work in a laundry when Clara was 13 or 14, the

---

[2] See Reference 1, p. 41.

4

TABLE 1

PHYSICAL CRITERIA OF ZYGOTIC ORIGIN
TWINS CLARA AND DORIS

Age 39 Years	Twin C	Twin D
Height (stocking feet)	156.6 cm.	154.4 cm.
Head breadth	15.2 cm.	14.9 cm.
Head length	17.9 cm.	18.1 cm.
Cephalic index	85	83
	Sudden declivity in skull from same point	
Interpupillary distance	6.2 cm.	5.9 cm. (approx.)
Eye color (Martin chart)	3	3
Need for glasses	Yes	Yes
Hair:		
Medullation	About 15%	About 2%
Type	Discontinuous	Discontinuous
Pigment granule pattern	Denser	More dispersed
Average diameter shaft	75 microns	75 microns
Cortical fusi	Numerous	Numerous
Cuticular scales	Alike	
Skin (freckles)	None	None
Oral cavity:		
Tongue furrows	None	None
Form of ear	Similar shape	
Feet:		
Size of shoe	6 to 7	5 to 6
Shape	Toe slightly curved	Toe deformity
Hands:		
Size	Similar	
Nails	Similar	
Mid-digital hair	None	None
Downy hair:		
Face	Lip	Lip
Arms	To middle of arm	To middle of arm, lighter
Handedness	Right	Right and left; can use left to sew

Fingerprints

	R		L		R		L	
Thumb	L^u	8	L^u	8	L^u	15	L^u	12
Index	A	0	A	0	L^u	7	A	
Middle	L^u	5	A		L^u	5	A	
Ring	W	8–1	L^u	10	L^u	10	L^u	11
Little	L^u	2	L^u	1	L^u		A	
Total ridge count		24		19		37		23

Differences in ridge counts:
  bilateral, 19
  homolateral, 17
  heterolateral, 19

girl was able to do the housework and cooking. An aunt, who usually shared a room with Clara, was also a member of the household. The family were Baptists and did very little entertaining.

Clara seems to have had a fairly happy childhood; according to her account her parents spoiled her but taught her to be polite. She had no set duties about the house, but spent much time with her foster father, helping him make fences and chicken coops. Her foster mother seems to have been somewhat compulsive about her housework, and kept Clara closely at home, permitting only her special chum to come into the house very much. Clara was never punished and her parents were generous with her. They could not understand it when she wished to leave school, but they did not "fuss at her," although her father had hoped she would learn to become a bookkeeper in his store.

Doris, the other twin, had a much less fortunate experience. Her foster parents already had two daughters and a son who later died, when they took her shortly before one of the daughters left home. Doris says that she "can't see why" they took her and she adds that they tried three times after she was adopted to get rid of her. She had very weak feet and ankles, and they thought she would always be a burden to them. The foster father was a carpenter. The family were Seventh Day Adventists, who said family prayers and observed Saturday very strictly. Doris "had to sit down on Saturday and didn't dare sneeze after Friday evening."

She was punished severely, and frequently. There was practically no entertaining at home, although Doris remembered that once church people were there and she and her foster mother's grand-daughter were told not to open their mouths. This granddaughter had been taken into the home with Doris because her mother (D's foster sister) beat her severely, which is interesting in view of the foster mother's own generally harsh attitude. Both children worked hard around the house. Doris' only memory of any affection from her foster mother was after "things happened" and her foster father was put out of the church; it was at this time that her foster mother gave her some sex information. It is not clear whether this incident had any connection with the fact that her foster father indulged in considerable sex play with her. Doris' first child was born before her marriage, but there is no suggestion of any sexual deviation since that time.

Education. Clara got as far as fifth grade in school, but did not learn to read and write, although she did well at cooking. Her last two years in school she spent in ungraded classes. She left school finally at 12. Her family were disappointed in her school record, but did not punish her, and provided dancing and piano lessons for her.

Doris started her schooling in a one-room school when she was six. She went to school very little and hated it. She made mistakes and was often kept after school, and this usually provoked a whipping and being put to bed with nothing to eat until noon the next day. Her foster parents got a tutor for her when she was 11, but this had little effect. She said she really learned nothing at school, but picked up what little she knew from working in educated families and seeing their magazines, etc. But she did learn to write and later taught Clara to do so.

Occupational history. Clara began

work in a factory when she was 15 or 16, making $19 a week, but left after a while because she got mad at a fellow worker. Her foster parents would have preferred to have her continue at school and made it clear that she did not have to work; but she wished to do so. At 17 she worked for a while in a hospital, washing dishes, but soon left to marry.

Doris began at 12 to look after children, and to take care of confinement cases whenever she could get the work. At 17 she worked in a sanitarium, making $9 a week at such jobs as bottle washing. Her mother took her pay from her until she went to live at the sanitarium. Then she worked at a printing company, doing laundry, and in various other jobs. After she married, at 23, she was employed for a time in a candy factory and then again at taking care of children.

Health history. Both had measles and mumps but did not remember other childhood diseases. Both reported severe "growing pains" before their teens. Menarche for both was at 11 years. Clara reported having headaches regularly with her periods, but Doris did not have them seriously until she was about 34. Clara was later than Doris in having her tonsils removed—at 23—while Doris had lost hers at 4 or 5. Menopause began for Clara at 38; Doris had both ovaries removed at 29.

Both had suffered from hysterical loss of voice upon occasion; C only once, when tired and worried over her children's getting home, D apparently several times, since she stated that her hearing was good "except when she lost her voice." C said of her hearing that "the right side was better than the left at night." C had worn glasses since she was five because of a severe astigmatism. D said she should have had them as a

child but her mother would not get them. At the time of the study she wore them to correct farsightedness.

Both had been troubled with eczema. C always developed it from eating potatoes; D had it on her mouth as a child, and at the time of the study had had it on her fingers for some years. Both had many sties as children, but neither had had them since marriage; D had also had numerous boils.

C noted that at 23 she was hospitalized for bronchitis; and at 37 was in bed for some time with pleurisy following influenza. At 32 she had lacerations repaired and part of her uterus removed, and at 39 a nerve tumor was removed from her arm. Apart from these incidents, however, her health had been uniformly good.

D, however, suffered from many additional troubles. She underwent an operation for adhesions at 14 following a kick by a child; she contracted typhoid at 20; at 25 a cervical tumor was removed; at 29 a laparotomy was performed, and apparently her ovaries were removed; at 36 she suffered a fractured coccyx, was in the hospital for a long time, and had bladder trouble for some time following this. At 38 D had another operation to free adhesions which had caused partial intestinal obstruction. About a year later she again was admitted to a hospital with vaginal bleeding and low back pain. At this time the diagnosis was "neurotic: intestinal spasm." She had always had "nervous spells," and after her hospitalization for a broken back she was referred to the neuropsychiatric division of the hospital because of her behavior. Here the diagnosis of "psychosis with psychopathic personality; unformed psychotic reactions of paranoid and depressive nature;

marked psychoneurotic admixtures" was entered in D's record, and she was discharged to await hospitalization at a state institution. If she actually was admitted temporarily to a state hospital at that time, the records do not show this. In any case, when Dr. Burks first saw her, about two years later, Doris was at home, making a fairly good physical recovery from a second paralytic stroke. The following year, just before a second visit by Dr. Burks, D was admitted to a state hospital for observation and treatment for an indefinite period with a diagnosis of manic-depressive insanity.[3]

SITUATION AT TIME OF STUDY (1942)

The twins were 39 years of age at the time of the study. At 17 Clara had married an older man, the only one with whom she had gone about. Her older daughter was born a year later, and four years later a second daughter. Six and eight years later her sons were born. Both of the girls were married before the study was made. All of the children were healthy and seemed reasonably well adjusted. All of them had had difficulty with reading in school but all were proficient in arithmetic. Apparently they lived the ordinary life of a family in the lower economic class. Clara had joined the Lutheran church with her husband, attended the Ladies' Aid Society, and belonged to two lodges. Her favorite recreation was driving the car and looking at picture magazines. She liked funny movies, but read almost not at all. She handled her children easily, was not at all strict with them,

and gave them a good deal of freedom. They always had birthday parties, and their friends came to the house freely. Clara used a good many clichés in speaking. She cried easily and was somewhat excitable; was easily disturbed if things went wrong, or if she had been unable to plan ahead. Both she and Doris liked older people, and each of them found in her own neighborhood an older couple who could be depended on for talk and advice.

Doris married at 23, in what was perhaps an attempt to escape from her unhappy home situation. Unfortunately her husband was a shell-shocked veteran of the first World War, who was able to work only intermittently, and they always had great difficulty in getting along financially. Doris was his third wife. Her oldest child, a boy, was born before the marriage, and there were two other children, a girl two years younger, and a boy five years younger. The older boy finished ninth grade at 14 and had been working since. At the time of the interview the daughter was in ninth grade, but was helping out very little at home. The youngest at 11 was in fifth grade, but found school work difficult, especially reading. Doris was always very nervous, very uncertain with people, and unable to go with groups, for if anyone "looked at her" she cried and felt hurt. When things did not go well, she cuffed at her children. She had always been inconsiderate of others, and she insisted on talking loudly. She was "crazy about cats and dogs," commenting, "They can't answer back." She professed to prefer them to children. She had always been impulsive and whimsical in her conduct. Her favorite recreations were the same as her sister's, riding and pictures. She did, however, read a newspaper occasionally.

[3] During this year Doris wrote frequently to Dr. Burks and obviously derived very great support from this contact. Dr. Burks did a great many things for her and the family; she interceded with the Red Cross to aid Doris' husband in obtaining a better pension, corresponded with various welfare workers about them, and herself contributed to getting help in the home.

With all her own illnesses, whatever their etiology, and with her husband's disability, she had certainly had an extremely difficult time. When she was bedfast it was hard to get help in the house and the children tended to be ineffectual, although it is difficult to see how they could have learned to be otherwise. Her discovery of her twin sister and the ensuing friendly relations between them became steadying factors in her life.

TESTS, RATINGS, AND OBSERVATIONS

Intelligence tests. On the Kuhlmann-Stanford test given when the twins were 39, C received a mental age of 11 years, 2 months, an I.Q. of 70; D a mental age of 9 years, 9 months, an I.Q. of 61. (Three years earlier the university hospital had recorded D's mental age as 12 years, 4 months. It should be remembered that she had had two strokes in the intervening period.) Both had a basal age of 7 and Vocabulary at 10 years. C could repeat 8 Digits Forward, 3 Digits Backward; D gave 6 Digits Forward, 3 Digits Backward. C failed the Ball-and-field test altogether, while D gave a superior performance on it. Both succeeded with Abstract Words and Picture Interpretation at the 12 year level; these, with the Ball-and-field were D's highest level performance, but C succeeded with Problems of Fact at 14 and Digits Forward at 18. So far as is indicated, Dr. Burks considered C's test representative and valid, but she noted that she would expect D to score an additional 11 to 15 months "if not fatigued or excited."

Descriptive rating scale. Twelve items were rated by Dr. Burks on the basis of direct observations made during the interview. These items were: physique (body build apart from height); manner (impression of masculinity-femininity); expression (clarity); talkativeness; neatness (in dress or person); courtesy; alertness; frankness; friendliness; poise; cheerfulness; emotional expressiveness.

A 5-point scale was used for these ratings, called a "Descriptive Rating Scale." The rating 1 in each case was the high end of the scale. These scales are given in Appendix A.

On 7 of the 12 items, C and D received the same ratings. Table 2 shows the items where differences appeared.

Trait ratings. In Table 3 are recorded a series of trait ratings for the twins, made by Clara's daughters and Doris'

TABLE 2

DESCRIPTIVE RATING SCALE COMPARISONS
TWINS CLARA AND DORIS

Characteristic	Twin C		Twin D		Steps (Diff.)
	Rating	Description	Rating	Description	
Physique	1	Overweight	3	Neither sturdy nor frail	2
Talkativeness	1	Extremely talkative	2	Quite talkative	1
Poise	2	Good self-control	4	Easily upset, often seems on verge of going to pieces	2
Cheerfulness	2	Light hearted	4	Rather sombre, pessimistic	2
Emotional expressiveness	2	Spontaneous	1	Extreme, almost no inhibition	1

TABLE 3
Trait Ratings of Twins Clara and Doris
Made by Clara's Daughters and Doris' Son

Trait	Rater	Degree				
		1	2	3	4	5
General health	C's daughters			C		D
	D's son			C		D
Physical energy	C's daughters			C		
	D's son		C		D	
Amount of activity	C's daughters	D		C		
	D's son	C D				
Sleep depth	C's daughters					C D
	D's son					C D
Reaction to pain	C's daughters		D		C	
	D's son		D		C	
Sympathy for family	C's daughters	C D				
	D's son		C D			
Sympathy for friends	C's daughters	C	D			
	D's son		C D			
Perseverance	C's daughters	C				
	D's son		C D			
Self-assertion at home	C's daughters	D	C			
	D's son	D	C			
Self-assertion in group	C's daughters					
	D's son		C		D	
Talkativeness at home	C's daughters	C D				
	D's son	C	D			
Talkativeness in group	C's daughters	C			D	
	D's son			C D		
Promptness	C's daughters	C	D			
	D's son	D		C		
Speed of decision	C's daughters		C D			
	D's son		D	C		
Generosity	C's daughters	C D ·				
	D's son					
Self-consciousness	C's daughters	D		C		
	D's son		D	C		
Sense of responsibility	C's daughters	C		D		
	D's son		C D			
Sense of humor	C's daughters		C D			
	D's son				C D	
Irritability	C's daughters	D	C			
	D's son		C	D		
Cheerfulness	C's daughters			C	D	
	D's son			C	D	

TABLE 3—(*continued*)

Trait	Rater	Degree 1	2	3	4	5
Courage (physical)	C's daughters	D	C			
	D's son		D		C	
Courage (móral)	C's daughters			C D		
	D's son	D		C		
Facing facts	C's daughters				C D	
	D's son		C D			
Trustfulness	C's daughters	C		D		
	D's son	D		C		
Sociality neighbors	C's daughters	C		D		
	D's son	D	C			
Sociality strangers	C's daughters	C				D
	D's son		C			
Leadership	C's daughters					D
	D's son		C			D
Popularity same sex	C's daughters	C		D		
	D's son	C D				
Emotional dependence on family	C's daughters	D		C		
	D's son					C D

son, the former working together. Hence there are two ratings of each twin on each trait. The following description of this schedule is taken from Burks' "A Study of Identical Twins Reared Apart."[4]

". . . . For the present study each 'trait' was set up in five descriptive steps; the concept of 'Average' was not used. With behavior (e.g., talkativeness, self-assertion) that, on the basis of clinical experience, the writer believed to be situational (i.e., to represent adaptations in defined social groups) and with behavior capacities that experimental work in psychology has shown to be mainly specific (e.g., memory), the trait descriptions were narrowed down. With behavior believed on clinical grounds to be 'focal' in Allport's sense, the 'steps' were carefully defined but were not limited in a situational sense. Examples from the schedule:

"Physical energy: S D 1. abounding vitality, seldom tires. 2. Large amount but sometimes 'overdoes.' 3. Good endurance for routine activity but soon fatigued by strenuous activity. 4. Unable to carry on any strenuous activities.

5. Tires at slight exertion; exhausted at end of day.

"Competitiveness: S D 1. Extremely eager to win games, unhappy when he loses. 2. Very eager to win but not discouraged by losing. 3. Fairly eager to win but enjoys the success of others. 4. Indifferent to winning; cares only for fun of game. 5. Prefers to play with and learn from players better than himself."

The complete rating schedule on physical and sensory traits is given in Appendix B.

As is quickly seen from Table 3, there is considerable discrepancy in the ratings. In some instances it is fairly clear that the son or daughters are favoring their own mother. Of the 25 pairs of ratings by C's daughters, 8 are the same, 6 are one step apart, 9 are two steps apart, 1 is three steps apart, and 1 is four steps apart. Of the 27 pairs of ratings of the twins by D's son, the twins receive the same rating 11 times, ratings differing

---

[4] See Reference 1.

by one step 7 times, by two steps 8 times, and by three steps once.

Both sets of ratings agree that the twins are *alike* in sleeping very lightly, in sympathy for their family, in their sense of humor, and in the way in which they face facts, although the numerical ratings assigned by the two sets of raters are different except in the first instance. C and D are probably very alike also in their sympathy for friends, in talkativeness at home, and in speed of decision. (Based on closeness of agreement of averaged ratings where original ratings were not more than one step discrepant.)

Both sets of ratings agree that the twins are *unlike* (ratings discrepant by two steps or more) in health and reaction to pain, with agreement by both raters that Doris is the more stoical of the two. There is no agreement on other points. Although it does not come out clearly in the ratings, in part because of some omissions, the twins appear to be also very unlike in their reactions to persons new to them, and in their general social behavior outside their close circles of family and friends, Clara being judged as the more sociable of the two. Neither has any special artistic, musical, or mechanical aptitudes.

Rorschach test. The Rorschach test as administered by Dr. Burks at the time of her first visit in 1940 did not include the standard Inquiry nor full identifying notes on the areas of the blots to which responses were made (location). The protocols were reviewed by Helen Davidson, Ruth Valentine, and Anne Roe. All three were in agreement that at the time of the test Clara was more disturbed than Doris. This finding is of interest in view of the fact that D was later hospitalized with the diagnosis of manic-depressive psychosis. It gives evidence that

at the time of the test D was not in either a manic or depressive episode. It suggests that both twins were emotionally unstable, though manifestations of this instability differed.

Dr. Davidson's comments on C's Rorschach were: "Very disturbed; average intelligence or a little better." Her comments on D: "Average intelligence or better; rather rigid, flat, but adjustment seems adequate (?)."

The responses are recorded in Table 4. Although the inadequacies in the recording of the protocols make scoring and interpretation highly tentative, Dr. Valentine proposed the psychograms given in Appendix C and the following comments as approximate:

"There are striking similarities in the two psychograms: below average number of responses; proportion of correct Form responses near lower border of normal range; number of Popular responses below average; narrow range of Content; absence of Movement responses; great difficulty with Card X. There are some similarities in phrasing content (Cards VI and VIII, and possibly II), but the similarity in VIII is the usual "popular" response of the climbing animal, and the response "colored rocks" occurs fairly frequently. Neither has any Form-Color response. Intelligence of both is probably low average, at best.

"Differences are that C, compared to D, pays less attention to the obvious details of the cards; C has four possible Shading responses, whereas D has only one. C uses Color in the cards more than D.

"At the time these records were taken C was more disturbed than D. She appears to be an anxious, very insecure, and dependent person though she tries ineffectually to do what is expected of her. Greatly in need of reassurance, she has little or no feeling of confidence in her relations with others, unless they are fostering and helpful. The world to her is a frightening place; only the simplest situations can she deal with alone. She easily becomes bewildered and uncertain. But she does not completely give up the struggle. She blunders along, unsure of herself, hoping that someone will come to her rescue. With fostering care and supervision she can make a social adjustment, but left to herself she is more liable to make a wrong than a right

TABLE 4

RORSCHACH PROTOCOLS
TWINS CLARA AND DORIS

Twin C	Twin D
I. (5″) 1. If it had an opening, make it you think of Hallowe'en mask. 2. Or parts of body like in here; what do you see in books like lungs in chicken. 3. Over it is much look like face. ⋁	I. (4″) 1. Pair of dogs that is all I'd say. 2. In middle a crab like. Don't look like dog poison?
1¼ min.	¼ min.
II. (3″) 1. Oh, gravy! only thing, parts of elephant with trunks together, a quick sketch (turns) nose and ears. <Something trying to catch it? 2. If looked at quick, like Scotty dog.	II. (3″) 1. Two dogs right enough. Smelling at something. Ain't eating. Hurting, bleeding.
1¼ min.	¼ min.
III. (Immed.) 1. Oh, lord save me! Nothing. Like spurs or claws, chicken foot. 2. If look quick, like chicken with sore foot and wing up back. Other one reversed.	III. (4″) 1. Ducks on edge of pond. Something like that.
¾ min.	¼ min.
IV. (5″) ⋁1. Some pieces of your body internally, or like chicken, or human person; some parts of body by chest.	IV. (12″) 1. Hm. Couldn't tell you nothing. Bear or something.
½ min.	½ min.
V. (Immed.) 1. Oh, that reminds you of one of these butterflies that has large noses on.	V. (3″) 1. Butterflies. >2. Heads or. 3. Lambs leg.
¼ min.	¾ min.
VI. (Immed.) 1. Oh, gravy! Not anything that I can see. A caterpillar if didn't have such long neck. Some kind of bug.	VI. 1. Worm, big fuzzy worm. That's all.
¾ min.	¼ min.
VII. (7″) 1. Not anything. ⋁ Nothing but large sketches or something unless clouds drifting along.	VII. (15″) 1. Like lion's head a little. (middle)
½ min.	¾ min.
VIII. (7″) 1. That makes you think of bear going up over some colored stones. > Same this way.	VIII. (5″) 1. Like a bear climbing over rocks, different colored rocks.
½ min.	¼ min.
IX. (10″) 1. Not anything, for that matter, that I can see. Unless it happened to be light and dark clouds or something like that.	IX. (10″) ⋁ 1. Picture of man (red profile) rest of it don't know.
¾ min.	¼ min.
X. (20″) 1. Oh, dear, ⋁ not anything that I can see on this problem. Nothing but little dab of this and dab of that.	X. (25″) ⋀ ⋁ 1. Don't know what you'd call it, some kind of scene hitched together, skies conj (sic) together.
¾ min.	(no time)

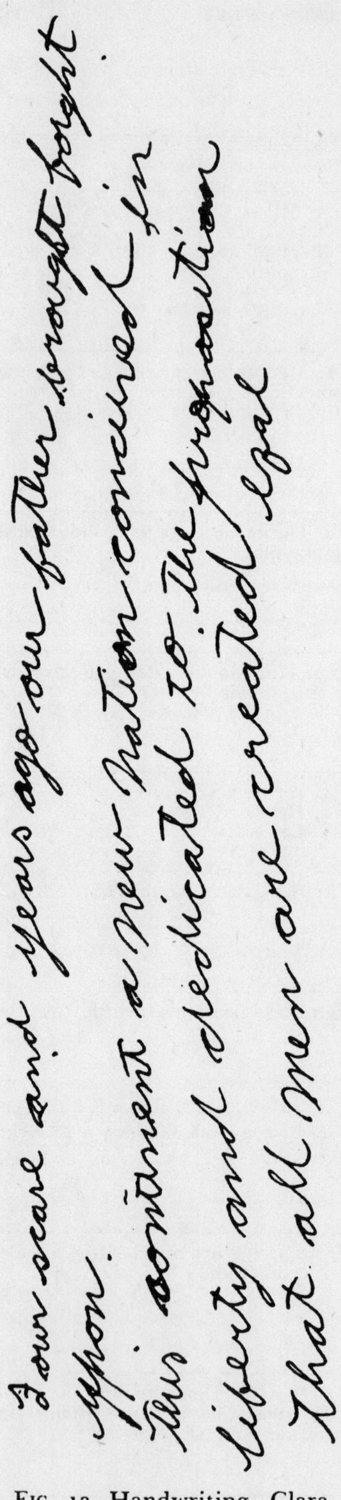

Fig. 1a. Handwriting. Clara.
Time: 5' 05".

Fig. 1b. Handwriting. Doris. Time:
5' 30", including nervous pause.

choice. She is not psychotic but is a person inadequate to deal with the problems of adult life except in a simplified and undemanding environment.

"D, though less disturbed at the time the Rorschach was administered, may have more potentialities for conflict with others. She seems to be more crude and less dependent than C. Less anxious, she appears to be socially a more intractable person. Her impulses, not held in check as are C's, by anxiety, may lead to difficulties with people—resentments, hostilities, emotional vagaries which are directed more against others than are C's. Superficially, D has a 'take it or leave it' attitude, whereas C will be more placating and anxious, using her helplessness as a bid for support. But with D, one suspects that this attitude of 'take me as I am' is defensive and that underneath this she is as desirous of affection and help as is C."

It is of interest to note that this interpretation of Clara's insecurity in her relations with people, based on her Rorschach record, resembles strikingly in some respects the overt behavior of Doris in her relations with others.

Handwriting. The two handwriting specimens reproduced in Figures 1a and 1b show very great similarities. But it should be remembered, of course, that Doris taught Clara to write.

SUMMARY

The twins Clara and Doris, among the youngest of 14 siblings whose history includes numerous instances of unstable maladjusted behavior, were separated when less than two years of age, and shortly afterward adopted by two different families. The chief environmental differences were as follows: for Clara (Twin C), residence in moderate sized city, only child of fond foster parents, extremely mild discipline, regular school attendance until fifth grade, marriage at 17 to stable older man; for Doris (Twin D), residence in large city, one of three children, in household with harsh foster parents, extremely strict discipline, intermittent school attendance, marriage at

23 to shell-shocked veteran. Neither C nor D did well in school, though D did manage to learn reading and writing. Both C and D left school at the age of about 12, and both held a series of odd jobs until they were married. The socio-economic status of their families was similar.

In their developmental histories the twins showed some striking similarities. Both reported "growing pains," early menarche, menstrual headaches, "nervousness," hysterical loss of voice, childhood sties, eczema and eye strain from an early age, and gynecological repairs. D's medical history is much more extensive than C's, however, including a series of subsequent operations and ailments some of which were presumed to be of neurotic origin.

Tests, interviews, and ratings were obtained when the twins were 39 years of age. At this time the twins were living in the same community and were close friends. Clara was engaged in a normal, moderately active life with her husband and two unmarried sons. Doris was discontented with her lot, and irritable with her children. She had been diagnosed as "psychotic" and a year later was hospitalized as "manic-depressive." The twins both scored well below average in intelligence, and neither gave evidence of any special abilities.

Despite their markedly different upbringing, the twins were judged by the interviewer to be "the same" on more than half of the 12 social and emotional characteristics which she rated, the chief differences being that D (psychotic, maltreated in childhood) is pictured as more easily upset, more pessimistic, and more free from inhibitions. Less consistency is found in the ratings of physical and sensory traits made by C's and D's children, partly perhaps because of personal prejudices found in these raters.

Certain striking similarities in response to the Rorschach test were noted and evidences of emotional instability were present in both records, though that of C showed the more disturbance at the time.

CHAPTER III

TWINS EARL AND FRANK

THE TWINS Earl and Frank were born in a large Midwestern city in 1904. Their parents were unmarried, and according to Earl's account, neither had ever had much formal education. The father worked for a utility company. He and the mother later married and had two other children, but the twins never had any meaningful contact with them after the age of about six months. It was at this age that the babies were turned over to the mother's sister, Fern, who kept Frank and placed Earl with a family who had advertised their wish to board a baby. This family soon assumed full responsibility for Earl and took him to a city in the Northwest without consulting Fern or her husband, although later they got in touch with them again.

Frank remained with his Aunt Fern, who was fond of both twins and who, along with other members of the family, wished she could arrange for Earl to return so the two could grow up together. The foster families kept in touch with one another and the boys were led to believe that they were cousins. When they were 15, Frank made a trip to the West Coast to visit Earl, but it was not until eight years later, when Earl returned the visit, that the boys learned they were twins. They seem to have accepted the family history with equanimity.

EVIDENCE FOR MONOZYGOTIC ORIGIN OF THE TWINS

Again, comparison of E and F on physical traits leads to the conclusion that they are monozygotic. As indicated in Table 5, the twins at 37 were of practically identical height, and although F was 24 pounds heavier than E, they looked very much alike. Both were getting bald in the same front central area pattern (like their father). Both were righthanded. E stated that he stuttered until he was in the second year of college; he was sent to a speech school but finally "worked out of it" himself. He said that so far as he knew his handedness had not changed. He explained the speech difficulty as due to the fact that he thought faster than he could speak.

ENVIRONMENTAL SURROUNDINGS AND HISTORY

Community. Earl's foster parents moved to a large Northwestern city not long after they took him. They remained there for a few years and then moved elsewhere in the West, where Earl went through a big city high school and a nearby university.

Frank was brought up in the Midwestern city where he was born, and remained there until his visit to the West when he was 15. After about six months with Earl, he returned home for two years. Then he went to a Midwestern city to work and "for adventure." He never lived outside of an urban community.

The foster homes. Earl was brought up as an only child. His foster father was a college graduate, his foster mother a high school graduate. His foster father was a salesman, apparently fairly successful, as the family always lived in a detached house with a yard, and Earl indicated that there had been no economic stress in his youth.

According to his own account, he was brought up in a comfortable home,

TABLE 5
PHYSICAL CRITERIA OF ZYGOTIC ORIGIN
TWINS EARL AND FRANK

Age 37 years	Twin E	Twin F
Height (stocking feet)	164.6 cm.	164.4 cm.
Weight (with clothing)	163 lb.	187 lb.
Head breadth	15.0 cm.	15.3 cm.
Head length	19.2 cm.	19.3 cm.
Cephalic index	78	79
Head circumference	22.0 inches	22.6 inches
Interpupillary distance		
Left reading (3)	5.8 cm.	5.6 cm.
Right reading (3)	5.7 cm.	5.1? cm.
Eye color (Martin chart)	5	5
Inner zone		Wider
Outer zone	Brown center	
Need for glasses	Never	Never
Hair:		
Form	Straight	Same
Medullation	6%	2%
Type	Discontinuous	Discontinuous
Pigment granule pattern	Same	
Color	Light brown	Slightly lighter
Average diameter shaft	90 microns	60 microns
Cortical fusi	Few and slender	Markedly more numerous
Cortical scales	No form differences	
	Same baldness pattern, front central area	
Oral cavity:		
Occlusion	Imperfect overlap	Better overlap
Tongue furrows	None	None
Form of ear	Same shape	
Feet:		
Size of shoe	6	6
Hands:		
Mid-digital hair	R4?	None
Downy hair:		
Arms	Thick and black	Same
Chest	Thick and black	Same
Handedness	Right	Right

Fingerprints:	R	L	R	L
Thumb	L^u 27	L^u 24	TL 26-1	TL 20-1
Index	L^u 5	L^u 11	L^u 4	L^u 11
Middle	L^u 12	L^v 7	L^u 7	L^u 3
Ring	L^u 14	L^u 17	L^u 19	L^u 15
Little	L^u 13	L^u 15	L^u 15	L^u 8
Total ridge counts	71	74	72	58

Diff. in ridge counts:
bilateral, 17
homolateral, 17
heterolateral, 15

by parents who were happily married, and who handled him without particular strain. They took him with them when they went visiting, welcomed his friends at any time, gave parties for him. He enjoyed being with them and felt free to confide in them. He was expected to feed the chickens, cut the lawn, and take some part in caring for pets, and he was taught to obey. He could "work" his mother but not his father, who always punished him when he said he would. These punishments were rare, though, and it is apparent that discipline was not at all severe. He had no regular allowance but was given what he needed. His pleasantest memories were of the family's being together and talking happily about the day's routine, and of trips they took together. His only unpleasant memories were of some occasions when the father drank too heavily with his customers. Earl was sent to Sunday School, probably for the sake of social conformity rather than because of any strong religious feeling. The family library included children's books which he enjoyed, and he had violin lessons from the age of 14 to 17 years. At the time of the study he played occasionally, and he commented, "I take to it more now than I did then."

Frank lived with his Aunt Fern and her husband, a streetcar conductor, in one room. They moved from one rooming house to another, but stayed in the same neighborhood where the twins were born. There were no other children in the family. Fern and her husband were separated when Frank was about 12, and after that he spent a good deal of time with his grandmother. Frank's report indicates a reasonably happy childhood. His foster mother was extremely attached to him. (Frank and his wife later named their daughter Fern.) He helped with domestic tasks such as wiping dishes, scrubbing floors, and hauling coal, for which he was paid "haphazardly" but was never cheated. He had no regular allowance. He was punished only "when he deserved it," as when he came home late. His mother whipped him; his father "talked to him." But he remembered both as being consistent in their rules about what he could and could not do. He always had cats and kittens and took full charge of them. When he was about 12 his parents arranged for him to have violin lessons. These did not "take," however, and were soon abandoned.

Education. Earl went to city schools in the Northwest and West and through a large university from which he graduated in 1930 at the age of 26. The next year he spent as a hospital orderly, with the idea that he might return to the university to study medicine. His foster parents hoped he would do so, but according to E, these plans were thwarted the following year by the illness and death of his foster father, whom he cared for at home. Earl did do some postgraduate work, with the thought of becoming a teacher, but gave up this goal when he failed to be appointed to the local city schools. E spoke defensively of this failure, blaming it on a system of rating which unduly weighted the experience he lacked. It is probable that his professional aspirations were too high; they tended to lessen appreciably the pleasure he took in the success of his business operations.

Frank had considerably less schooling than Earl, and was perhaps in poorer schools. He graduated from grammar school at 15, having had to take a summer make-up course in arithmetic after sixth grade. The following year, while visiting his brother in the West, he attended high school for about six months. This he reported to be about the extent of his high school experience, although many years later, after his daughter was born, he attended night school for four years, taking courses in typing, welding, and chemistry.

Both twins were poor spellers, and transposed letters, as did Frank's daughter.

Occupational history. During his school days Earl had various jobs, during summers or after school hours. His position as hospital orderly the year following graduation from college has already been mentioned. E did not return to nursing as a profession, however, because he considered its future financially uncertain. Instead, he acquired a service station which he owned and operated for some years, then sold at a profit. He spent another two years selling service station equipment. About a year and a half before the study was made he gave up his selling job in the city to take over the management of a suburban cafe. It is interesting that his brother was the one who found this particular cafe and called Earl's attention to it. This was his job at the time of the study. He was more satisfied with this than with his previous occupations but talked of selling out, taking a trip, and looking around.

Frank began work when he left school at 16 or 17, and had a number of jobs, most of them, until the one he held when interviewed, as tire serviceman or salesman or garageman. During the depression he was unemployed for nine months and there were undoubtedly some difficult times. He moved to the West when he was 26, and had continued to live there. At the time of the study he was living in the same suburban community as Earl, having held his job as a modestly paid laborer with a utilities company for the seven preceding years.

Health history. The reports of Earl and Frank indicate histories notably similar and free from health problems. Both had measles and whooping cough in childhood, but neither had any serious illnesses, except for one severe attack of bronchitis, which F had at 34. Each of the twins stated that his own general health was good, that he seldom became tired, and rarely had colds or headaches. Both reported good hearing, and neither had ever needed glasses.

SITUATION AT TIME OF STUDY (1941)

When the twins were interviewed Earl was working hard, and with reasonable contentment, at running his suburban cafe. He took considerable pride in his success; he seemed almost defensively self-satisfied. He had married at 27 a laboratory technician in the hospital in which he was then working as relief orderly. His wife was a college graduate. They had no children, but it seems to have been a successful marriage. They had some friends nearby, people they met when they first came to the restaurant, but most of their friends were in the larger city from which they had moved. They made trips to the city every three or four weeks, and friends from there came to visit them. They saw Frank about one night a week. Neither E nor his wife participated in community life in any particular way, and both spent their leisure time reading, or driving, or playing cards with another couple. E's wife said he was of a "steady temperament," but one of his friends described him as "moody." His wife added, "Earl doesn't stew about decisions, and there's no turning back when he makes up his mind."

Frank was also married, to a girl from the neighborhood of his childhood. Their daughter, Fern, was 13 at the time of the interviews. The family relationships seemed to be very warm and close and the home atmosphere relaxed and comfortable. F's wife had completed three years of high school and had then worked as a telephone operator, continuing for a couple of years after their marriage when she was 20. He was fairly contented with his job, except that opportunities for advancement were not many. He got on well with his neighbors, but most of his friends were people he worked with. He played handball quite regularly with a group of men and "loved" to play cards—especially poker. He greatly enjoyed his friends, and liked nothing better than to visit with them for an evening. He occasionally played his violin, chiefly by ear, but only if others played too. E played with him sometimes. The family usually took a camping trip once a year with friends. Their daughter had originally accompanied them, but later on preferred her own friends, a fact which her parents accepted with equanimity. F's wife said he was calm about decisions and did not worry about things. He was a little quick-tempered, sometimes unexpectedly, but was shortly over it. Both twins liked prize-fights and often attended together.

Earl and Frank seem rather well characterized by their responses when asked what three things they wished most.

Earl wanted: "1. A good business of some kind, a wholesale line of some kind with men working for you. 2. A comfortable living and home; we've got a home but don't live in it. 3. Travel, around the U.S. We've been around the U.S. but we'd do it more thoroughly, a week here, stop and work if found a job."

Frank wanted: "1. Happiness of my family. I don't want to be wealthy, just for them to be taken care of. 2. Betterment of this country. [Interviewer's note: This was said simply and with apparently sincere feeling.] And for 3, he turned to his wife and said, "I'll let you wish this time." When his wife turned it back to him, Frank thought a while, then said, "I'm easy pleased."

TESTS, RATINGS, AND OBSERVATIONS

Intelligence tests. On the Stanford-Binet (1916) E passed all the tests through 12 years, failed all at 18, and reached a Mental Age of 15 years, 4 months, with an I.Q. of 96. At the 14-year level he failed 7 Digits forward and at 16 years the Difference between Abstract Words and the Code. His Vocabulary was at the 16-year level (67 words); he repeated 6 Digits forward and the same number backward.

F's basal year was 10 and he failed all tests at 18 years; his Mental Age was 13 years, 4 months, his I.Q. 83. Of the 12 year tests he failed the Dissected Sentences and Digits backward; at 14 years he failed Induction, President-and-king, and Arithmetical Reasoning (over time), and at 16 years he succeeded only in the Fables and the Difference between Abstract Words (which E failed). His Vocabulary was at the 14 year level (58 words); he repeated 4 Digits backward. On Digits forward only the failure at 18 years is recorded.

Descriptive rating scale. Dr. Burks' ratings on the 12 items on the descriptive rating scale are identical for the twins in all but three instances, where the discrepancies are slight. For clarity of expression and talkativeness, E is rated 2.5

in each instance and F is rated 3. On emotional expressiveness E is rated 4, F 3, that is, somewhat less reserved.

Mrs. Newman,[5] who also interviewed these twins, rated them differently on physique (E 1, F 2); manner (E 1, F 2); courtesy (E 2, F 3); frankness (E 2, F 1); cheerfulness (E 3, F 2); and emotional expressiveness (E 4, F 2).

On the 24 ratings of the two men, the two raters agreed in 8 instances for E and only 5 for F. There were no disagreements greater than one step.

Trait ratings. Ratings on physical and sensory traits were made by the wives of the twins for each twin and recorded by Mrs. Newman. They are shown in Table 6. Examination of the table shows that F's wife had a strong tendency to give higher ratings[6] to both men, the tendency being a little stronger with regard to her own husband. Since these higher ratings are usually somewhat more approving, or at least more positive ones, they probably reflect fairly marked differences in the personalities of the two raters. Apart from this tendency, it is clear that the wives agreed that their husbands were alike in health, energy, appetite, reaction to pain, sympathy for family and friends, self-assertiveness at home, promptness, irritability, physical courage, facing facts, popularity with both men and women, and emotional dependence on their families. They agreed that they were notably different in sociality, with F the more outgoing of the two. They also agreed that F was more "trustful" than E, a judgment which appears consistent with E's

---

[5] Frances Burks Newman accompanied Dr. Burks when she visited the twins Earl and Frank in 1941.
[6] "Higher" here refers to a more marked manifestation of a trait; on the scale the rating "1" is "high," "5" is "low."

"defensiveness" as noted by the interviewers.

Some interesting sidelights on the ratings are contained in comments by Mrs. Newman based on conversations, observations, and joint discussion with Dr. Burks at the time of the study:

"Earl, with whom all preliminary arrangements for the interviews and tests were handled by correspondence, from the first spoke of his brother with condescension. Before Frank was scheduled to arrive at the cafe, Earl took us aside to warn us that he had not broached the subject of our visit to Frank, and that he did not know how F might feel about it, implying that F might be edgy and uncooperative. Thus on our guard, and armed with all the tact at our command, we were more than surprised to find F if anything readier to cooperate than E. F. was more relaxed and unpretentiously friendly in his contacts. E's assumed apprehensions regarding his brother's behavior seem to be part of a whole pattern of life he has adopted, in which his status as a highly educated, successful gentleman figures very prominently and must be carefully preserved. He never forgets the burden of *noblesse oblige* he has shouldered along with his superior educational and social advantages."

In addition to the resemblances and differences indicated by the ratings, it was noted that both E and F played a little on the violin, enjoyed the same kind of music, liked natural beauty, had considerable mechanical ability, enjoyed working around cars, and the like. On the other hand, neither of the twins had any marked interest in art, neither sang, wrote, nor manifested any special talent, and neither of them indulged in or developed skill in any physical activity, except that F played handball.

Strong Vocational Interest Blank. In Figure 2 are shown the vocational interest patterns of E and F, at the age of 37. The profiles show striking similarity and parallel each other closely, in spite of the fact that the most outstanding differences in the upbringing of E and F were related to vocational and social

STRONG VOCATIONAL INTEREST PATTERNS
FOR TWINS E. AND F. AT AGE 37
E.= —— F.= ----

OCC. GROUP	OCCUPATION	TWINS E.	TWINS F.
I	Artist	11	11
	Psychologist	16	-1
	Architect	5	13
	Physician	16	18
	Dentist	15	31
II	Mathematician	-1	-3
	Engineer	15	21
	Chemist	14	35
	Aviator	31	45
III	Production Mgr.	47	44
IV	Farmer	35	45
	Carpenter	23	48
	Printer	37	50
	Math.-Sci. Teacher	41	40
	Policeman	42	59
	Forest Service	31	34
V	Y.M.C.A. Phys. Dir.	48	50
	Personnel Mgr.	51	38
	Y.M.C.A. Secy.	46	35
	Soc.-Sci. Teacher	57	44
	City School Supt.	33	10
	Minister	34	23
VI	Musician	28	31
VII	C.P.A.	19	9
VIII	Accountant	36	35
	Office Worker	44	53
	Purchasing Agt.	31	40
	Banker	29	34
IX	Sales Manager	40	41
	Real Estate Sales	35	45
	Life Ins. Salesman	38	43
X	Advertising Man	28	26
	Lawyer	17	16
	Author-Journalist	19	17
	Pres. Mfg. Concern	24	25
	Occupational Level*	45	39
	Masc.-Femin.	49	52
	Interest Maturity	69	59

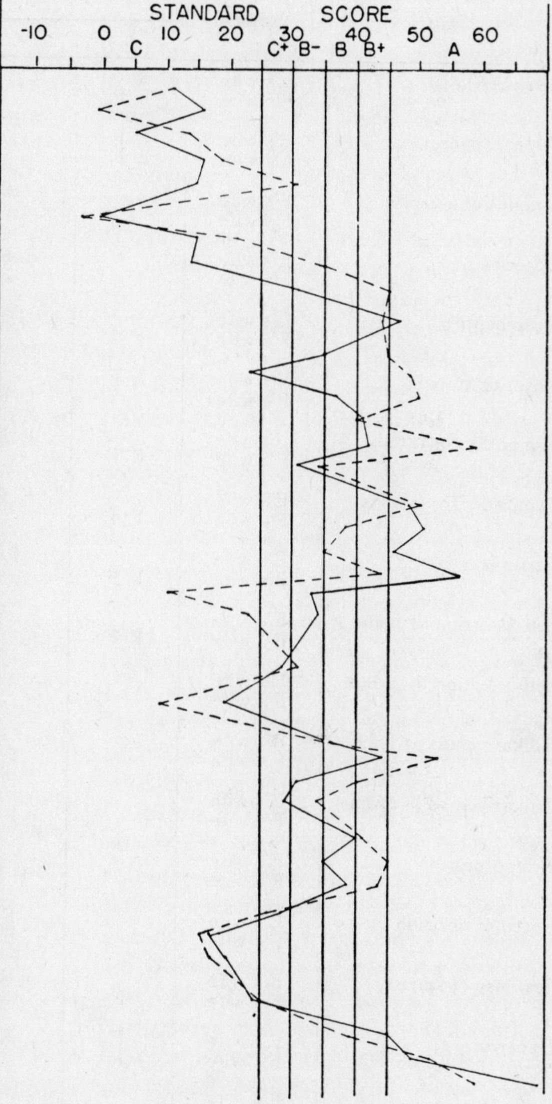

STANDARD SCORE: -10 0 10 20 30 40 50 60 C C+ B- B B+ A

* Occupational level is a measure of the amount a given score differs from the average of unskilled laborers. Hence a high score means one's interests are "elite" in the sense that they are like those of professional men rather than laborers.

FIG. 2. Vocational interest patterns, Earl and Frank.

TABLE 6
TRAIT RATINGS OF TWINS EARL AND FRANK
MADE BY THEIR WIVES

Trait	Rater	Degree 1	2	3	4	5
General health	E's wife		E. F			
	F's wife	E F				
Physical energy	E's wife	E F				
	F's wife	E F				
Amount of activity	E's wife			E	F	
	F's wife	E		F		
Appetite	E's wife		E F			
	F's wife		E F			
Sleep depth	E's wife		F?	F?		E
	F's wife				F	
Reaction to pain	E's wife	E F				
	F's wife		E F			
Sympathy for family	E's wife		E F			
	F's wife	E F				
Sympathy for friends	E's wife		E F			
	F's wife	E F				
Perseverance	E's wife		E	F?		
	F's wife	E F				
Self-assertion at home	E's wife			E F		
	F's wife	E F				
Self-assertion in group	E's wife			E F		
	F's wife					
Talkativeness at home	E's wife			E	F	
	F's wife		F	E		
Talkativeness in group	E's wife			E	F	
	F's wife		F	E		
Promptness	E's wife			E F		
	F's wife		E F			
Speed of decision	E's wife		F	E		
	F's wife		F	E		
Jealousy of spouse	E's wife		E F?			
	F's wife	F				
Generosity	E's wife	F	E			
	F's wife	F	E?	E?		
Self-consciousness	E's wife				E F	F
	F's wife				E	
Competitiveness	E's wife		F		E	
	F's wife		E F			
Sense of responsibility	E's wife	E	F			
	F's wife	F				

TABLE 6—(*continued*)

Trait	Rater	Degree				
		1	2	3	4	5
Sense of humor	E's wife	E F				
	F's wife	F	E			
Irritability	E's wife					E F
	F's wife			E F		
Cheerfulness	E's wife		E F			
	F's wife	F				
Courage (physical)	E's wife		E∤F			
	F's wife		E F			
Courage (moral)	E's wife	E				
	F's wife	E F				
Facing facts	E's wife	E F?				
	F's wife		E‚F			
Trustfulness	E's wife		F	E		
	F's wife	F			E	
Sociality	E's wife	F		E		
	F's wife	F		E		
Leadership	E's wife		E			
	F's wife	E F				
Popularity same sex	E's wife		E F			
	F's wife	E F				
Popularity opposite sex	E's wife		E F			
	F's wife	E F				
Athletic interests	E's wife		F	E		
	F's wife	F			E?	
Emotional dependence on family	E's wife			E F		
	F's wife		E F			

ambitions, so that we might expect to find some of the greatest differences between the twins to be in this area.

Of the 38 pairs of scores, 25 differ by no more than 10 points of standard score, which is one standard deviation of the distribution of the criterion group. Seventeen pairs are within 5 points standard score of each other. Only three pairs differ by as much as 20 points in standard score, or 2.0 standard deviations of the criterion group distribution.

In "A Study of Identical Twins Reared Apart" Dr. Burks notes the markedly greater similarity in the vocational interest schedules of Twins A and B at age 18 than at age 12, and she suggests that "interest patterns, as maturity is approached, not only become stabilized but actually have a closer relation to native potentialities than do interests in early adolescence."

In the light of this hypothesis of Dr. Burks, attention may be called to the close parallelism of vocational interests in these mature twins E and F, despite

the background influences which might
have been expected to steer them in
different directions.

Rorschach test. The Rorschach tests
were administered by Dr. Burks. There
is no Inquiry for either E or F, although
some locations for E's responses have
been indicated on a "location chart"
with some elaboration of his responses.
These, however, add little to the protocol
for they are chiefly inaccurate anatomical details. The protocols of Earl and
Frank are given in Table 7.

Dr. Davidson's comments on E's Rorschach were: "Above average intelligence; poor affective relationships, rigid;
self-conscious; very weak ego; adjustment
fair." Her comments on F's Rorschach:
"Above average intelligence; very insecure about himself (see Card III), weak
ego; responsive; probably adequately ad-
justing (?)."

Dr. Valentine agrees, with one major
exception: she would infer that neither
E nor F was more than average in intelligence. She also infers that F's ego is
less vulnerable than E's. She has sub-
mitted approximate psychograms for E
and F, given in Appendix D, and has
added the following comments:

"The chief similarities in these two psychograms are: below average number of responses;
narrow range of Content; preponderance of
Whole responses at the expense of the usual
Details; absence of Movement responses; absence
of Form-Color responses.

"Differences in the psychograms are: E has
a much lower percentage of good Form responses than F, fewer Popular responses, more
Color responses, and a more limited range of content.

"Qualitatively, the striking difference between
E and F is the strained effort of E to impress,
to show that he is above the common run of
people. But there is a wide gap between his
aspirations and his ability to make these good.
F, on the other hand, is more simple and un-
pretentious, less eager to impress people, somewhat more capable of easy relations with them.
Both are of average intelligence but E wishes

to be accepted as superior; he is 'cagey' and
unwilling to give himself away, hides his inadequacies under a rather empty pomposity. He
appears to be more emotionally unstable than
F and to make an attempt to deal intellectually
with his feelings whereas F tends to accept his.
F shows humility about himself—which he possibly uses as a technique of ingratiation."

Handwriting. The samples of the
handwriting of these twins are reproduced in Figures 3a and 3b. Although
these are superficially much less alike
than those of the first pair of twins, there
are a number of points of similarity.

SUMMARY

The monozygotic twins Earl and
Frank, born out of wedlock of parents
with little education, were separated at
the age of six months and raised by adoptive parents in different areas of the
country. They did not see each other
again until the age of 15. The chief environmental differences were as follows:
Earl (Twin E) lived in cities in the
Northwest and West, in comfort and
economic security, and was encouraged to
attend college and to embrace professional ambitions somewhat beyond his
intellectual capacities. Frank (Twin F)
was brought up by a maternal aunt and
her husband in the economic and social
milieu in which the twins were born,
with little economic security or even
physical comfort but with marked affection from his aunt. F had considerably
less schooling than E and was not pushed
toward ambitious achievements. Similar
environmental influences were that both
twins enjoyed reasonably happy childhood homes and moderate discipline,
though F's training may have been somewhat more consistent. Both twins were
exposed to violin lessons.

Developmental and health histories
were very similar; each twin commented
on his own good general health and high

TABLE 7

RORSCHACH PROTOCOLS
TWINS EARL AND FRANK

Twin E	Twin F
I. (at once) A pelvic bone . . . V (can I turn)? . . . it still does.	I. Bat V Some emblem of some sort.
(no time)	1 min.
II. (10″) Looks like a type of bug of some kind.	II. (15″) V < Basis of these monsters. . . . Looks like a cat that's scared, a bobtailed cat.
(no time)	¾ min.
III. (12″) A spider.	III. (10″) V Are these supposed to represent something? A sea horse Butterfly Also the features of a man's head with mouth open.
(no time)	1¼ min.
IV. (at once) A bat.	IV. (10″) Has the features of some sort of worms. Don't know whether to call him cousin of bat or not (laughs).
(no time)	¾ min.
V. A butterfly.	V. (20″) Don't believe I ever saw anything like it . . . afraid I'm kind of dumb. Animal life . . . could be cousin of a bat.
(no time)	¾ min.
VI. (15″) (turns around) A skin of some animal.	VI. (20″) More like a rug to me. Lacking head, could be a bear rug.
(no time)	¾ min.
VII. (turns around) (40″) That one I wouldn't say much; similar to islands geographically.	VII. (15″) Sort of like clouds. Could be looking down from airplane at ridge of mountains.
¾ min.	¾ min.
VIII. (at once) Looks like a cross section of some embryo, stained . . . microtome section, different types of tissue.	VIII. (15″) Looks like animals trying to hang on to something . . . color effects are very pretty (smiles).
(no time)	¾ min.
IX. (30″); (turns around) Some type of deep sea life.	IX. (15″) Earl Carroll's(?) night club. Have colors just about like that. Looks like fountain and neon lights.
(no time)	¾ min.
X. (15″) Same thing, cross section of some animal, types of tissue taking different stains.	X. (8″) Without colors would say in a stream of water where bugs are floating around (turns)
(no time)	½ min.

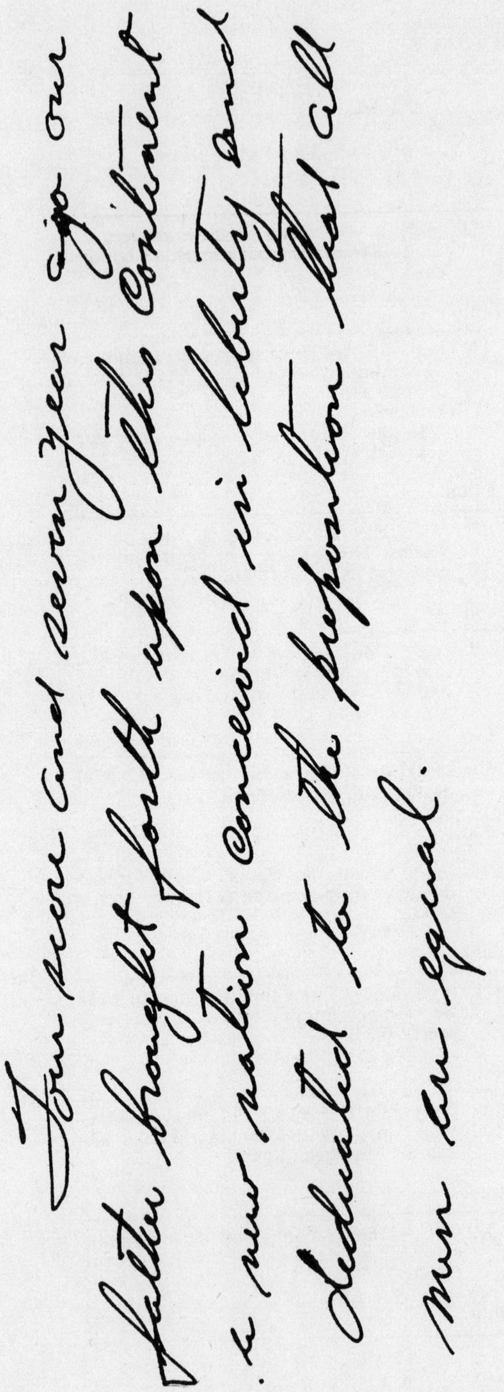

Four score and seven years ago our
fathers brought forth upon this continent
a new nation conceived in liberty and
dedicated to the proposition that all
men are equal.

FIG. 3a. Handwriting. Earl.

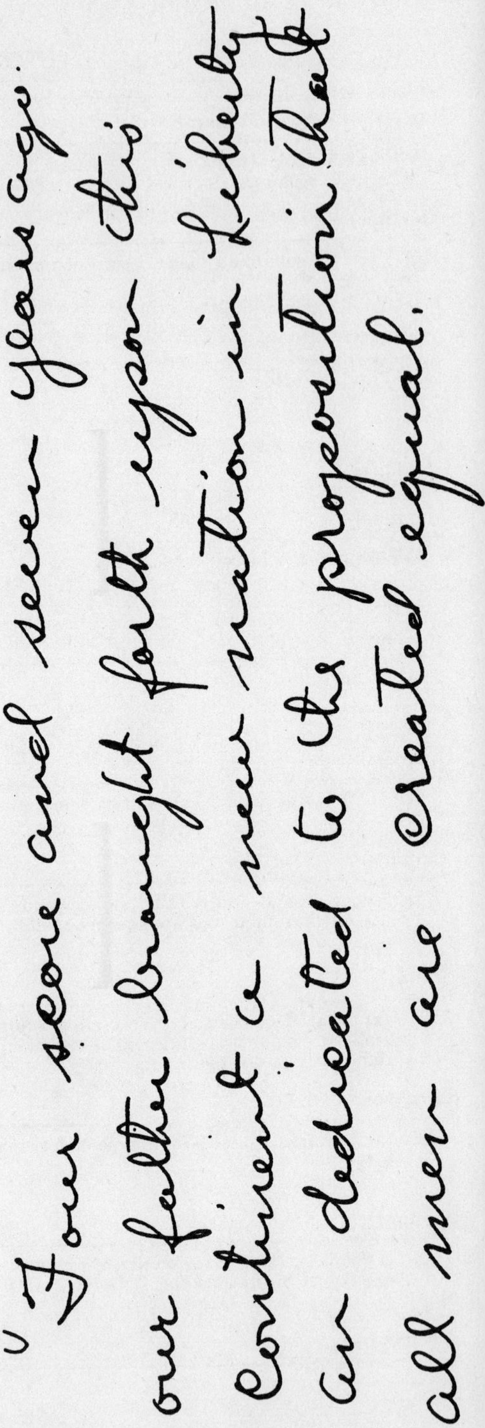

"Four score and seven years ago.
our father brought forth upon this
continent a new nation in liberty
an dedicated to the proposition that
all men are created equal.

FIG. 3b. Handwriting. Frank.

energy level. In appearance they were markedly alike.

When studied at the age of 37 both twins were living and working in the West, E running successfully a suburban cafe, F employed as a laborer in a utilities company—an occupation which was that of his own father. Both were married, both had friends with whom they liked to associate. E's ambitions and desire for worldly success were strong and not entirely satisfied, while F was more relaxed and contented with his lot.

Intelligence tests showed E's I.Q. to be in the normal range, F's in the low normal. Ratings by Dr. Burks on characteristics observed during the interviews were identical in three fourths of the items. Ratings by the two wives of the twins on certain physical and sensory traits showed agreement that both E and F were alike in many points and notably different only in two: sociality and trustfulness of others, F being the more outgoing and trustful of the two, and warmer in his personal relations.

CHAPTER IV

TWINS GERTRUDE AND HELEN

THE TWINS Gertrude and Helen were the two survivors of a set of triplets (the third triplet lived only a few months) born in the Northwest in 1889. Each weighed about three pounds at birth. The parents were Finnish immigrants. The father was well educated, but the mother illiterate. Gertrude was taken by foster parents when she was about a year old, while Helen remained with her own parents who went to a remote farm. The motives of the parents in placing Gertrude for adoption are not clear, since later they had two younger children, but perhaps the difficulties of caring for twin babies made it seem to them desirable.

Gertrude did not know she was adopted for some years, but when she was about 13 she spent two weeks with her own family and after that Helen usually came and stayed with her for a while twice a year.

EVIDENCE FOR MONOZYGOTIC ORIGIN OF THE TWINS

Here again the available evidence bearing on the zygotic origin of the twins G and H, given in Table 8, suggests that they are monozygotic.

ENVIRONMENTAL SURROUNDINGS AND HISTORY

Community. The twins were brought up in the same part of the country, a very remote district in the Northwest. Both lived on farms during childhood.

The homes. Gertrude was brought up as an only child. Her foster father was Finnish, the foster mother Danish. According to her daughter, Gertrude was warmly cared for during her early childhood, provided with suitable clothes, and presented with gifts on holidays. When she was nine her foster mother died, and after that she kept house for her foster father. Gertrude's account indicates a consistently good relationship with her foster father even though he sometimes indulged in heavy drinking bouts, especially on his occasional trips to town. He did the cooking, but she had many farm chores. She played largely by herself or with the children of the family across the river, with whom she went berry picking and swimming. She remembered that they had frequent fights, but did not remember what they were about. After her marriage her foster father lived alone, on an inland ranch, but when he became feeble and childish, her husband persuaded him to come and live with them where Gertrude could care for him. He lived to be 96 years old.

There is little information about Helen's childhood with her own parents. She was not given chores to do, and did not remember having had home training of any sort. Apparently the children were just left alone. They were never punished. The father and maternal grandmother who lived with them were inclined to be mean and hard to get along with. There were no holiday celebrations except rice pudding at Christmas.

Education. Neither girl had much schooling. Both attended the county school for a few months a year, and Gertrude once went to a boarding school for nine months, but she did not finish the seventh grade and Helen stopped before the fifth grade.

Occupational history. Before her mar-

TABLE 8

Physical Criteria of Zygotic Origin
Twins Gertrude and Helen

Age 52	Twin G	Twin H
Height (stocking feet)	161.1 cm.	161.4 cm.
Head breadth	16.4 cm.	15.7 cm.
Head length	19.4 cm.	17.7 cm.
Cephalic index	84	88
Head circumference	23.0 inches	21.5 inches
Interpupillary distance		
Left reading	6.55 cm.	6.62 cm.
Right reading	6.6 cm.	5.95 cm.
Eye color (Martin chart)	³ Brown flecks around center, bluer	Rim wider ³
Need for glasses	Reading	Reading
Hair:		
Color	Brown and gray	More gray
Form	Straight	Straight
Texture	Coarse	Less coarse
Thickness	Thick	Less thick
Medullation	75%	75%
Type	Discontinuous	Same but islands not so heavy and more dispersed
Pigment granule pattern	Same	
Average diameter shafts	85 microns	78 microns
Cortical fusi	Normal, but interspersed with irregular ones (due to waving?)	Normal, few in number
Cutical scales	Same	
Skin color:	Light	Light
Freckles	A few on forehead	Same
Oral cavity:		
Teeth color	Yellow	Yellow
Condition of gums	Reddish	Same
Tongue furrows	None	None
Feet:		
Size of shoe	6E or EEE	6 less wide
Hands:		
Mid-digital hair	L4 RO	L4 R4
Downy hair:		
Face	Light over lips and chin	Same
Arms	Light	Same
Handedness	Right	Right

Fingerprints	R	L	R	L
Thumb	W 23-30	L^u 16	W 21-?	L^u 13
Index	W 15-17	W 23-12	W 21-22	W 30-15
Middle	L^u 15	W 17-20	L^u 15	W 25*-19
Ring	W 29-19	W 20-25	W 27-26	W 13-25
Little	L^u 18	L^u 20?	L^u 25	L^u 23
Total ridge count	166	153*	165*	163*

* Estimated.

riage, Gertrude worked only on her foster father's farm and after marriage she had occasionally done similar work; for example, she and Helen picked hops one summer. At the time of the study Gertrude ran a rooming house and grocery store on the water front of a small town.

Helen did outdoor work on farms before her marriage, and enjoyed it. After her marriage, she occasionally sewed for others. This had not brought in much income, however, because she enjoyed making clothes for little girls so much that she would charge almost nothing for it. (She had only boys of her own and always wanted girls.)

Health history. As has been noted, both were very small at birth, about three pounds in weight. At the time of the study both were very much overweight; one weighed 236 and one 222 pounds. Each had been small until she began having children, but gained with each child and never lost thereafter. During childhood both had measles and mumps, but no other diseases which they remembered, and their health and general energy were excellent. After they became adult, both had severe cases of yellow jaundice at the same time, although they were then living some distance apart and had not seen each other for two years. Hearing was fair; both wore reading glasses. Age at menopause was early for both, for Gertrude 36, for Helen 34.

The health of both remained generally excellent until each developed rheumatism. When Gertrude was 47, she spent almost a month in the hospital with rheumatism, but her condition improved after she went to a hot springs, except for periodic swelling of the ankles. At 51, Helen spent about two months in the hospital with the same difficulty, and never was really well after that. She was unable to walk for a long time, and a year later went again to the hospital with a heart disturbance. She died there from dropsy, a few months after Dr. Burks' visit.

SITUATION AT TIME OF STUDY (1942)

The twins were 52 years of age at the time of the study. After going around with a number of boys, Gertrude at 22 married a man much older than herself, who had much the same drinking pattern as that shown by her foster father. They lived on a ranch for some years and after that lived in a succession of small towns. There were three children: a daughter and two sons. Both boys died of flu and the daughter became blind at that same time, at the age of six. Gertrude's daughter said that when she was young the children had to do as they were told or they were whipped. But they were taught to be sympathetic, and if they slapped an animal, Gertrude slapped them. Gertrude's daughter did not confide in her mother at any time. At the time of the study, G was living in a small town in the Northwest, where she ran a rooming house and grocery store, as has been mentioned. She did not like the community in which she lived and did not engage in an active social life. She belonged to a card club and occasionally went to the movies and read a few "pulps." She rarely went to church. Her daughter was married and had a child of her own at this time. They lived nearby, and G spent a good deal of her time with them. G's emotional tone was far from cheerful. She said, "I don't see why we're put in this world, no pleasure, but as long as we're here, make the best of it. . . . We [the triplets] should never have been born."

Helen married at 20 the first man she

had ever gone with and had ten children, of whom six sons survived. Her marital relations were somewhat happier and more affectionate than Gertrude's. Helen's niece said that she seldom punished the children, but she would sometimes go off on trips and leave them to fend for themselves and habitually left them to cook and wash for themselves. Her husband put it that she "tried never to interfere" with the children. All had seventh or eighth grade education, one attended high school. The youngest son played truant from school and finally was sent to a training school. Helen and her husband always had difficulty getting along financially, although both were hard working. They always had good relations with their neighbors and Helen had many friends. The family went to church occasionally, and Helen belonged to three organizations, although she was never an officer in any of them. She was fond of embroidery and sewing, and liked to listen to the radio, but she read only local news, never books nor magazines. At the time of the study H was in a hospital about 80 miles away from her home. In spite of this distance, however, her many friends did not neglect her, and she had visitors every day.

TESTS, RATINGS, AND OBSERVATIONS

Intelligence tests. On the Kuhlmann-Stanford G did somewhat the better of the two. Her Mental Age was 10 years, 6 months, her I.Q. 66, but her performance was erratic and her scatter very wide. Her basal year was 6. She failed at 7 years Digits forward, at 9 years Comprehension (but passed it at 10), Making change, and Rhymes, at 10 years Digits forward. She passed, however, at the 12 year level Abstract Words, Digits backward and Pictures, and at 14 years the

Induction test. Vocabulary was at the 10 year level. The irregularities in her performance in repeating digits were striking: she was able to repeat 5 Digits backward but only 4 Digits forward.

H was ill at the time the test was given, shortly before her death. Dr. Burks noted that her attention was good and that she did not seem fatigued during the test, but was too tired to continue the interview afterward. Her basal year was 7. She failed the Ball-and-field, Comprehension, and Definitions at 8 years, Words and Rhymes at 9 years, and all of the 10 year tests. Vocabulary score was 23 words; she repeated 5 Digits forward (6 were not tried apparently) and 4 backward. Her Mental Age was 8 years, 2 months, her I.Q. 51.

Descriptive rating scale. On the descriptive rating scale filled out by Dr. Burks, the sisters received the same ratings on 10 out of the 12 items. On two they differed: Helen was rated as "quite masculine," her sister as "neither masculine nor feminine," and Dr. Burks added on Helen's record, "Speech profane, briefer, more clipped than Gertrude's. Similar in body handling." On cheerfulness, Helen was rated 4, rather sombre, pessimistic, and Gertrude 3, neither sombre nor gay, but with the note that Helen's hospital situation should be considered, and that she laughed occasionally and suddenly just as her sister did.

In the light of the earlier quotation of Gertrude's and the somewhat dreary mood suggested by it, a similar rating of 4, "sombre, pessimistic" for both twins would seem to have been justified.

Trait ratings. Ratings on physical and sensory traits are shown in Table 9. Ratings were made by Gertrude's daughter for both G and H and by Helen's husband for as many traits as he felt able to

TABLE 9

TRAIT RATINGS OF TWINS GERTRUDE AND HELEN
MADE BY GERTRUDE'S DAUGHTER AND HELEN'S HUSBAND

Trait	Rater	Degree				
		1	2	3	4	5
General health (until recently)	G's daughter	G H				
	H's husband					
Physical energy (when young)	G's daughter	G H				
	H's husband					G H now
Amount of activity	G's daughter	G H†				
	H's husband					
Appetite	G's daughter	H	G			
	H's husband		G H			
Sleep depth	G's daughter					G H†
	H's husband					G H
Reaction to pain*	G's daughter					G H†
	H's husband					G H
Sympathy for family	G's daughter		G		H	
	H's husband					
Sympathy for friends	G's daughter		G H			
	H's husband					
Perseverance	G's daughter		H†	G†		
	H's husband					
Self-assertion	G's daughter			G H		
	H's husband			G H		
Talkativeness	G's daughter				G H	
	H's husband					
Promptness	G's daughter		G			H
	H's husband			G†	H	
Speed of decision	G's daughter			G		
	H's husband					
Jealousy	G's daughter			G H		
	H's husband		H			
Generosity	G's daughter		G	H		
	H's husband			G H		
Self-consciousness	G's daughter			G H		
	H's husband					
Competitiveness	G's daughter	G			H	
	H's husband					
Sense of responsibility	G's daughter	G			H	
	H's husband					
Sense of humor	G's daughter		G H			
	H's husband				G H	

* G's daughter notes, "Both hurt so easy, if you touch them, scream. Arms bruise easily but scratches don't react. Both rave if sick and in pain."
† Ratings made on basis of Dr. Burks' notes.

TABLE 9—*(continued)*

Trait	Rater	Degree 1	2	3	4	5
Irritability	G's daughter		G		H	
	H's husband			G_H		
Cheerfulness	G's daughter			G H		
	H's husband			G H		
Courage (physical)	G's daughter					G H
	H's husband				G H	
Courage (moral)	G's daughter	G H				
	H's husband	G H				
Facing facts	G's daughter			H†	G†	
	H's husband		G H			
Trustfulness	G's daughter	G H				
	H's husband	G H				
Sociality	G's daughter			G	H	
	H's husband			G H		
Leadership	G's daughter			G		H
	H's husband					H
Popularity	G's daughter			G	H	
	H's husband	H				
Emotional dependence on family	G's daughter			G H		
	H's husband					

rate. According to G's daughter, who rated both twins on 28 items, they were alike in 16 traits; she rated them as different by one step in 6 traits, by two steps in 4, and by three steps in 2 traits. H's husband, rating them both on 15 items, rated them the same in 14 traits and different in 1. The only marked discrepancy in ratings by the two was for H's popularity, which her husband rated as 1 and her niece (i.e. Gertrude's daughter) as 4. It was apparent that H's niece did not approve of her and this attitude was probably reflected in the ratings.

Rorschach test. The Rorschach protocols are given in Table 10. The tests were administered by Dr. Burks. An Inquiry is recorded for G's test but only a brief one for H's.

Dr. Davidson's comments on G's Rorschach were: "Insecure; deteriorated; poor adjustment." On H's test she comments: "Sick, inadequate personality; deteriorated; very poor adjustment." Dr. Valentine agrees and in addition submits an approximate psychogram, given in Appendix E, and makes the following comments:

"So far as their Rorschach protocols are concerned, these would indicate that both twins G and H are sadly impaired in functioning. Whether their poor performances are the result of deterioration or an indication of a life-long poor adjustment and level of functioning it would be hazardous to guess on the basis of these records. Those responses which are poor Form are not bizarre but rather vague anatomy perseverations. Once started, it is easier so to continue than for them to exert themselves to see anything else.

"There are similarities in the two psychograms: below average number of responses;

TABLE 10

RORSCHACH PROTOCOLS
TWINS GERTRUDE AND HELEN

Twin G	Twin H
I. (8″) Might be a skeleton of bug or bat, isn't that right? That's what I think it would be (cautious). No.	I. (2″) Butterfly, isn't it? (turns). Kind of man's picture face.
1¾ min.	1 min.
II. ∨ (15″) I don't know what that would be. Might be a backbone or something, would it? I don't know what it would be. It might be a giant or something with backbone.	II. (3″) Man's front breast through here, and neck.
2¼ min.	(no time)
III. (10″) I don't know. ∨ What is it supposed to be? a drawing? Might be a stone image or anything living? I don't know what it would be; might it be part of a person's body? I don't know what it would be.	III. (6″) Some kind of people's body I think.
3 min.	½ min.
IV. (15″) Might be a skeleton of sea fish or something. That's what it looks like to me.	IV. (12″) I don't know, that's just a shoulder or something, some kind of body like a rabbit, isn't it? ∨
¾ min.	¾ min.
V. (5″) A bat (laughs) I'd say more like a bat than anything I could figure out. Is this to try your eyesight?	V. (6″) I don't know. ∨∧ (30″) . . . unless across the spine here.
1½ min.	(no time)
VI. (8″) Cow hide (laughs, then giggles loudly). I don't know if that's what it's supposed to be.	VI. (10″) All people's bodies or what? Like the backbone I guess, looks something like it.
1 min.	¾ min.
VII. (8″) Goodness, I'd say cloud or something in the sky, you see clouds sometimes, funny shapes. They don't represent anything do they?	VII. (10″) I don't know. Looks like some (30″) kind of meat (laughs). I don't know at all. It's something. Some kind of flesh I guess.
1½ min.	(no time)
VIII. (10″) I don't know what that would be. Another one of them things, I don't know what it would be. I don't know.	VIII. (10″) A little bit like a chest. Little ribs a-sticking here. Looks pretty much like it.
¾ min.	¼ min.
IX. (25″) I don't know either. It wouldn't supposed to be a person's lungs would it? I don't see that it would be anything. Sort of funny things.	IX. (12″) I guess some part of human's body. >∨ . . . What did G call them?
1½ min.	(no time)
X. (25″) In a way it sort of looks like a person's system all inflamed. I bet I don't get any of them right.	X. (10″) Looks like a person's neck (top gray). Some kind of person.
1 min.	¾ min.

TABLE 10—(*continued*)

Twin G	Twin H
INQUIRY	
I. Whole.	I. Butterfly: whole. Man's face: side edge Dd profile.
II. "Middle is where spine would go (space), the red ones where nerves would come."	II. Breast: upper part of black. Adds: neck is red (top).
III. Image: man's torso; stone: usual leg; "are red splotches supposed to be blood or what?"	X. Neck: center stalk of top gray points out pink as ribs side blue as shoulder, lower green as spine.
IV. Whole. "So many jellyfish when they dry up, kind of like that."	
V. Whole.	
VI. Whole. "If I'd know what it was I could see something else."	
VII. Whole. "Just the way they come up over mountain or in sky some times, funny shapes."	
VIII. "It doesn't look like anything. No. It might be a couple of bears climbing somewhere . . . 4 legs."	
IX. Lungs: "I imagine that's the way they'd look if they'd be inflamed or anything like that."	

percentage of anatomical responses greater than animal responses; percentage of good Form responses below normal; Popular responses below normal (only 1 in the case of H); the majority of their perceptions are poor and vague Whole responses.

"Differences are that G's percentage of good Form responses is somewhat higher than H's; G has more Popular responses, and a lower percentage of responses with anatomical content.

"In protocols such as these the lack of a thorough Inquiry prevents more than the briefest and most tentative observations. However, G seems to be capable of a slightly more adequate adjustment than H; she has somewhat more awareness of and conformity with accepted social conventions; she is less concerned with her body and its functioning, whereas H is very much preoccupied with this. G seems more capable of emotional interplay with others, although always with egocentric emphasis."

Handwriting. Samples of their handwriting are given in Figures 4a and 4b. Helen was ill at the time, but even so the similarity is very apparent.

SUMMARY

The twins Gertrude and Helen, two survivors of triplets born to Finnish immigrants, were separated at about one year of age. Gertrude (Twin G) was taken by foster parents, while Helen (Twin H) remained in her own home. Both were raised on farms in the Northwest.

The chief environmental difference was the warmth with which G was surrounded in her relations with her foster mother, and after her foster mother's death with her foster father. H on the other hand was brought up in a hit-or-miss fashion, with little of tenderness, ease, or discipline. Neither twin had much schooling. Both had done farm work occasionally before their marriage. The developmental histories had strik-

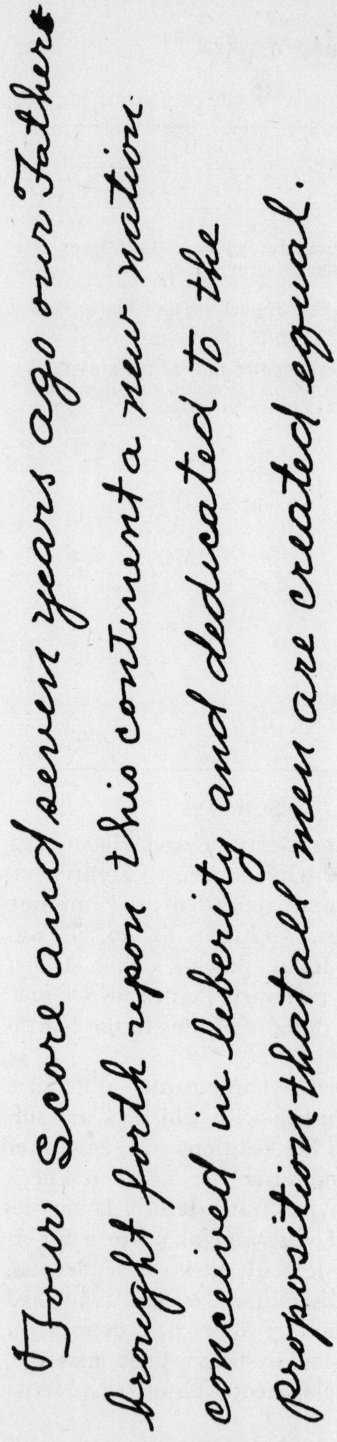

Four Score and seven years ago our Fathers
brought forth upon this continent a new nation:
conceived in liberity and dedicated to the
Proposition that all men are created equal.

FIG. 4a. Handwriting. Gertrude.
Time: 3' 40".

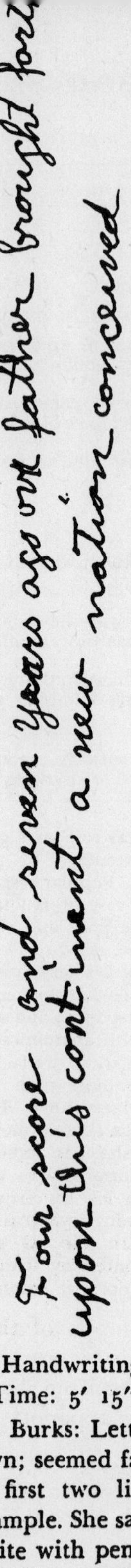

Four score and seven years ago our father brought forth
upon this continent a new nation conceived

FIG. 4b. Handwriting. Helen
Time: 5' 15".

Note by Dr. Burks: Letters were pain-
stakingly drawn; seemed fatigued, so Ex.
told her the first two lines would be
enough of a sample. She said it made her
nervous to write with pen, she was only
used to pencil. She was ill at this time.

ing similarities. Each weighed only three pounds at birth. At the time of the study, at the age of 52, both were greatly overweight, having gained at time of childbirth. Both reported measles and mumps in childhood and severe yellow jaundice in adulthood. Both reached menopause at an early age. Both suffered from acute rheumatic conditions. At the time of the study both twins were married and G had borne three children (one living), H ten (six living).

On the intelligence test, administered at the time of the study, G's performance was better than H's. But H was then ill and died of dropsy shortly thereafter. The difference in Mental Age could be attributed largely to this circumstance. Ratings both on characteristics that could be observed during the interview and on physical and sensory traits were markedly similar, as were the Rorschach records and handwriting samples of these twins.

CHAPTER V

TWINS JAMES AND KEITH

THE TWIN boys James and Keith were born in 1933, the illegitimate children of American-born Lithuanian parents. The putative father had been a boxer and farm worker, and was said to be friendly and kind. The mother had worked as domestic and nursemaid, after two years in high school. She was described as honest, dependable, good-natured and even-tempered, but "man crazy." She is said to have had later another illegitimate child. She was committed to a training school for girls, where her Stanford-Binet Mental Age is given as 13 years; Pintner-Paterson 14 years, 6 months; Porteus Maze 17 years; and Healy II 18 years, 8 months.

The twins did not remain with her for any length of time. For the first ten months of their lives the babies were placed in various boarding homes, under the supervision of the Department of Public Welfare. At one of these boarding homes records were kept of the birth weights and of certain other measurements and notations made at one year of age. These data are given in Table 11 and may be compared for the two boys.

The similarities are striking. The general condition of both was said to be "fair." A note to "watch James' right knee," however, indicates that there was already evidence of the condition which at 14 months was diagnosed as tuberculosis of the knee. This necessitated placing James in the hospital of an orphanage, where he was living at the time of the study. Keith continued to be placed in various homes until finally at the age of five or six he was adopted.

EVIDENCE FOR MONOZYGOTIC ORIGIN OF THE TWINS

Available data bearing on the zygotic origin of the twins are given in Table 12. In the records of the adoption agency is the statement of a physician, who had been present at the birth of the children, that they were not identical twins. This note was dated two years after the birth of the twins, and the basis for this opinion was not given nor was it possi-

TABLE 11

PHYSICAL MEASUREMENTS AND OBSERVATIONS ON
TWINS JAMES AND KEITH AT ONE YEAR

	Twin J	Twin K
Birth weight	4 lbs.	3 lbs.
Present weight	16½ lbs.	16½ lbs.
Height	28 inches	27½ inches
Chest		
insp.	17¼	17½
exp.	16	16¾
	Sleeps well	Poor sleeper
	Some constipation	Constipated
	Two teeth	No teeth
	Face seems fuller, larger	Sweet mouth and dimple in chin

Both have light hair, very little, inclined to be sandy; look much alike; well shaped heads; nice blue eyes; Wassermanns are negative.

40

TABLE 12

PHYSICAL CRITERIA OF ZYGOTIC ORIGIN
TWINS JAMES AND KEITH

Age 7 Years	Twin J		Twin K	
Hair:				
Medullation			More shafts medullated	
Type	Discontinuous		Discontinuous	
Pigment granule pattern		Same		
Average diameter shaft	80 microns		70 microns	
Cuticular scales		Same		
Cortical fusi		Very few and small		
Fingerprints:	R	L	R	L
Thumb	W 25-17	L^u 22	L^u 23	L^u 17
Index	W 7-8	W 8-8	A^t 0	L^u 16
Middle	L^u 9	L^u 8	L^u 8	L^u 1
Ring	W 27-7	W 2-27	L^u 4	L^u 8
Little	L^u 24	L^u 21	L^u 8	L^u 11
Total ridge counts	124	96	43	53
Diff. in ridge counts:				
bilateral, 36				
homolateral, 12				
heterolateral, 118				

ble to obtain any additional information from the physician. Dr. D. C. Rife, on the basis of the fingerprints, also felt that these twins were probably not monozygotic, though he did not consider the evidence sufficient to rule out the possibility. Dr. Burks herself believed that this pair, as well as the other three pairs, were monozygotic.

SITUATION AT TIME OF STUDY (1940)

Until the age of eight, James remained in the orphanage hospital to which he had been sent at 14 months. After this he was placed in a foster home. (Dr. Burks' study occurred just before this placement.) Life at the hospital was highly institutionalized, and much of the routine was designed for the convenience of those in charge rather than for the better development of the children. The lack of stimulation to learning in the environment may account for James' backwardness in such matters as speech, self-care, dressing and bathing, assumption of responsibility, etc. He was not

without affection, however, as the Sister in charge of him when he was a baby gave him a good deal of personal affection, and he continued to visit her daily even after he was moved to the Boys' House. These visits were apparently made possible only by the fact that he had to report to the hospital daily to have his knee cared for, since generally there was no provision whatever for individual recognition of the children.

Keith on the other hand was the only child in his foster family and was apparently treated affectionately. He was able to dress himself; his foster mother reported that he could bathe himself but that his father liked to do it. He lived in a moderate-sized Eastern city, where he was kept fairly closely at home, except when his parents were with him. They took him out a good deal, though, for fishing and swimming, and he enjoyed "helping" his father with carpentry about the house.

School record. In their first year at school neither boy did very well, but

Keith improved considerably in the second term. Teachers of both boys, as well as all other adults who came into contact with them, noted that their attention-span was very much less than normal, which of course would retard learning.

Association with other children. Although both boys were described as always cheerful and happy, and seldom resentful, neither got along well with other children. James' teacher reported that he had no sense of responsibility, forgot to do things he was told, and often did things very impulsively without waiting to see how they should be done. He often hit other children without any particular reason, or tripped them up.

Keith's teacher noted: "He is constantly in trouble on the playground, quarrels with the children, is very mean to them and often vicious in that he throws things that hurt them badly. He is also very underhanded and sly about doing things and trying to shift the blame on other children. He is very unruly." His foster mother, however, found him very appreciative, affectionate, and helpful.

James' irresponsible behavior might be due to considerable insecurity, of which there is other evidence. He was at the time of the study very much preoccupied with his status as an orphan, and apparently fantasied very extensively about his mother. Keith's foster home situation would be expected to have given him increasing security, and it is possible that his aggressive behavior toward other children was a temporary carry-over from an earlier period.

Health history. James had always had trouble with his tuberculous right knee. In addition he had had measles, mumps, and chicken pox, and at five and seven recurrent ear infections. At the time of the study his hearing was definitely defective.

Data on Keith's health history are lacking.

TESTS, RATINGS, AND OBSERVATIONS

Intelligence tests. Dr. Burks gave James the 1916 form of the Stanford-Binet test when he was 7 years and 2 months old. He attained a Mental Age of 5 years, 3 months, an I.Q. of 73. She noted: "The I.Q. alone would suggest borderline deficiency, but the wide scatter suggests the influence of emotional blocking or specific limitations of experience or both. Moreover, James has learned to read this winter, an attainment seldom reached under a Mental Age of 6 or 6½. In view of an earlier reported I.Q. of 96 at 4 years, 4 months, he might be expected to come up to low average range if he could have the individual care of a boarding home. It is possible that poor hearing also accounts in part for the low level of functioning and for his indistinct infantile speech, which is not due to any impediment as far as can be judged."

Dr. Burks did not test Keith, but the record shows that Stanford-Binet tests on various occasions gave the following results: at 4 years, 1 month, an I.Q. of 86; at 5 years, 1 month an I.Q. of 95; and at 6 years, 6 months, an I.Q. of 91.

Goodenough Nonverbal Test. The drawings reproduced in Figures 5a and 5b were obtained by Dr. Burks when the twins were 6 years, 9 months old. James scored a Mental Age of 5 years, an I.Q. of 74, and Keith a Mental Age of 7 years, 6 months, an I.Q. of 111. About six months later, their scores were 5 years, 9 months and 7 years, 3 months.

FIG. 5a. Drawing by James.
C.A.6-9; M.A. 5-0; I.Q. 74.

TABLE 13
VINELAND SOCIAL MATURITY SCALE
TWINS JAMES AND KEITH

	Twin J	Twin K
III to IV Years		
Item		
45. Walks downstairs 1 step per tread	Plus	
46. Plays cooperatively at kindergarten level		
47. Buttons coat or dress	Plus Minus	Plus
48. Helps at little household tasks	None	Plus
49. "Performs" for others		Plus
50. Washes hands unaided	Plus	Plus
IV to V Years		
51. Cares for self at toilet	Plus	Plus
52. Washes face unassisted	Plus	Plus
53. Goes about neighborhood unattended	No chance	Minus
54. Dresses self except tying	Plus Minus	Plus
55. Uses pencil or crayon for drawing	Plus	Plus
65. Goes to bed unassisted	Plus	

In the drawings reproduced here and in others in the record, the animation in Keith's is quite extraordinary.

Vineland Social Maturity Scale. Results for the two boys at 6 years, 9 months are given in Table 13. Omitted items were failed by both, or not scored. It is clear that Keith was ahead of James in this measure of maturity. Undoubtedly some of the difference reflects differences in opportunity to learn.

Dramatic play with toys. The dramatic play situation was developed as follows:

FIG. 5b. Drawing by Keith.
C.A.6-9; M.A. 7-6; I.Q. 111.

Metal toys, representing people, animals, furniture, and vehicles adaptable for imaginative play, were wrapped separately in paper and then placed on a desk in front of the children. Notes taken by Dr. Burks, the examiner, (*Ex.*) described the child's reactions to each toy, including a verbatim account of his remarks. The striking differences in spontaneity between the two boys is evident from their records which are reproduced below in full.

Twin J

The toys were placed on the desk before J, who enjoyed unwrapping them but showed no interest in examining them further. In order to stimulate further reaction the examiner sought to focus his attention upon each toy as it was unwrapped with such questions as: "What is this?" "What is it for?" or "What does it do?"

1. (Red car)
   A car. For play with.
2. (Cowboy and pony)
   He rides.
   He wrestles with somebody.
3. (Airplane)
   An airplane.
   Ride up in the sky.
4. (Traffic policeman)
   A soldier.
   Ex: What does he do?
   He's marching.

Ex: Do you think it is a policeman?
Yes. He's doing this (gesture with hand).
Ex: What does he tell people?
He's doing this.
5. (Old man)
A man's got a cane.
Ex: Is he a young man?
Yes.
6. (Motor policeman)
A cop on a motorcycle.
Ex: Where is he going?
To his house.
7. (Man with coat over arm)
He's holding a coat.
Ex: Who is?
A man.
8. (Woman with tennis racket)
She's holding a pocketbook.
Ex: Who is?
A lady.
9. (Boy)
A man.
Ex: Is it a man or is it a boy?
Yes.
10. (Boy)
They are just the same. He is holding something.
11. (Woman with dog)
A lady with a doggie.
12. (Girl)
A little girl with a doll.
13. (Dog)
A little horse.
Ex: Are you sure it is a horse?
A dog.

After all the toys had been unwrapped J lined them up in a row, dropping several as he did so. He asked about the woman figure, pointing to tennis racket, "What is that?" He then moved all the figures in another double row naming them: two little boys, two big men, two big ladies, one little girl, a cowboy, etc. He put the girl on the car and the lady on the airplane.

Ex: What do you call this? (pointing to the propeller of the toy airplane)
The wing.
Ex: What does it do for an airplane?
The wing.

J now removed all of the toys except the family group of father, mother, two boys, and dog. J put the dog on the hat of the man, but showed no other initiative with the toys.

Ex then set up and described a situation. The father was going to work, the mother was going to the store, and the boys were going to school. J moved the toys appropriately but did not develop the theme.

Ex: Now it's time to come home, etc.
He comes home; they come (moving toys).
Ex: What does the mother say when they come home?
J places one boy by the father, one boy by the mother.
Ex: What do they say?
I don't know.
(Manipulates the toys aimlessly and then says he wants to make another picture.)

Ex then gave J paper and crayons. Using the man as a model he attempted to copy it.

Ex: What's this? (producing a toy bed)
A bed.
Ex: It's a bed for the boys. What do they do?
J piles all the toy dolls including the dog into bed, then removes them.
Ex: It's bedtime for the boys.
J puts the boys in the bed.
Ex: Does anyone say good night to them?
Yes.
Ex: The father?
J brings the father doll over but does not develop the situation.

Twin K

The examiner took out the small metal toys each wrapped in a separate paper and put them on the desk for Keith to open. He enjoyed doing this and as soon as he opened one he immediately seemed to know what he wanted to do with it; arranged it in a very definite way and had it enter into the game.

1. (Red car)
K responded immediately.
A mail car. (In the city where K lived special deliveries were made in red cars.)
Ran car over desk for a while.
2. (Traffic policeman)
Soon had policeman signaling the car to stop and start.
3. (Motor policeman)
This is a cop, too!
Soon had the motor cop chasing the red car.
4. (Nurse)
Oh, a nurse! We'll put her over here (puts her to one side).
Is there a hospital here?
Ex: There probably is one in the city.
5. (Dog)
K had dog following policeman.
6. (Woman)
We'll have the woman walking along the street.
7. (Man)
This is a father.
8. (Boys)
Places one boy with mother; other going to school.

9. (Cowboy on pony)
   K delighted.
   I play cowboys, too!
   Plays with cowboy on the pony for several
   minutes.
10. (Girl)
   A girl. We'll have her play out in the yard.
11. (Dog)
   I wonder who's going to take that dog.
12. (Man) What will I have him do? Go to
   work, I guess. Begins playing with the cowboy again.

K had all the metal toys arranged according
to his desire and played having them cross the
street, and being stopped by the policeman. He
referred to the cowboy as "The Texas Ranger."
He enjoyed these toys and when the examiner
began to put them away, she suggested that he
might like to keep the little red car as he had
opened that first. With apparent pleasure, he put
the car with his book. A man, a woman, and
a little boy were left out and he continued to
play with these. The figure of the man left
out had a coat over his arm. K decided that
the man, to whom he referred as father, was
going to take his coat to the cleaner, and from
here he went on into play, talking all the time.
"The father is going to take his coat to the
cleaner and the mother is going with him. She
is going to buy the groceries. The boy says,
'Can I go too?' and the father says, 'Yes.' 'Can
we have supper downtown, too?' 'O.K.,' says the
mother. The father goes to the cleaner and the
boy goes along with him while the mother says,
'I'll go buy the groceries and meet you. Where
will I meet you?' 'We will meet you on the
corner.'" And then K had them meet and
have their supper, go to the show, and go home.
At this point the bed was presented and K
said, "The little boy goes to bed first and then
we'll put him in the middle so he won't fall
out." "Now it's morning," said K, "and the
mother gets up to get the breakfast and then
she calls the father to get up. The father says,
'O.K.' and he goes into the bathroom to wash.
Then the mother calls the boy that breakfast
is ready and he gets up and they have breakfast, and the father goes to work and the boy
goes to school."
The differences in the children's behavior in
the dramatic play situation are marked and
demonstrate clearly the differences in their attitudes. James wanted to rush on to each new
toy without an examination of the one just
opened. When his attention was focused briefly
by the examiner's questions, e.g., "What is it?"
his paucity of ideas in relation to the toys
became evident. We know that in James' institutional environment there had been little if any
opportunity to play with toys of this kind, or

in general to give free expression to his imagination. Keith, on the other hand, exhibited a
lively interest in the toys and reflected in his
dramatization an easy identification with normal
family activities.

SUMMARY

The twins James and Keith were illegitimate sons of working-class parents.
At an early age, under the supervision
of the Department of Public Welfare,
they were placed in boarding homes. Of
the four sets of twins included in this
study, this is the only pair about whose
monozygotic origin there seems to be
some difference of opinion. The boys
were first seen by Dr. Burks not long
before their seventh birthday, but records
covering earlier history are available
from several sources. Measurements at
the age of one year were very similar
with respect to height, weight, and chest
circumference. Both twins were described
as attractive babies with nice blue eyes
and well-shaped heads, looking much
alike, though James' face seemed fuller.
James (Twin J) had two teeth and slept
well; Keith (Twin K) had no teeth and
was a poor sleeper.

The most outstanding differences in
the twins' first seven years are as follows:
J from the age of 14 months was subjected to a highly institutionalized existence in an orphanage because of treatment needed for a tuberculous knee;
had hearing impairment due to recurrent
ear infections; received no individual
affection except from one of the hospital
nurses. K lived in boarding homes until
the age of about 6, then was adopted as
the only child of protective, affectionate
foster parents. Both twins had difficulty
at school, and were noted as having a
very short attention-span, though K
showed some improvement in his second
term.

The records obtained at the age of

seven indicate marked similarities chiefly in the area of social behavior. Both J and K were described as cheerful and happy; they were, however, also thought not to get along well with other children, with whom they were aggressive, unruly, and lacking in a sense of responsibility.

Very pronounced at this age were the differences between the twins in mental test performance, and also in their response to a dramatic play situation. In these test situations, J's handicaps both from his history of ill health and from his circumscribed institutional existence were strongly in evidence. Dr. Burks questioned the validity of J's I.Q. of 73 and tended to attribute his low level of functioning to emotional blocking or specific limitations of experience or both. J was also noted as being backward for his age in matters of speech, dressing, assuming responsibility, etc. This again could be a reflection of the limited environment of his orphanage, where older children were assigned the job of helping to dress and bathe youngsters of J's age. James' retardation is further evidenced in his drawings and in his rating on the Vineland Maturity Scale. K's mental test performance (for which Dr. Burks obtained three earlier records) placed him well within the normal range.

In the dramatic play situation, J's inhibition and apparent blocking in relation to the development of play fantasy is in marked contrast to K's spontaneity in expressing his imaginative ideas centering around normal child life activities.

In view of the early developmental data collected by Dr. Burks, further study of these twins is much to be desired, especially after James' placement in a foster home where presumably a more stimulating environment may have helped to counteract results of the early deprivation.

CHAPTER VI

SUMMARY AND CONCLUSIONS

IT WOULD be too much to expect any far-reaching conclusions from the records available for these four twin-pairs, but the following summary on various aspects of the study may serve to high-light some of the more important findings. Table 14 gives comparative data for the four pairs of twins.

1. *The question of zygosity.* The available physical data pertaining to the zygosity of these pairs of twins have been included in the case records. There seems to be little reason to doubt the monozygosity of any of the pairs except possibly James and Keith. Dr. Burks was convinced that all were monozygotic. Dr. Leon Hausmann, who examined the hair samples, did not question the monozygosity of any set. Dr. D. C. Rife, who very kindly contributed the analysis of the fingerprints which Dr. Burks had taken, believes on the basis of the fingerprints that the first three sets reported here are identical, but questions the monozygosity of the fourth set, though he considers the evidence insufficient to rule out the possibility. The differences shown in the physical and anthropometric schedules are in the main quite small. In the case of Earl and Frank there was a difference of 24 pounds in weight and some difference in eye pigmentation, hair diameter, and dental occlusion, but differences of the magnitudes found have been noted in other studies of identical twins. In view of what is known about the difficulty of diagnosis based upon examination of fetal membranes, the opinion expressed by the physician who delivered James and Keith (that these twins were not identicals) can be disregarded.

2. *Length and completeness of separation.* The age at time of separation, although not always stated in months, seems to have been close to one year for each pair. Clara and Doris, after they were separated, had no contact with each other until the age of 30, but were in close touch for the following nine years. Earl and Frank after their separation did not meet until they were 15, but their foster families had kept in touch with each other. Gertrude and Helen had their first remembered contact at 13 and thereafter visited each other about twice a year. No mention is made of contact between James and Keith from the time they were separated at about 14 months. For the adult pairs, at least, the separation was long enough and complete enough to permit marked environmental differences to operate.

3. *The magnitude of environmental differences.* For none of the four pairs was there a very extreme difference in the cultural or social-economic level of the environments compared. The greatest difference was in the case of Earl and Frank. Earl's foster father was a college graduate and Frank's was a streetcar conductor of unstated amount of education. Earl graduated from college; Frank attended high school only six months, though later he attended night school for four years. Numerous differences less extreme have been noted in the text and in sections 7 and 8 of this summary.

4. *Differences in tested intelligence.* The Binet mental ages of the three adult pairs differed 17 months for Clara and Doris, 24 months for Earl and Frank, and 28 months for Gertrude and Helen. The respective I.Q. differences are about 10,

TABLE 14

COMPARATIVE DATA FOR FOUR PAIRS OF TWINS

Twins	C	D	E	F	G	H	J	K
Age when tested	39	36	37	37	52	52	4-4, 7	6-6
M.A. (Stanford-Binet)	11-2	9-9[a]	15-4	13-4	10-6	8-2[a]	5-3[b]	5-11[b]
I.Q.	70	61	96	83	66	51	73	91
Community where reared	Moderate size (Urban)	Large Eastern (Urban)	West Coast (Urban, large)	Middle West (Urban, large)	Remote rural	Remote rural	Moderate size Eastern city	Moderate size Eastern city
Home: Child	Only child in foster home; cherished	2 other children in foster home; maltreated	Only child in foster home; well treated; financially secure	Only child in foster home; strong bond with foster mother; financially pressed	Only child in foster home; strong bond with foster mother	Own parents, 2 other children; neglected	Orphanage until after study	Boarding homes; later, only child with protective foster parents
Adult	Stable marriage, 4 children	Shell-shocked husband, 3 children	Successful marriage, no children	Warm marriage ties, 1 child	Drinking husband, 3 children	Fairly stable marriage, 10 children		
Education	5th grade; D taught C to write	Intermittent, barely literate	College graduate	9th grade, night school	6th grade; Intermittent	4th grade; Intermittent	2nd grade orphanage	2nd grade
Health	Similar in childhood; sties, eczema, loss of voice, eye strain, etc.	Many operations; diagnosed psychotic	Similar good health; childhood diseases; hearing and eyesight good	childhood diseases;	Very similar; severe jaundice, rheumatism at same time, extreme obesity.	Died at age 52 of dropsy	Tuberculous knee, recurrent ear infections, defective; Short attention span	Not known
Behavior	Extremely talkative / Cheerful / Spontaneous / Self-controlled / Sociable; Similar in sympathy, sleeping lightly, frankness, neatness, alertness, etc.	Slightly less talkative / More sombre / No inhibitions / Easily upset / Less sociable	Reserved / Moderately sociable / Not trustful / Defensive regarding unfulfilled ambitions[c]; Similar in energy, sympathy, cheerfulness, popularity, etc.	Less reserved / Very sociable / Trustful / Content with modest status[c]	Neither gay nor sombre / Fairly prompt / Speech more extensive; Similar in body handling;[c] occasional sudden laughter	More sombre / Less prompt / Speech more clipped, profane	Similarly unruly, irresponsible, aggressive toward other children[c]; Dramatic play inhibited	Dramatic play spontaneous, imaginative
Miscellaneous	Rorschach indicates disturbance	Rorschach indicates less disturbance	Vocational interest ratings notably similar		Rorschach indicates similar poor adjustment, possible deterioration			

[a] Probably invalid.
[b] The Goodenough test, given to J and K at the age of 6-9, yielded I.Q.'s of 74 and 111, respectively.
[c] Not rated on scale.

13, and 15 points. The differences between Clara and Doris and between Gertrude and Helen may be largely spurious; Doris was tested when she was recovering from a second stroke, and Helen was tested shortly before her death from dropsy. The I.Q. difference of some 13 points between Earl and Frank in all probability reflects the difference in the cultural level of their foster homes and in the amount of schooling they had had. The I.Q. difference between James and Keith varies considerably from test to test. There was some reason to question the validity of J's I.Q. at the time he was studied.

5. *School records.* Although no achievement tests were administered to any of the subjects, it is evident from the records that only Earl and Frank made anything like normal school progress. We have noted above that E graduated from college and that F attended high school briefly and night school for four years. Both Clara and Doris attended school about six years without learning to read or write. D had a tutor for a time when she was 11 but made no progress. After leaving school she worked in educated families and learned to write by her own efforts; many years later (after age 30) she taught C to write. Neither Gertrude nor Helen had much schooling; G completed only the sixth grade and H only the fifth. James and Keith, aged 7 when they were studied, both had poor school records during the first term but K was showing some improvement in his second term.

6. *Occupational histories.* The occupational histories of the three sets of adult twins were about what one would expect in view of their school records and their cultural backgrounds. Clara worked in a factory for a time and later in a hospital; Doris looked after children, washed bottles in a sanitarium, and had various other jobs at a similar level. Earl, after graduating from college, worked one year as a hospital orderly, owned and ran a gas station for some years, later became a salesman, and at the time of the study was manager of a fairly prosperous suburban cafe; his twin, Frank, held various jobs after leaving school at 16, a number of them as tire serviceman or garageman, and for 7 years preceding the time of the study he had been working as a laborer with a utilities company.

The twins Gertrude and Helen did only farm work prior to marriage; after marriage they both picked hops one summer and Helen worked occasionally making clothes for little girls. When they were studied Gertrude was running a rooming house and a grocery store in a small town and Helen was hospitalized with dropsy.

7. *Health histories.* The health histories of Clara and Doris are interesting because of the many similarities and many differences. Common to both were measles, mumps, tonsillectomies, growing pains, menarche at age 11, eczema, sties, visual correction, nervousness, excitability, hysterectomy, and hysterical loss of voice. In addition, C had acute bronchitis at 23, pleurisy and surgical repair of lacerations at 37, and removal of a nerve tumor on the arm at 39. D had a long history of operations and hospitilizations, including removal of adhesions at 14, laparotomy and ovariotomy at 29, fractured coccyx at 36, removal of intestinal adhesions at 38, two strokes at about 39, and hospitalization as a manic-depressive at 40. Three or four years earlier her condition had been diagnosed as "psychosis with psychopathic personality." The illnesses not common to both, though exceptionally numerous for iden-

tical twins, could probably all be accounted for in non-genetic terms if the medical records had been complete.

Earl and Frank were both exceptionally free from ill health of every kind, though Frank had experienced one attack of bronchitis.

The health histories of Gertrude and Helen were strikingly similar: both were small until first pregnancy and thereafter became more and more overweight; both had measles, mumps, and yellow jaundice (this at the same time while living apart); both reached menopause at an early age (36 and 34), and both had acute rheumatism (ages 47 and 51). The one important difference was Helen's heart condition and dropsy, from which she died.

The only significant difference in the health records of the young twins, James and Keith, was J's hospitilization from the age of 14 months to 7 or 8 years with tuberculosis of the knee. It is worth noting, however, that when they were in a boarding home at about the age of one year it was recorded that one slept well, the other poorly, and that one had two teeth, the other none.

8. *Similarities and differences in personality.* The data on personality for the three adult pairs included descriptive ratings and comments by Dr. Burks on 12 traits, ratings of each subject on 24 traits by two or more persons, and the Rorschach protocols. Less information was available for the young pair, James and Keith.

Clara and Doris were much alike in 7 of the 12 descriptive traits and markedly unlike in health, poise, and mood. In the trait ratings they were judged by both raters as markedly unlike only in health, reaction to pain, and trustfulness. Surprisingly, it was Doris who appeared

"less disturbed" as judged by the Rorschach responses; it suggests that when the test was given she was not in either phase of her manic-depressive cycle. Why Doris became insane and suffered strokes cannot be determined from the records available. It will be recalled, however, that as a child she was treated harshly and punished severely, that her marriage was less happy than Clara's, and that she had many more illnesses and surgical operations than Clara.

Earl and Frank did not differ greatly on any of the 12 descriptive traits, but on the trait ratings given by their wives it appears that Frank is the more social and outgoing in his attitudes. On the Rorschach both are judged by one Rorschach worker to be above average in intelligence (another worker questions this), and "fairly well" to "probably adequately" adjusted. "Weak ego" is also noted for both, but Earl is characterized as self-conscious and Frank as responsive. For these twins, scores on the Strong Vocational Interest Test are available. Both made scores of from A to B— for the occupations of Y.M.C.A. physical director, production manager, social-science teacher, mathematics-science teacher, policeman, office worker, and sales manager. Earl's scores were higher by two or more scale-steps for Y.M.C.A. secretary, personnel manager, and city school superintendent; Frank's were higher by two or more scale-steps for carpenter, chemist, aviator, printer, farmer, real estate salesman, and purchasing agent. The scores for occupational level and for masculinity-femininity were closely similar. Altogether, the proportion of large differences in the Strong scores was very small.

Gertrude and Helen showed no marked differences either in the descriptive or in the trait ratings. On the Rorschach both were judged to be "poorly adjusted"; and one Rorschach worker noted evidences of "deterioration"; Gertrude was characterized as "insecure" and Helen as "sick" and "inadequate" as to personality. (The test was given not long before Helen's death from dropsy.) Helen's marriage was happier than Gertrude's, notwithstanding the greater financial strain resulting from her much larger family.

James and Keith were not rated on personality traits, but it is noted both were described as very aggressive toward other children. Keith was a little more self sufficient in terms of the Vineland Social Maturity Scale, and in dramatic play with toys he showed far more initiative, imaginativeness, and tendency to verbalization. These differences could well have been due to James' long illness and hospitalization.

9. In conclusion it may be said that despite the fairly long-continued separation of the twin pairs, the data reviewed do not offer any very dramatic evidence of the relative influences of nature and nurture. The physical similarities are more numerous and more marked than are commonly found for fraternal twins of the same sex and thus confirm the conclusions from earlier studies regarding the operation of genetic factors. There are several instances also of the presumptive influence of environmental factors, and these would probably have been more numerous if the intra-pair environments had differed more radically. The one difference in tested intelligence that seems clearly associated with cultural difrences in the foster homes is found for Earl and Frank. The fact that Doris became a manic-depressive mental patient while her twin did not could have been the result of environmental factors. The same may be said regarding the heart condition and dropsy which Helen contracted but which her twin escaped. As both had suffered acute rheumatism, a disease which sometimes does and sometimes does not involve heart complications, it is probable that Helen's heart condition had this origin and that her dropsy was a cardiac edema. That James but not Keith contracted a tubercular infection certainly need not imply a constitutional difference. In the case of all the adult pairs there is plausible evidence of linkage between minor personality differences and intra-pair differences in experiences encountered in childhood and youth. This is especially true of Clara and Doris, and, to a lesser extent, of Gertrude and Helen.

Number   Name   Date
Interviewer

DESCRIPTIVE RATING SCALE
Based on direct observation during interview

PHYSIQUE (Body build apart from height)
1. Strikingly overweight or obese
2. Sturdy
3. Neither sturdy nor frail
4. Rather frail
5. Very frail and underweight

MANNER (Impression of masculinity-femininity)
1. Markedly masculine (direct, assertive, decisive, economy of gesture, etc.)
2. Quite masculine
3. Neither masculine nor feminine
4. Quite feminine
5. Markedly feminine (coy approach, tentative, helpless, fluttery, etc.)

EXPRESSION (Clarity)
1. Excellent vocabulary, precise meanings
2. Good and rather accurate choice of words
3. No trouble making himself understood
4. Poor use of words
5. Very confused mode of speech

TALKATIVENESS
1. Extremely talkative; hard for interviewer to find opening
2. Quite talkative; volunteers considerable information
3. Gives full verbal responses, but initiates little
4. Laconic; brief replies
5. Very inarticulate; hard for interviewer to elicit responses

NEATNESS (in dress and person)
1. Fastidious
2. Rather painstaking
3. Neat and clean
4. Careless, disorderly
5. Unkempt; shabby

COURTESY
1. Elegant
2. Attends to social forms of courtesy
3. Good manners, but no emphasis on social forms
4. Sometimes discourteous
5. Aggressively rude

ALERTNESS
1. Highly stimulated by interview; follows every point intently
2. Wide-awake, good contact with situation
3. Interest fluctuates; has to be aroused by interviewer
4. Rather abstracted and sluggish
5. Continually absorbed and preoccupied; little contact established

FRANKNESS
1. Very frank and open
2. Few topics evaded; usually quite frank
3. Frank on a few topics, evasive on others
4. Seldom speaks openly
5. Marked sense of privacy; resistance to interview

FRIENDLINESS

1. Eager to please; tries to elicit approval
2. Quite friendly; outgoing; enjoys interview
3. Neither friendly nor unfriendly
4. Shows occasional hostility toward interviewer
5. Marked hostility during interview

POISE

1. Very well-poised and calm
2. Good self-control; occasional hesitancy in speech or fidgety gesture
3. Somewhat over-active; defensive or over-anxious etc. in speech
4. Easily upset; often seems on verge of going to pieces
5. Disorganized behavior; severe agitation during considerable part of interview

CHEERFULNESS

1. Constant gaiety and over-optimism
2. Light-hearted; cheerful tone
3. Neither sombre nor gay
4. Rather sombre; pessimistic
5. Very sombre or sad; difficult to elicit smile or laugh

EMOTIONAL EXPRESSIVENESS

1. Extreme emotional expressiveness; almost no inhibition
2. Spontaneous in expression of anger, joy, desires, etc.
3. Fairly expressive, but few visible signs of excitement
4. Rather reserved; seems to avoid emotional expression, but occasionally unbends
5. Extremely reserved and inhibited

APPENDIX B

Number   Name   Date
Interviewer

Rated by
Relation (Parent, Friend, etc.)

TRAIT RATING SCALE

PHYSICAL AND SENSORY TRAITS

General health: S D.*

  1. Very robust
  2. No general health handicaps, not affected by variations in sleep or diet
  3. Good except when subjected to unusual strain
  4. Requires considerable special attention
  5. Health is serious problem

Physical energy: S D.

  1. Abounding vitality, seldom tires
  2. Large amount but sometimes "overdoes"
  3. Good endurance for routine activity but soon fatigued by strenuous activity
  4. Unable to carry out any strenuous activities
  5. Tires at slight exertion, exhausted at end of day

Amount of activity: S D.

  1. Extremely restless and fidgety, almost never still when awake
  2. Decidedly restless and fidgety but has short periods of repose
  3. Free from restlessness for an hour or more when absorbed in an occupation
  4. Restless and fidgety only at special times (when tired, etc.)
  5. Almost never restless and fidgety

Appetite: S D.

  1. Comes to table ravenous, looks forward to meals
  2. Excellent appetite, eats with gusto
  3. Ordinary, shows mild enjoyment of food
  4. Indifferent to food
  5. Constant effort to get him to eat

Food preferences: S D.

Food aversions: S D.

Allergies (foods, pollen, animals, other)

Sleep (depth): S D. An hour or two after falling asleep:

  1. Can be roused only with great difficulty
  2. Not disturbed by ordinary activity in his room
  3. Not disturbed by ordinary activity outside his closed door
  4. Distant noises of household waken him
  5. Wakens at slight rustle

Sleep (amount): S D. Hours

Vision: S D.

Hearing: S D.

Reaction to pain: S D.

  1. Stoical even if badly hurt
  2. Shows signs of distress only when badly hurt (broken bone, operation, stunning blow)
  3. Shows mild signs of distress at ordinary mishaps (cut finger, hot food, etc.)
  4. Reacts strongly to ordinary mishaps
  5. Shows signs of distress at pin prick, light pinch, etc.

---

* S denotes similar; D, different.

GENERAL CHARACTERISTICS

Sympathy (for family) (for friends): S D.

1. Strongly aroused by suffering, abhors cruelty
2. Goes out of his way to help another in trouble
3. Fairly sympathetic, but easily distracted from suffering
4. Usually unmoved by the predicaments of others
5. Often enjoys the predicaments of others

Perseverance: S D.

1. Seldom abandons even a distasteful task which he feels obligated to complete
2. Works for weeks on a task which interests him
3. Works for only a few days on an interesting task
4. Seldom shows day to day continuity
5. Gives up at slightest difficulty

Self-assertion (at home) (in group): S D.

1. Eager to take charge of affairs and impose own will
2. Enjoys managing, but not against their will
3. Stands up for own desires, but does not try to manage others
4. Submissive, concedes to wishes of others
5. Extremely submissive, follows suggestions without question

Talkativeness (at home) (in group): S D.

1. Chatters almost continually
2. Very talkative, volunteers something many times a day
3. Fairly talkative, responds to overtures of others
4. Talks rather little
5. Speech has to be "dragged out of him."

Promptness: S D.

1. Likes to get things done ahead of time
2. Almost always prompt
3. Occasionally delays a little
4. Late about as often as prompt
5. Habitually tardy

Speed of decision: S D.

1. Extremely impulsive, seldom stops to think before he acts
2. Makes up his mind after brief consideration
3. Weighs various possibilities deliberately
4. Goes over and over possibilities
5. Puts off decision as long as he can

Jealousy (spouse): S D.

1. Usually pleased at interest shown in others
2. Seldom shows resentment of interest shown in others
3. Occasionally resentful if he feels left out
4. Often shows resentment of interest in others
5. Persistent and intense attitude of jealousy.

Generosity: S D.

1. Enjoys sharing or giving away possessions or money
2. Enjoys sharing only with his close associates
3. Fairly generous in small matters but hesitates to give up valued possessions
4. Rather possessive, has to be urged to share
5. Very possessive, difficult to get him to share or give

Self-consciousness: S D.

1. Extremely shy and bashful of strangers
2. Shy at first, less so after 5 or 10 minutes
3. Slightly reticent in presence of strangers

4. Responsive, no noticeable signs of self-consciousness
5. Forgets himself completely, entering into occasion

Competitiveness: S D.

1. Extremely eager to win games, unhappy when he loses
2. Very eager to win, but not discouraged by losing
3. Fairly eager to win, but enjoys the success of others
4. Indifferent to winning, cares only for fun of game
5. Prefers to play with and learn from players better than himself

Sense of responsibility: S D.

1. Eager to take responsibility and carry it to successful conclusion
2. Assumes responsibility when necessary
3. Usually responsible when impressed with importance of obligation, but lax on minor matters
4. Rather irresponsible, often forgets his obligations
5. Has to be constantly reminded to carry out his obligations

Sense of humor: S D.

1. Very quick to see the funny side of things even when the joke is on himself
2. Enjoys funny stories and episodes, less amused by jokes on himself
3. Usually sees the point of a joke
4. Often has to have funny stories explained to him
5. Serious-minded, almost nothing seems funny to him

Irritability: S D.

1. Extremely quick-tempered, often flies off the handle over small irritations
2. Loses temper easily, but not without some provocation
3. Loses temper when others deliberately annoy him
4. Will endure many annoyances without losing temper
5. Almost never loses temper

Cheerfulness: S D.

1. Prevailing mood radiant, great zest
2. Cheerful and optimistic
3. Fairly contented, rarely complains
4. Tends to be dissatisfied, often complains
5. Unhappy, wistful, or dissatisfied with life

Courage (physical): S D.

1. Extremely daring, seldom deterred by risks
2. Meets situations courageously but avoids unnecessary risks
3. Fairly courageous in ordinary situations, loses courage in danger
4. Rather timid, tends to avoid risks
5. Very timid, apprehensive of trivial risks.

Courage (moral): S D.

1. Stands up for what he believes in, regardless of consequences
2. Will suffer considerable antagonism for sake of convictions
3. Doesn't mind upholding convictions if others don't ridicule, etc.
4. Seldom upholds convictions against others who differ
5. Shrinks from having others differ with him.

Facing facts: S D.

1. Unusual capacity to accept disappointments, recognize own limitations
2. Tries to be reasonable but emotions interfere with thinking just at the start
3. Occasionally resorts to pretences, daydreams, temper, etc. to avoid unpleasant necessities
4. Marked reluctance to face unpleasant facts
5. Almost never faces unpleasant facts squarely

Trustfulness: S D.

1. Trusts other people's motives so thoroughly that others can often impose on him
2. Very trustful unless given strong cause for distrust

3. Fairly trustful, but quick to see false motives
4. Rather distrustful, has to be "shown" first
5. Misinterprets motives, looks for trouble

INTERESTS AND ATTITUDES

Sociality: S D.

1. Extremely social, wants to be with friends in nearly all leisure time
2. Very social, wants to spend much time with friends
3. Fairly social, but content with own resources
4. Rather unsocial, prefers solitary occupations
5. Very unsocial, prefers solitude and objects to spending time with others

Leadership: S D.

1. Extremely successful in getting others to follow his plans
2. Others usually welcome his suggestions
3. Others usually take the lead
4. Rarely exerts influence upon plans of associates
5. Quite lacking in leadership traits

Popularity (associates of same sex): S D.

1. Very much sought after, has many close friends
2. Often sought after, well liked by most
3. Others usually welcome his company
4. Others usually indifferent to his presence
5. Others usually manage to leave him out

Popularity (associates of opposite sex): S D.

1. Very much sought after, has many close friends
2. Often sought after, well liked by most
3. Others usually welcome his company
4. Others usually indifferent to his presence
5. Others usually manage to leave him out

Attitude toward opposite sex:

Athletic interests: S D.

1. Would rather play at outdoor games and sports than anything else
2. Very fond of athletics, often participates
3. Likes to play three or four times a month
4. Indifferent, plays only when urged
5. Dislikes athletics, avoids sports

Emotional dependence on family: S D.

1. Seems almost indifferent to sympathy, encouragement or advice
2. Not dependent, but values companionship
3. Occasionally seeks encouragement, etc.
4. Usually seeks this several times a day
5. Very dependent, feels lost when presence of family is withdrawn

Special abilities in any of the following: (Describe)

Art work
Art appreciation
Singing
Playing an instrument
Musical appreciation
Appreciation of natural beauty
Mechanical ability
Dramatic art
Literary composition
Athletics
Domestic Arts
Other special abilities

APPENDIX C

Rorschach Psychograms
Twins Clara and Doris

Twin C		Twin D	
R	15?/3?	R	15/4
RT	7¼'/2'	RT	3½' plus ½' plus
F+ %	70?,	F+%	72?
F%	60?	F%	60?
A%	60	A%	66
P	3 (plus 1 doubtful)	P	4
W	5?	W	3
W(S)	1?	W(S)	0
D	8?	D	12
Dd	1?	Dd	0
F	10? (3 are poor form)	F	11 (3 are poor Form)
M	0 (1 movement tendency)	M	0 (2 movement tendencies?)
CF	1, or more	CF	3?
F(C)	2?	F(C)	1?
COF	2?	COF	0
A	5	A	8
Ad	4	Ad	2
A anat	1	Hd	2
Anat	1	Nat	2
Nat.	3	Blood	1
Mask	1		

1 failure (X)
Approach .... W-(D)-Dd(?)

Succession .... ?,

Experience balance ...oM(2MT):
         1 or more Sum C

1 near failure (X)
Approach .... (W)-D

Succession .... ?

Experience balance .... oM(1MT?):
         1 Sum C

APPENDIX D

Rorschach Psychograms
Twins Earl and Frank

Twin E		Twin F	
R 10/3		R 14/3	
RT ....?		RT ....8'/2'	
F+ % 66		F+ % 88	
F% 60		F% 57	
A% 50		A% 57	
P 2		P 4	(plus a near P in V)
W 10		W 9	
D 0		D 4	
		Unknown 1	
F 6	(2 are poor form)	F 9	(1 is poor form)
F(C) 1		F(C) ....2?	
FCO 0		FCO 1	
CF 1		CF 1	
C/F 2	("arbitrary" use of color)	C/F 0	
		Unknown 1	
A 4		A 7	
Ad 1		Ad 1	
Anat 3		Anat 0	
Geog 1		Geog 0	
Nat 1		Nat 2	
		Hd 1	
		Emblem 1	
		A scene 1	
		Scene 1	
Approach ......W!		Approach .... W-((D))	
Succession ....?		Succession ....?	
Experience balance ....O M: 3 sum color		Experience balance ....oM(2MT): 3 Sum C (?)	

Perspective used in VI
Color remark in VIII

APPENDIX E

Rorschach Psychograms
Twins Gertrude and Helen

Twin G		Twin H	
R	11/2	R	12/4
RT	15'/3¼'	RT	4' plus/1' plus
F+ %	50	F+ %	36
F%	54	F%	36
A%	18	A%	25
Anat%	27	Anat%	50
P	3 (plus near P in I)	P	1
W	7?	W	8
W(S)	1?	W(S)	0
D	2	D	0
Dd	0	Dd	3
S	0	S	1
Unknown	1	Unknown	0
F	6 (3 are poor Form)	F	11 (7 are poor Form?)
F(C)	1?	F(C)	1?
FCO	1	FCO	0
CF	2 (both poor Form)	CF	0
Unknown	1	Unknown	0
A	1	A	1
Ad	1	Ad	1?
Aanat	2	Aanat	0
(H)	2	(H)	0
Hd	0	Hd	2
Anat	3	Anat	6
Nat	2	Nat	0
		Meat	1

Twin G

1 failure .... (VIII)
Approach .... W-((D))
Succession .... ?

Experience balance ..... 0 M: 2 sum color?

Twin H

no failure
Approach .... W-Dd
                        =
Succession .... possible trend to confused?
Experience balance ..... 0 M: 0 color

BIBLIOGRAPHY

1. BURKS, BARBARA. A study of identical twins reared apart under differing types of family relationships. (In) McNemar, Q. and Merrill, M. A. (Editors). *Studies in personality*. New York, McGraw-Hill, 1942. Pp. 35-69.

2. CARTER, H. D. Ten years of research on twins: Contributions to the nature-nurture problem. *Yearbook*, Nat'l Soc. for Study of Education, 1940, Part I, pp. 235-255. Bloomington, Illinois, Public School Publishing Co.

3. CARTER, H. D. Case studies of mature identical twins. *Ped. Sem. and J. Genet. Psychol.*, 1934, 44, 154-174.

4. GALTON, F. *Inquiries into human faculty and its development*. New York, Macmillan, 1883.

5. GESELL, A. The developmental psychology of twins. (In) *A Handbook of child psychology*, C. Murchison (editor). Clark University Press, Worcester, Mass., 1931, pp. 158-203.

6. HILGARD, J. R. The effect of early and delayed practice on memory and motor performances studied by the method of co-twin control. *Genet. Psychol. Monog.*, 1933, 14, 493-567.

7. KOMAI, T. AND FUKUOKO, G. A set of dichorionic identical triplets. *J. Heredity*, 1931, 22, 233-243.

8. McGRAW, M. B. *Growth: a study of Johnny and Jimmy*. New York, Appleton-Century Co., 1935, p. 319.

9. McNEMAR, Q. Special review of Newman, Freeman, and Holzinger's *Twins: A study of heredity and environment. Psychol. Bull.*, 1938, 35, 237-249.

10. NEWMAN, H. H. Studies of human twins: I, methods of diagnosing monozygotic and dizygotic twins. *Biol. Bull.*, 1928, 55, 283-297.

11. NEWMAN, H. H., FREEMAN, F., and HOLZINGER, K. J. *Twins: A study of heredity and environment*. Univ. of Chicago Press, Chicago, 1937, p. 369.

12. ROSANOFF, A. J., HANDY, L. M., and PLESSET, I. R. The etiology of manic-depressive syndromes with special reference to their occurrence in twins. *Amer. J. Psychiat.*, 1935, 91, 725-762.

13. ROSANOFF, A. J., HANDY, L. M., and PLESSET, I. R. The etiology of mental deficiency with special reference to its occurrence in twins: A chapter in the genetic history of human intelligence. *Psychol. Monog.*, 1937, 48, pp. 1-137.

14. SONTAG, L. W., and NELSON, V. L. A study of identical triplets: Part I, Comparison of the physical and mental traits of a set of monozygotic dichorionic triplets. *J. Heredity*, 1933, 24, 474-480.

15. STRAYER, L. C. Language and growth: The relative efficacy of early and deferred vocabulary training, studied by the method of co-twin control. *Genet. Psychol. Monog.*, 1930, 8, 209-319.

A FINAL FOLLOW-UP STUDY OF
ONE HUNDRED ADOPTED CHILDREN

Marie Skodak
Harold M. Skeels

The Journal of Genetic Psychology, 1949, **75**, 85-125.

A FINAL FOLLOW-UP STUDY OF ONE HUNDRED ADOPTED CHILDREN[*][1]

Iowa Child Welfare Research Station, State University of Iowa

MARIE SKODAK AND HAROLD M. SKEELS

A. HISTORICAL BACKGROUND

While there have been a substantial number of studies reporting the intelligence status of foster children (16, 19, 20, 21, 28, 30) repeated evaluations of the same children into adolescence or early adulthood have been rare. This report constitutes what will probably be a final chapter in a long range study in which the same group of adopted children have had intelligence tests on four occasions. Reports of the results of the first three examinations (24, 25, 26) provoked a great deal of discussion and many questions regarding the *IQ* and the rôle of heredity in determining the eventual status of the children. The intensity of the debates over the relative functions of environment and heredity has dissipated in the past decade as evidence from other studies has shown that modifiability of intelligence is not an unusual phenomenon (13, 15, 22, 23, 28).

As it now appears unlikely that children in this study will be revisited, this report will include details and certain raw data which may be of value to others contemplating similar research. Many problems remain unsolved and an account of practical difficulties may expedite the inevitable preliminary steps in other studies.

The study originally began, not as a research, but as a service project. This difference in orientation accounts for some of the gaps in information, for the techniques selected and for the general planning, which might have been done otherwise had the project been conceived primarily as research. However, there is a practical question of whether the study could have been accomplished at all had it been weighted down with all the scientific safeguards which the perspective of 15 years of study might have suggested. Because of its simplicity and apparent innocuousness, the study was accepted by lay people, parents, and children with a minimum of explanation.

[*]Accepted for publication by Robert R. Sears of the Editorial Board, and received in the Editorial Office on December 30, 1948.

[1]This research was conducted under the auspices of the Iowa Child Welfare Research Station, State University of Iowa. Funds for this unit were provided by the Parents Institute, Inc.

85

This study was made possible when the Board of Control of State Institutions of Iowa instituted psychological services in connection with its Children's Division in 1934. The staff consisted of Harold M. Skeels, Director and Psychologist, and Marie Skodak, Assistant Psychologist. Liaison relations with the Child Welfare Research Station of the State University of Iowa were established through the half-time appointment of Dr. Skeels with that institution. Through coöperative relations with the staff of the Child Welfare Research Station it was possible to amass a substantial body of reliable data on the mental status of the residents of the children's institutions and also to free the regular staff members of the Children's Division for work outside the institutions.

One of the major extramural projects was the examination of all children who had been placed in foster homes and who were about to be legally adopted. While children of all ages were involved, by far the majority were younger children who had been placed as infants. The policies of the institution were determined by an appointed Board who were not selected for academic qualifications or experience in social work or psychology. At that time, neither the Board, nor the institutional staffs, nor the field workers who supervised the children included a single person who had had any formal training or who could be described as a "qualified trained social worker." The head of the Children's Division was a qualified person but was relatively powerless to institute so-called modern social work methods in the face of various pressures. The children were accepted for care in institutions, cared for while in the institutions, and placed in free, wage, or adopting homes largely on the basis of "good common sense" as well as the good judgment or whims of the workers as modified by prevailing pressures or policies. While this rather casual modus operandi produced miscarriages of optimum planning, these were not as numerous as might be feared. The general atmosphere with regard to the younger children was one of sentimental pity rather than punitive aggressiveness, though the latter was not uncommon with the older children. The pressure of physical overcrowding and the demand for children for adoption together with the generally unsophisticated and homey attitude, resulted in a tendency to place children in foster homes at the earliest possible time. Since there were no provisions for boarding funds, the following alternatives were available: (a) Wage homes, where in return for services the child received care and some weekly wage or allowance. These were obviously the older children who had usually had some preliminary training in the institution. (b) Free homes, where the child was "treated like one of the family" without legal adoption. He remained a ward of the state, could be removed at the discretion of the supervisor, be returned by the family, or eventually be adopted. Children of all ages were so placed, but the majority were in the elementary school ages. (*c*) Adoptive homes, wherein, after a year of probationary residence, the child was legally adopted. During the probationary residence the child was visited several times by the field worker to determine the adequacy of the care the child received, the compatibility of the parents and child, and to check on the child's development. While children of all ages were placed in adoptive homes, the great majority were infants and preschoolers and in the majority of cases legal adoption was completed within two years after placement. After adoption there were no more official relationships between the family and the institution or the Children's Division.

The extramural services of the psychologists on the one hand provided examination and consultation facilities for those homes where behavior problems were encountered, primarily with older children, and on the other hand offered psychological evaluation of children about to be adopted. The primary purpose of this was to guard against the adoption of mentally retarded children as well as to offer the services of a child development specialist to aid in problems which the adopting parents might encounter or might anticipate.

Through the coöperative arrangements with the University it was possible to offer a similar service during 1934-36 to the Iowa Children's Home Society, a private state-wide child placing agency. This organization, with a better trained staff and boarding home facilities, also placed a substantial number of children in early infancy and arranged for the pre-adoption examination as an additional service to the adopting parents.

Another extramural service performed by the psychologists was the examination of children, and occasionally the mothers of illegitimate infants, where there was a probability that the children would become wards of the state. This preliminary information facilitated the proper institutional assignment and subsequent planning for the children. Since the examinations were frequently conducted in the homes or at a nearby school, the psychologists had an invaluable opportunity to see at first hand the home, neighborhood, and often the relatives constituting the child's early environment or his social-economic heritage.

The foster homes into which the children were placed became available through a number of sources. The child-placing programs of the State Board of Control and the Iowa Children's Home Society were well known throughout the state since the majority of agency placements were made through them. Both organizations had travelling workers, assigned to certain areas whose duties included: (*a*) The supervision of children placed in wage, free, and adoptive homes to insure proper care, protection, education, and home relationships. (*b*) The evaluation of homes and foster families for children in terms of financial resources, physical set-up, attitudes toward children, future demands on children. (*c*) The development of community interest in child care, adoption, and placement.

Parents interested in adoption would write directly to the state office, the institution, agency, or one of the field workers. The application blanks contained only the minimum information regarding the type of child desired, the family's financial and vocational status, and the names of at least three references. The field worker would then visit the home, interview the applicants, evaluate the physical and emotional resources and the possible future demands with regard to education and vocation. References were contacted by mail, phone, or visit. The degree of investigation varied. Families who were well known or who were manifestly capable were accepted with less scrutiny than families in more modest circumstances or where there were questions regarding the present or future adequacy of the home. It is not known what proportion of applicants were rejected, but in many cases families were dissuaded from completing an application if it seemed unlikely that a child would be placed with them.

On the whole the foster families were above the average of their communities in economic security and educational and cultural status. They were highly regarded by the town's business, professional, and religious leaders and usually had demonstrated a long-time interest in children through church or community activities.

The placement procedure in both organizations was essentially similar. In the state agency after the application was accepted the family was placed on the waiting list and their name was considered at the monthly staff meetings when assignments were made. At these case conferences, attended by the head of the Children's Division, the superintendent of the institution, the psychologists, and head nurse, the available babies and available homes were discussed. Factors in the assignment included religion, sex, age, color or complexion, physique, medical history, and report of the family background. Pre-placement psychological examinations were not available for the children in this study. In many instances the information about the child's family background was so meagre that it was of little or no value. The primary factors in matching were the stipulations of the foster parents regarding religion, sex, and hair color in that order.

This method of placement of children from relatively inferior socio-economic backgrounds into substantial homes thus provided the setting for the study. Perusal of the child's social history as recorded in the institution and comparison with the field's agent's pre-placement evaluation of the adopting home was disheartening. It did not seem possible that children with such meager possibilities, as projected from the intellectual, academic, and occupational attainments of their parents, could measure up to the demands of cultured, educated parents. Yet careful examination of one child after another showed none of the retardation or misplacement which might have been anticipated. Following a preliminary survey of results (24) it was decided that a follow-up study was imperative, and the coöperation of the foster parents was solicited and received.

B. DESCRIPTION OF THE SAMPLE

A detailed report of the population of which the children in this study constitute a sample was presented in 1945 (26).

In general there are three levels of society from which children for adoptive placements originate. It is believed that children from culturally, socially, and educationally superior homes tend to be placed among relatives or in adoptive homes through various private sources. Because of the extreme difficulty of identifying and locating such placements, no studies have been made of the subsequent development or adjustment of these children, nor is the exact number of these children known to official agencies. At what may be described as the second socio-economic level, the children tend to become the charges of private or semi-private child caring or placing agencies. Many of these children's aid and protective societies exercise considerable control over their intake. Policies may, for instance, preclude the acceptance of children of mentally defective parents, or of other children who may be judged "unplaceable" or in need of care which that particular organization does not feel equipped to offer. These organizations tend to draw from the various middle economic classes but also have a fair number of children from extremely ineffective homes as the study by Roe and Burks indicates (21). The third group of children from the lowest socio-economic levels are usually known to various public welfare agencies. The public agencies, in contrast to the private ones, are usually obligated to accept all children committed to their care and naturally receive children no other agency feels able to accept. There is no doubt that the general social, vocational, and adjustment level of the parents of children committed to public agency care is substantially below that of children who become wards of private agencies or who are adopted through private channels.

It is necessary to differentiate between observations regarding the natural families of infants committed for care and the natural families of preschool or older children. All studies which have published reports on the education of the true parents of children placed in foster homes agree that the true parents of the older children are more apt to be inadequate, unstable, retarded, unemployed, in other words, less competent by any criterion of measurement which has been used. The social factors behind this difference are not difficult to identify. The youngest children, the infants, are primarily illegitimate children. In the first place, their parents are relatively younger. While parents-out-of-wedlock show various signs of emotional instability, the psychoses, alcoholism, and cumulating effects of maladjustment characterizing the parents of older dependent children have not yet indelibly affixed themselves. With the rest of their generation, the younger parents enjoy higher educational opportunities together with the dubious benefits of being "lifted" from grade to grade on the basis of physical size rather than academic accomplishment. Vocationally it is understandable that an 18-year-old youth is a farm hand or truck driver's helper, while an adult of 40 on the same job is prima facie scored well down on the scale of occupational success. The young illegitimate parents have not had the accumulating frustration of economic deprivation, children in unwanted numbers, and the growing weight of community disapproval of their inefficient way of living. For many it is the first, and often the only, social transgression and after this experience many, perhaps even the majority of illegitimate parents, go on to establish secure, socially acceptable homes and families. A study of what happens to illegitimate parents who decide to establish a family together, as compared to those who release their child, may shed some interesting light on the factors which operate to produce the poorer histories among the older children as compared to the younger. There is a significant socio-economic difference between the parents of the younger and older groups of children who become dependent. It does not necessarily follow, however, that this difference is genetically determined.

1. Subjects of This Study

The criteria for inclusion in this study were as follows: (a) The child was placed in an adoptive home under the age of six months. (b) The child had been given an intelligence test prior to November, 1936, and after one year's residence in the adoptive home. (c) Some information, though of variable amount and reliability, existed concerning the natural and the adoptive parents. (d) The child was white, of North European background (it so happened that no children of South European, Latin, or other social backgrounds met the other criteria either).

In this study all of the children were received for care as infants. The Iowa Soldiers' Orphan's Home, identified as the public agency, was the placing agency in 76 per cent of the cases and the Iowa Children's Home Society, a state-wide, private, non-sectarian organization placed 21 per cent. The remaining three children were privately placed and were included because they were available and met the criteria set up for the other children.

It was earlier pointed out (26) that 96.6 per cent of the 319 children committed to the two agencies under the age of six months between 1933-1937, were placed in adoptive homes. In only four cases was the child withheld from adoptive placement because of poor family history. The remaining seven had serious health problems. Since the majority of the children originally in the study had been placed during this period, and the remainder had been placed earlier during a time when the policies regarding family background had been even more lenient, it was concluded that the children in the study were representative of all those placed by these organizations.

During 1934-36, when the mental testing program was coördinated for the two agencies, and 1933-37 for the public agency alone, it was found that 90 per cent of the children placed under six months of age had been given at least one intelligence test. The mean IQ of this group was 119, slightly above the mean IQ of 116 achieved by the members of the follow-up group on the first examination during the same calendar years.

It was evident that the group of children who constituted the first sample were representative of the available children since there was no systematic withholding of numbers of children because of poor histories, nor was there a group with lower initial intelligence test scores who were excluded from the study.

In the first follow-up report (25), out of a total of 180 children who met the criteria of age at placement, race and date of examination, it was possible to retest 152 children during 1937-38. On the third examination 139 children were seen during 1940-41 (26) and the fourth and final visit in 1946 resulted in the present sample of 100. The major factor in the reduction of the size of the sample has been time and expense. The families, all originally in Iowa, are now scattered over many states and Canada. To locate and visit the 100 children in the 10 weeks available for the study, it was necessary to drive over 12,000 miles even though accurate addresses were available and careful preliminary arrangements had been made with planned appointments acceptable for the parents and the child.

a.   Losses between Test I and Test II.   A total of 180 children under six months of age had had an intelligence test prior to November, 1936. The first re-examinations were given between December of 1936 and October of 1937. A few children were excluded because less than a year had elapsed since the first examination, but the majority were dropped because travel schedules and the convenience of the family did not happen to coincide. Four families did not wish to coöperate further. Twenty-two families either could not be located, were known to have left the state, or could not be conveniently scheduled for retests.

b.   Losses between Test II and Test III.   Between 1937 and the third examination in the summers of 1939 and 1940, the sample decreased from 154 to 139. The 15 children who dropped out of the study at this point included 10 who had moved out of the state, four whose families refused to coöperate further, and one who was returned to the institution because of the cruelty and neglect of the foster parents.

c.   Losses between Test III and Test IV.   Between 1940 and 1946 World War II was fought, and research was immobilized by gas and tire rationing and the universal shortage of professional personnel. A fortunate combination of circumstances freed the author (M.S.) who has given the majority of the tests, for a 10-week period. The preliminary planning and a preliminary registered-mail inquiry, with a questionnaire to be returned by the family, facilitated the optimum utilization of time. A copy of the letter and questionnaire may be found in the Appendix. At the time of the fourth examination, seven additional families declined to coöperate further, eight had moved from the state, two were contacted but could not be scheduled because of various conflicts, and the remaining 22 did not respond or could not be reached by registered mail through their 1940 address. On the basis of the letters received from the parents who had moved and from previous knowledge of the families from whom no response was received, it is estimated that approximately 20 of these children could have been seen had time and funds permitted.

The comparisons between the continuous group of 100 and those who dropped out at the various retest points, are given in Table 1.

These figures account for the original 180 children who met the qualifications for age at placement in an adoptive home and date of first examination. Systematic selection which would influence the character of the final group of 100 is not evident from the comparisons between the mean *IQ*'s of the group

TABLE 1

	Test I	Test II	Test III
Continuous Group (N 100)	117	112	115
Dropped after 1940 (N 39)	113	107	110
Dropped after 1937 (N 15)	114	111	
Dropped after 1936 (N 26)	120		

at the various re-examination periods. The standard deviations for all means are large, ranging from 11.9 to 17.2, and none of the differences is statistically significant.

It may be concluded that this group of 100 children is probably representative of the total group placed by these agencies at comparable ages, and that conclusions based on the pattern of mental development of these children are probably applicable to others with similar experience and social backgrounds and placed under similar circumstances into comparable homes.

2. Test Techniques

The purpose throughout the study was to secure the most reliable and valid measure of the child's intellectual ability at the time of the examination. On first examination the children ranged from 11 months to six years in age with 78 per cent of the children between one and three years. Four children had been placed at a few days of age and were tested shortly before the expiration of the one-year observation period. The 1916 Stanford-Binet was suitable for use with the 19 per cent over three years of age and was occasionally used with younger children who were obviously accelerated in mental development. The Kuhlman Binet was routinely used with all children under three years, and occasionally as a clinical supplement with some children over three.

The re-examinations were begun in 1936 when the Revised Stanford-Binet was not generally available and the 1916 revision was consequently used. In this series of tests, although 17 per cent of the children were under 3-0 years of age, they were all over 2-6 and sufficiently accelerated to make the 1916 Stanford-Binet a usable test. Therefore, all test scores reported for the second examination were based on the 1916 revision.

When the third examination was scheduled in 1939-40, the question of "best test" was raised. From the standpoint of fatigue and future rapport, it seemed advisable to limit the number of tests given and the 1916 revision was again selected. Survey of the literature (7, 14, 18) showed that between 5 and 11 years, the ages of these children at the third examination, the results of the 1916 and 1937 scales were most nearly identical. Not only had the 1916 test been used in the earlier examinations, but it also had been used in examinations of the mothers and a few of the fathers of the children. Direct comparisons of test scores were thus made possible without getting into the knotty problems of comparability of standardization of the different revisions. The problems of such a long-time research underscore the need for an intelligence test which results in comparable scores at all ages.

When the fourth and last examination was scheduled in 1946, the children were between 11 and 17 years of age. In view of the problems surrounding the 1916 revision at these ages, it was decided to impose on the good nature of the subjects and give both the 1916 revision and Form L of the 1937 revision. This set up a program involving approximately two hours, often a great deal more, if there was marked scatter on either or both tests. Since there are a number of overlapping items, these were given and scored simultaneously. The 1916 revision was completed first and the 1937, Form L, second. Whatever advantage of practise effect there might have been, was judged to be cancelled by fatigue. Every effort was made to keep the interest and effort of the examinees at an optimum level. No subject refused to take the tests after an appointment was made and only two were openly antagonistic in typical adolescent behavior. Even these were persuaded to cooperate and no greater compliment to the intrinsic interests of the tests can be made than to say that in spite of themselves even these reluctant subjects became interested and made scores consistent with their earlier test results and their current school placements.

All of the third and fourth tests, and all but five or six of the first two tests were given in the foster homes. This made it possible to observe the relationships between child and parents, the fluctuation in family economic and cultural status over the 13-year period, and to sample the child's behavior in the home situation. A cordial relationship developed between the parents and the examiners as a result of these repeated visits. The first examination was usually a highly emotional experience for the parents, who understood that the psychologist's word was final in approving or disapproving the completion of adoption. In a sense this was even more crucial than the court action since as one parent stated "we were taking an examination in parenthood. Our success was shown by the results in our child." The majority of the families, located in areas where clinics and psychologists were not available but who were familiar with these resources through reading and the radio, availed themselves of the opportunity to discuss various child rearing problems. As would be anticipated, the character of the problems changed with age, and on the fourth visit dealt with problems of adolescence, vocational choices, educational plans, emancipation from the home, etc. There seemed to be no problem which was unique to this group of children as compared to any other group of similar age. The problem of information concerning their own adoption had been well solved by nearly all the families. Surprisingly enough two families had still not "told," but other evidence indicated that these children probably guessed. In two or three instances there had been community problems in which, despite the efforts of the foster parents, the children had had a very difficult adjustment to the adoptive status.

All the parents were aware of the research nature of the re-tests and were, on the whole, proud of the distinction. Through their contribution they felt they could facilitate early placement of children in adoptive homes and provide reassurance to families uncertain about adoption.

Relationships between the children and the examiners were more casual. Some of the children recalled the examiner's visits from one occasion to the next, and when they did, it was in terms of the fun of playing games with an unusually agreeable person. An explanation was made to all participants during the fourth examination following the general pattern that:

> When you were a younger boy, you were a member of a group of boys and girls all over the state who were given tests like this. We wanted to find out how well children could do different sorts of things, how well they could remember, figure things out and so on. Now that they are older, we would like to see how much they have changed and in what way. The tests are a little like a quiz program on the radio and most people find them rather fun.

In a few instances the question was raised as to whether children who were not adopted were also tested and the subjects were assured that children in many places also took similar tests. Two of the participants, one, the oldest subject, who had completed one year in college, and one a superior high school senior with decided research interests, were familiar with the published reports of the study and coöperated delightfully.

C. MENTAL DEVELOPMENT OF THE CHILDREN

All of the children had been seen on four occasions and a few for various reasons had been given additional tests. In these cases the test given at an age nearest the mean age for the group was selected for use in the major comparisons. Distribution of the ages at which the tests were given is presented in Table 2. The mean age at first examination was *2 years 2 months,* at second examination *4 years 3 months,* at third examination *7 years 0 months* and at fourth examination *13 years 6 months.*

TABLE 2
AGES OF 100 FOSTER CHILDREN AT TIME OF TEST

Chronological age	Test I	Test II	Test III	Test IV
0-6 to 0-11	3			
1-0 to 1-11	55			
2-0 to 2-11	23			
3-0 to 3-11	12	28		
4-0 to 4-11	4	33	2	
5-0 to 5-11	2	12	15	
6-0 to 6-11	1	4	53	
7-0 to 7-11		5	7	
8-0 to 8-11			14	
9-0 to 9-11		1	2	
10-0 to 10-11			6	
11-0 to 11-11			1	13
12-0 to 12-11				25
13-0 to 13-11				38
14-0 to 14-11				12
15-0 to 15-11				5
16-0 to 16-11				5
17-0 to 17-11				1
18-0 to 18-11				1
Number	100	100	100	100
Mean	2 years, 2.3 months	4 years, 3.4 months	7 years, .1 month	13 years, 5.8 months
Median	1 year 10.2 months	4 years, 1.9 months	6 years, 7.5 months	13 years, 4.8 months
Standard Deviation	13.08 (mo.)	16.4 (mo.)	17.0 (mo.)	16.3 (mo.)

The group included 60 girls and 40 boys. The range, median, and mean ages for both sexes were essentially the same.

Table 3 shows the results of the examination described earlier. Ages and results may be summarized for the 100 children as given in Table 4.

The mean *IQ* of this group of children has remained above the average for the general population throughout early childhood, school age, and into adolescence. It would be generally accepted that if major changes in intellectual functioning occur after this age, they probably result from psychiatric and emotional problems rather than from developmental abnormalities.

An interesting problem in test evaluation is posed by the results from the "simultaneous" administration of the 1916 and 1937 Stanford tests. Comparative studies of the 1916 and 1937 revisions support the general impression of clinicians that the 1937 revision tends to overrate the average or above average adolescent, while the 1916 revision tends to underrate him. This dilemma was frequently encountered in the examination of these children since differences of 15-20 points between the two tests were moderately

TABLE 3
IQ Distribution of Tests of Children in Follow-up Study

IQ	Test I	Test II	Test III	Test IV (1916-S.B.) (C.A to 16)	Test IV (1916-S.B.) (T-M Table)	Test IV (1937-S.B.) (Form L.)
150-154	1					1
145-149	0					1
140-144	3	2	2			3
135-139	6	1	2	1	1	7
130-134	5	3	3	0	0	12
125-129	15	9	4	2	2	6
120-124	14	5	16	7	11	14
115-119	15	8	6	11	9	13
110-114	12	8	16	12	16	14
105-109	10	20	17	12	9	10
100-104	8	17	13	15	16	9
95- 99	7	11	9	13	16	2
90- 94	1	5	6	10	4	3
85- 89	1	7	3	5	6	0
80- 84	2	4	2	5	4	3
75- 79			1	2	3	1
70- 74				2	1	
65- 69				1	2	1
Number	100	100	100	100	100	100
Mean	116.8	112.4	114.8	107.1	108.8	116.8
Median	117.5	111.0	114.2	107.85	108.9	117.2
SD	13.55	13.75	13.20	14.40	13.90	15.45

TABLE 4

Test	Age	Mean IQ	SD	Range	Median
I	2 yrs. 2 mo.	117	13.6	80-154	118
II	4 yrs. 3 mo.	112	13.8	85-149	111
III	7 yrs. 0 mo.	115	13.2	80-149	114
IV (1916)	13 yrs. 6 mo.	107	14.4	65-144	107
IV (1937)	13 yrs. 6 mo.	117	15.5	70-154	117

frequent. Years of clinical and guidance experience with young people of these ages provided a background against which the quality of their responses, their school achievement and their general intellectual maturity as evaluated from an interview could be projected. The result was a feeling of dissatisfaction with both tests and a fervent wish that a more adequate instrument were available.

The test results are presented here as they were obtained. In computing the IQ on the 1916 tests, 16 years was used as the maximum divisor, following Terman's instructions. In computing the IQ on Form L, the Terman-Merrill tables were used, which provide for a gradual rather than abrupt change in relationship between chronological and mental age. The next to last column in Table 3 shows the effect of using the same Terman-Merrill table with the mental age secured on the 1916 Stanford-Binet. There is a slight rise in mean IQ from the corrective effects of the table but this is not enough to account for the total difference between the two tests. The difference, however, is not statistically significant (CR 1.6) but its consistency and general character is shown in both Table 5 and the detailed presentation in the Appendix.

The general trend of IQ's where the tests are distributed by age, is shown in Table 5. IQ's reported for years one and two are based on the Kuhlmann scale, for years 3-10 the 1916 Stanford, and years 11-15 the 1916 and 1937 Stanford as indicated. Beyond 14 years of age the number of subjects in each age group was too small to warrant inclusion. The small number of cases at 10 and 11 years resulted from the long interval between third and fourth examinations. Repeated cross section analysis of the results shows that the group has consistently achieved a higher average mental age than would be found in a representative sampling of the total child population of the same age. Detailed statistical analysis of this material is not possible since every test for each child is presented, including some which are not used in the major comparisons. While fluctuations do occur, accentuated by the small numbers of cases at single age levels, the findings are essentially the same

TABLE 5
IQ BY AGE AT TEST

IQ	\multicolumn{9}{c}{Age—years}
	1	2	3	4	5	6	7	8	9
155-159									
150-154		1							
145-149	3		1	1		2			
140-144	3		1	1		1	1	1	
135-139	2	3	4	2		2	2		
130-134	7	2	1	6		1	4	1	1
125-129	6	7	4	4	3	5	1	1	2
120-124	4	6	6	2	4	4	2	2	1
115-119	4	7	5	3	4	7	6	2	2
110-114	6	9	3	6	4	9	5	1	1
105-109	3	4	1	5	6	7	4	1	1
100-104	1	4	4	6	1	5	2	2	1
95- 99		3	1	2	3	1	2	1	
90- 94			1	4	2	1	2	1	
85- 89				3		1		1	
80- 84									
75- 79									
70- 74									
65- 69									
60- 64									
Number	39	46	33	45	27	46	29	16	10
Mean	120.10	117.45	113.95	113.35	111.25	115.50	112.35	108.85	115.5
Median	120.75	116.64	114.92	111.58	111.38	113.94	110.75	112.0	114.5
SD	12.20	11.85	14.65	16.0	10.35	13.80	12.10	14.55	10.95

TABLE 5 (continued)

		Age—years							
	10	**11** SB'16	**11** SB'37	**12** SB'16	**12** SB'37	**13** SB'16	**13** SB'37	**14** SB'16	**14** SB'37
155-159									
150-154									
145-149									1
140-144			1			1	1		
135-139			2	1	1		1		1
130-134	1	1			3		2	1	1
125-129		3	1	2		2	5	2	
120-124	2		1	3	3	8	4		5
115-119		1		1	3	7	5	5	4
110-114		1		5	4	2	3	3	3
105-109	2	2	1	4	2	5	4	4	2
100-104				1	1	3	2		5
95- 99				1	1				1
90- 94		1				3			
85- 89		1						5	1
80- 84						1	1		
75- 79							1	1	1
70- 74						1			
65- 69									
60- 64									
Number	5	10	7	19	18	34	34	25	25
Mean	114.0	110.5	127.0	110.4	117.30	111.25	120.10	102.40	112.80
Median	115.75	109.5	127.0	108.0	116.17	115.21	120.75	102.63	113.67
SD	7.15	16.75	11.65	10.25	10.75	14.0	15.90	12.40	13.55

as in the earlier reports. The mean *IQ* of this group has remained consistently above the average of the population as a whole at each age level.

TABLE 6
CHANGES IN *IQ* BETWEEN TESTS

	Between Test I and II Number	Between Test II and III Number	Between Test III and IV '16 Number	Between Test III and IV '37 Number
+36 to +40				
+26 to +35	1	4		
+16 to +25	7	7	1	1
+ 6 to +15	11	26	12	14
— 5 to + 5	34	42	30	32
— 6 to —15	25	17	30	34
—16 to —25	18	4	25	18
—26 to —35	3		2	1
—36 to —45				
—46 to —50	1			
Total	100	100	100	100

	Between Tests I and III Number	Between Tests I and IV '16 Number	Between Tests III and IV '37 Number
+36 to +40	2		
+26 to +35	2	2	2
+16 to +25	5	5	5
+ 6 to +15	21	12	14
— 5 to + 5	30	19	21
— 6 to —15	23	29	29
—16 to —25	13	16	14
—26 to —35	3	11	10
—36 to —45	1	6	5
—46 to —50			
Total	100	100	100

	Between Tests II and IV '16 Number	Between Tests II and IV '37 Number
+36 to +40		
+26 to +35		1
+16 to +25	8	8
+ 6 to +15	15	17
— 5 to + 5	22	26
— 6 to —15	31	31
—16 to —25	21	14
—26 to —35	3	3
—36 to —45		
—46 to —50		
Total	100	100

Rather wide fluctuations in *IQ* between tests were found throughout the entire period. Table 6 summarizes the changes found. The general trend is toward losses when the first test is taken as the basis of comparison, as the mean *IQ* on succeeding tests would indicate. Since the total number of cases is 100, the percentages may be computed automatically and only the actual number of cases is given in the table.

These results, together with the correlations reported later, are consistent with findings from other studies, (3, 4, 13, 23) which show that *IQ* fluctuations of considerable magnitude are found among children who live with their own parents. The greater the time span between tests the greater the probability of wide difference between successive test scores. From a clinical standpoint this serves as an additional caution in the use of a single test score in long range prediction of intellectual attainment. Yet inspection of the raw data for individuals, as shown in the Appendix, gives somewhat more assurance. By and large the children did not change their positions relative to the population as a whole as drastically as these figures might lead one to conclude. When marked changes occurred there were related factors which could usually be identified in the individual instances.

Correlations between successive tests may be summarized as given in Table 7.

TABLE 7

	Test II	Test III	Test IV '16	Test IV '37
Test I	.54±.05	.44±.06	.35±.06	.35±.06
Test II		.70±.03	.58±.05	.59±.04
Test III			.71±.03	.75±.03
Test IV '16				.92±.01

These correlations do not differ markedly from those reported in other studies (2, 11) where the retests are separated by similar time intervals. From the standpoint of prediction of individual status in terms of the child's future *IQ*, the early tests may be considered disappointing, yet this group is not unique in its variability or its fluctuation from one examination to the next.

Of special interest are those children whose early mental development was average and who as adolescents are below 85 *IQ*. These cases, numbered 41G, 47G, 48G, 76G, 81G, 82G, 23B in the Appendix, include five children who occasioned concern from the beginning of the study. Three of them have been seen by psychiatrists at the initiative of the parents and are the only children in the group who have been referred for such help. No. 41G is a shy, diffident compulsive neurotic who is described as a meticulous housekeeper, who doesn't leave a task until it is complete in every detail. Characteristically she does poorly wherever there is a time limit and fails all tests at school though her homework is perfect and her individual reports to the teachers are good. She repeated the eighth grade, but in a medium sized high school she is a B student. It was felt that the 1916 Stanford-Binet *IQ* of 79 did not adequately represent her functional level. Nos. 82G and 76G are two of the disturbed children in the study. They have long histories of inexplicable erratic behavior similar to that seen in some post encephalitis cases. The tests have shown consistently wide scatter reflecting the difficulties in concentration, the short interest span, the erratic achievement of which teachers invariably complained to the parents. School progress has been based on other factors than achievement. As adolescents both have shown somewhat improved stability. In both cases it was felt that the test results adequately represented present functioning levels. Children 47G and 48G succeeded in making average scores as younger children, but the quality of their responses was consistently poor. These were the only children in this study whose legal adoption had been deferred a year since it was feared that their development might not prove to be normal in spite of an *IQ* of 100 on the Kuhlmann tests. Both have been unusually prone to severe accidents and illnesses including a skull fracture for 48G. They have been frail, thin children and on the basis of their physical health and interrupted schooling have attended special classes. It was felt that the tests adequately represented their present intellectual and academic ability. However, they have had splendid home training, are competent dancers and musicians, are socially poised, and thus give an impression of ability beyond the test scores.

Cases 81G and 23B are children in very simple home environments, where the intellectual stimulation is limited. In one home the father is dead, in the other extremely busy. Children of low average academic ability satisfy the aspiration levels of the parents. In neither case are the children encouraged to attain maturity or independence.

D. Relationships between Mental Development of Adopted Children and Characteristics of Their Foster Parents

1. *Occupational Level*

In the selection of foster homes all agencies give preference to families who not only have sufficient financial resources to assure adequate care for the child, but who show signs of culture, refinement, and intellectual and emotional understanding of the needs of children and the special problems of adoption.

The occupational level of foster families reflects this initial selection
and has remained consistently well above the average for the general population. Table 8 shows the foster father and the true father occupations com-

TABLE 8
DISTRIBUTIONS OF TRUE AND FOSTER FATHER OCCUPATIONS

Occupational classification	General U. S. population employed males, 1930 Per cent	True fathers Number	Per cent	Foster fathers Number	Per cent
I. Professional	3.1	2	2.7	14	14.0
II. Semiprofessional and managerial	5.2	3	4.1	17	17.0
III. Skilled trades	15.0	9	12.3	27	27.0
IV. Farmers	15.3	5	6.8	29	29.0
V. Semiskilled	30.6	10	13.7	8	8.0
VI. Slightly skilled	11.3	9	12.3	5	5.0
VII. Day laborers	19.5	35	48.0		
Number	100.0	73		100	
Mean	4.8	6.47		2.85	
Median	5	6		3	
Standard deviation	1.5	1.77		1.33	

pared with the occupational distribution of the population as a whole,
based on the 1930 census and classified according to Goodenough's seven-
point scale (9). Figures for the 1940 census are not directly comparable
because of differences in classification method, particularly in the clerical,
sales, skilled, and slightly skilled occupations.

In 1940 in the U. S. as a whole, 4.4 per cent of employed males were
in professional occupations. In Iowa they constituted 3.7 per cent of the
employed population while 14 per cent of the foster fathers were so employed.
Although only 14 per cent of employed U. S. males are farm proprietors
or managers, 29.5 per cent of Iowa men and 29 per cent of the foster
fathers are so employed, thus farmers were adequately represented. In the
U. S. approximately 17 per cent of men and in Iowa 19 per cent are unskilled laborers. None of the foster fathers, but 48 per cent of the natural
fathers are so classified.

Further comparison between the figures for the foster parents, the general
population, and the data for 73 true fathers for whom occupational information was available shows that the foster fathers are not only above the average of the population with a mean scale score of 2.85 as against 4.8 for
the U. S. as a whole, but are conspicuously above the mean for the true
fathers. The latter are, in addition, well below the mean for the total

population with an average scale score of 6.47, equivalent to the status of an unskilled or very slightly skilled workman. The children whose natural parents, as a group, come from one extreme of the population were placed in foster homes representing the opposite extreme in occupational status.

Observation of the homes over the 13-year period showed that, although they were above the average in culture, resources, and financial security at the time the child was placed, they were, on the whole, even more prosperous at the end of the study. Only two fathers had been in military service, one as a professional man and one as a non-commissioned draftee. While some had benefited from high war wages, others on fixed incomes had been at a slight disadvantage. The general economic prosperity of 1945-47 was evident in most cases.

In a number of families rather serious changes in total family constellations had occurred. Among the 100 children five foster fathers and one foster mother had died by the time the children reached adolescence. None of the surviving foster parents had remarried and none seemed to plan to do so. No two families were affected by the bereavement in the same way. In four instances the foster mothers and the children seemed to be closer than they had been before. In only one case did this seem to have an undesirable emotional consequence for the child. In two instances there appeared to be increasing difficulty in relationships between the surviving foster parent and the children. In both cases there had been marked attachment to the deceased parent and a rather unsatisfactory plan for care and supervision or financial support after the death of the favored parent. Both children were becoming resentful, uncoöperative, and failing in school.

Serious illnesses, affecting family income and security, had occurred in six families. One foster mother, whose instability had been noticed in 1937, finally became psychotic and was hospitalized. The foster daughter of 15 has been keeping house very well for herself and the foster father. This is a family with one of the lowest cash incomes in the group but standards of cleanliness and order were very good. One father has been under periodic psychiatric treatment but has maintained a prosperous business. Another was absent from the home for several years as a wandering alcoholic, but has returned and is making a good adjustment. One father, suffering from a brain injury, and another father and a mother suffering from chronic heart disease have been invalids at home. There was no indication that the presence of these major health problems has had an unusual affect on the children. The general attitude was one of acceptance and understanding on the part of the children. The parents in good health were apt to be over anxious about insuring the continuance of education and economic and emotional security for the child.

In three of the 100 families the foster parents had been divorced. In all three instances the foster mothers had deserted and left the boys with the foster fathers. Two of the foster fathers had remarried and in both instances the foster mothers were sincerely interested in the children and showed more insight and intelligence than the original foster mothers had demonstrated during the earlier contacts. The boy whose father had not remarried was living with an elderly relative who disapproved of the foster father and the apparent exploitation of the boy's athletic skills. All three of these boys were having much difficulty in school and were having a generally difficult adolescence, but were neither delinquents nor seriously disturbed emotionally.

Relationships between the child's IQ and foster father's occupation are obscured because the personal qualities, the cultural opportunities and intellectual stimulation of the homes are not directly reflected by the occupational classification of the families. The opportunities of many of the farm (Class IV) and skilled trades (Class III) homes exceeded some of the teachers', physicians', and managerial homes (Classes I and II). The results, however, summarized in Table 9, show persistent slight differences in favor of homes in the upper three categories. Comparisons for all years except the first two are based on the 1916 Stanford-Binet. Since all available test scores were utilized and the number of cases at any year is small, detailed analysis is not attempted.

It can be concluded that, on the whole, children in homes in the higher occupational categories tend to have somewhat higher mean IQ's at all ages. However, all the children, including those in homes of lesser occupational levels, are above the mean for the total population at all age levels where the number of cases is sufficient to warrant consideration.

2. Education

The distribution of educational attainment of the natural and foster parents is shown in Table 10. The average school attainment of the foster parents as recorded on the application record and verified in 1946 showed that mean and median attainment for the foster parents was high school graduation, with 15 per cent having completed college. According to the 1940 census figures the median education for native Iowans in a comparable age group (35-44 years of age in 1940) was 8.8 for males and 9.3 for females. In general, urban populations have an average of one more year of education than rural populations.

TABLE 9

COMPARISONS OF MEAN *IQ* AT AGES 1-16 FOR 100 CHILDREN PLACED IN UPPER THREE AND LOWER FOUR OCCUPATIONAL CATEGORIES

	Ages															
	1	2	3	4	5	6	7	8	9	10	11	12	13	14	15	16
Mean *IQ* Upper 3	121	114	115	115	116	115	113	113	—	103	121	108	112	103	98	98
Mean *IQ* Lower 4	117	114	114	107	107	116	87	113	105	82	112	106	111	99	86	—
Number Upper 3	37	23	24	24	20	30	11	9	0	5	16	30	44	16	6	10
Number Lower 4	23	15	16	15	9	28	1	5	3	1	10	21	30	10	4	0
SD Upper 3	13.5	11.7	13.0	14.4	10.0	14.1	14.3	9.7	—	13.6	10.4	9.0	16.4	11.3	10.6	13.5
SD Lower 4	10.0	15.3	12.9	14.1	12.2	13.0	—	11.6	6.3	—	9.0	10.9	11.3	9.5	10.3	—

TABLE 10
DISTRIBUTION OF TRUE AND FOSTER PARENT EDUCATION

School attainment	True fathers No.	%	True mothers No.	%	Foster fathers No.	%	Foster mothers No.	%
20					3	3.0		
19							1	1.0
18					6	6.0		
17					2	2.0	1	1.0
16	2	3.4			10	10.0	14	14.0
15	1	1.7			7	7.0	9	9.0
14	2	3.4	2	2.2	2	2.0	10	10.0
13	3	5.0	6	6.5	14	14.0	16	16.0
12	15	25.4	24	26.0	16	16.0	18	18.0
11	7	11.8	9	9.8	3	3.0	5	5.0
10	3	5.0	7	7.6	6	6.0	8	8.0
9	3	5.0	9	9.8	5	5.0	3	3.0
8	13	22.0	23	25.0	23	23.0	9	9.0
7	5	8.5	8	8.7	2	2.0	4	4.0
6	2	3.4	2	2.2			1	1.0
5	2	3.4						
Less than 4	1		2	2.2	1	1.0	1	1.0
Unknown	41		8				1	
Number	59		92		100		100	
Mean	10.05		9.80		12.09		12.31	
Median	10.57		9.78		12.13		12.56	
SD	2.73		2.31		3.54		2.89	

The educational status of the true parents is significantly below that of the foster parents and is below the average of a comparable age group for the state. The 1940 census showed that native Iowans 25-34 years of age had a mean education of 10.2 for the males and 11.0 for the females. While the information on the education of foster parents is reasonably accurate, there is evidence that the education of the natural mother has been overstated by an average of one year (12, 26).

These data again show that while the education of the foster parents is superior to the average for their age and region, the natural parents' education is below the average for their age and region.

Correlations between foster parent education and child *IQ* on successive tests are summarized in Table 11.

Earlier reports on somewhat larger numbers of children showed a slight positive correlation between foster child *IQ* and foster parent education (24, 25, 26). In this array of correlations there is no discernible trend except a consistent lack of statistical relationship. Inspection of the original scatter diagrams confirms the lack of relationship. However, it should be pointed out that both the *IQ*'s and the educations represented here are confined to the upper segment of the total possible range. As long as the parents

TABLE 11

	Foster mother education	Foster father education
Child's Test I	—.03±.07	.05±.07
Child's Test II	+.04±.07	.03±.07
Child's Test III	.10±.07	.03±.07
Child's Test IV (1916)	.04±.07	.06±.07
Child's Test IV (1937)	.02±.07	.00±.07

are highly selected, and the children as a group also have a limited range of *IQ*'s and are in the upper half of the total population, it is not likely that repetition of similar studies will produce any more significant correlations. Increasing the number of cases may extend the range and sharpen the focus on what little difference exists. These figures are lower than correlations generally reported in the literature for both foster child-foster parent and own-child-parent correlations. However, in other cases the range for both distributions has been wider.

The only conclusions which may be drawn from these data are that the foster parents are above the average of their age and regional group in education and that the children in these homes are above the average in mental development. The differences between these adoptive parents in amount of formal education completed are not reflected in differences in intelligence between the children.

E. Relationships between Mental Development of Adopted Children and Characteristics of Their True Parents

1. *Intelligence*

Intelligence test results were available for 63 of the true mothers. All were based on the 1916 Stanford-Binet except one Terman Group Test, two Otis, and one Wechsler-Bellevue. Since the scores on these tests were consistent with other evidence on the mental adequacy of the mothers, the scores were included. The tests were given by trained examiners, under ordinary testing conditions, usually after the mother had decided to release the baby for adoption. The release was not contingent on the mother's test score and examinations were not made when the mother was ill or obviously upset emotionally.

Table 12 shows the distribution of the true-mother *IQ*'s and child *IQ*'s at a mean age of 13.6 based on the 1916 Stanford-Binet. This test was selected since it offered the maximum available degree of comparability for parent and child intelligence test scores. The mean *IQ* of these children

TABLE 12
COMPARISON BETWEEN DISTRIBUTION OF *IQ*'s (1916 STANFORD-BINET) OF TRUE MOTHERS
AND THEIR CHILDREN

IQ	Mothers		Children	
	No.	%	No.	%
130-134	—	—	2	3
125-129	1	1	6	10
120-124	—	—	6	10
115-119	—	—	7	11
110-114	2	3	6	10
105-109	5	8	7	11
100-104	5	8	10	16
95- 99	6	10	8	13
90- 94	8	13	3	5
85- 89	7	11	3	5
80- 84	5	8	1	1
75- 79	8	13	1	1
70- 74	5	8	2	3
65- 69	5	8	1	1
60- 64	4	6	—	—
55- 59	—	—	—	—
50- 54	2	3	—	—
Number	63		63	
Mean	85.7		106	
Median	86.3		107	
Standard Deviation	15.75		15.10	

on the 1937 revision is 10 points higher than on the 1916 revision. If a correction were to be made for the *IQ*'s of the mothers, as some investigators have suggested, the 1937 test scores of the children would be used, with the same relative difference between the two arrays of scores.

A difference of 20 points between the means of mothers and children is not only a statistically reliable difference (*CR* 9.2) but is also of considerable social consequence.

Previous analysis (26) showed that there was no difference between the mean *IQ*'s of children whose mothers had been examined and those whose mothers' *IQ*'s were unknown. This was confirmed by examination of the present data (see Appendix).

Relationships between mother-child pairs, with regard to *IQ*, expressed in terms of correlation coefficients on 63 cases, are summarized in Table 13.

TABLE 13

Test I	.00±.09
Test II	.28±.08*
Test III	.35±.07**
Test IV (1916)	.38±.07**
Test IV (1937)	.44±.07**

*Reliable at the 5 per cent level of confidence (17, p. 212).
**Reliable at the 1 per cent level of confidence (Ibid.).

It is apparent that the above tabulation contains more questions than it answers and can be the source of considerable controversy. Certain conclusions can be drawn, however. Among these are the following: Test scores of children secured during the first two years of life bear no statistical relationship to the scores of their mothers, nor, it should be noted, do they show a very high relationship to their own later scores ($r = .35$). By seven years of age a substantial correlation with true mother's IQ is reached which remains of the same magnitude in adolescence provided the 1916 Stanford-Binet test is used with both children and mothers. The correlation is still further increased if the 1937 revision of the Binet is used.

Many reasons can and have been advanced for the low correlation between infant tests and later measures which will not be reviewed here. There is considerable evidence for the position that as a group these children received maximal stimulation in infancy with optimum security and affection following placement at an average of three months of age. The quality and amount of this stimulation during early childhood seemed to have little relation to the foster family's educational and cultural status.

The available data which can be statistically used—occupational classification and formal education—are not sufficiently sensitive to be useful in measuring these less tangible differences in child rearing practises. This point is important for the interpretation of the correlations between the child's IQ and his mother's IQ because it is possible to throw the weight of interpretation in the direction of either genetic or environmental determinants. If the former point of view is accepted, then the mother's mental level at the time of her examination is considered to reflect her fundamental genetic constitution, and ignores the effects of whatever environmental deprivations or advantages may have influenced her own mental development. Thus it would be assumed that the children of brighter mothers would in turn be brighter than the children of less capable mothers regardless of the type of foster home in which they were placed. The increasing correlation might be interpreted to support this point of view, since the occupational differences between foster parents are not large. It is, however, inconsistent with the evidence that the children's IQ's substantially exceed those of their mothers and that none of them are mentally defective even though a number of the mothers were institutional residents. The rôle of the unknown fathers adds to the complication although the evidence indicates that the fathers resembled their unwed partners in mental level and education (1).

If the so-called environmental point of view is accepted, then the question is raised whether the increasing correlation between child and true mother *IQ* possibly reflects the tendency to place the children of brighter mothers in the more outstanding foster homes, and the influence of these homes becomes increasingly prominent as the child grows older.

The question regarding selective placement can be approached in at least two ways. The first is an inspection of the relationships between such characteristics of the true and foster families as education and occupation. Using these crude measures, correlations of .24 between true mother *IQ* and foster parent education and .27 between true mother and foster parent education were found in this sample. Comparisons between true mother characteristics and foster father occupation for the present sampling are summarized in Table 14.

TABLE 14

| | Foster father occupation | | | | | |
	I	II	III	IV	V	VI
No. of foster fathers	14	17	27	29	2	5
Mean *IQ* of mothers of children in these homes	86	89	87	83	77	90
Number of cases	9	13	20	15	4	2
Mean education of mothers of children in these homes	10	10	10	8	8	8
Number of cases	12	16	28	25	9	2

It is apparent from both types of analyses that while a trend existed, selective placement, as evaluated by these measures was not consistently practiced.

Another approach to this problem of relationship is to examine the data for two contrasting groups of children. Selected for this purpose were: (*a*) Those children whose mothers were known to be mentally defective, with other evidence supporting the known *IQ* of under 70 ($N = 11$). (*b*) Those children whose mothers were above average in intelligence as measured by tests. Since there were only three cases above 110 *IQ,* the next five, in the 105-109 *IQ* range, were also included ($N = 8$).

Comparisons between the two groups are shown in Table 15. It is evident from the table that there is a marked difference between the intelligence and education of the true mothers of children in Groups (*a*) and (*b*). On the basis of education and occupation the foster parents of both groups are essentially similar, with perhaps a slight advantage for Group (*b*). On the first examination both groups of children were above average. By seven years of age a marked difference in mental level between the two groups is observable which persists into adolescence and is reflected by both the 1916 and 1937 Stanford-Binet tests. While children in Group (*a*) show average mental development as a group, the children in (*b*) show superior mental

TABLE 15

COMPARISONS BETWEEN CHILDREN OF MOTHERS OF INFERIOR AND OF ABOVE AVERAGE INTELLIGENCE

Case No.	True mother's IQ	True mother's Educ.	Foster mid-par. educ.	Foster father occup.	Test I	Test II	Child's IQ Test III	Test IV	Test IV '37
Group A									
8B	64	8	16	I	126	125	114	96	106
10B	64	11	8	III	125	109	96	87	100
18B	65	8	9	VI	114	102	112	122	118
53G	63	8	13	III	127	121	119	101	111
54G	67	9	12	III	116	113	113	91	102
58G	54	8	13	III	117	114	119	98	113
60G	66	8	10	V	105	109	90	105	115
67G	65	6	12	IV	110	111	114	95	103
70G	63	1	10	II	110	113	107	101	118
76G	67	7	15	I	109	92	87	74	84
82G	53	3	12	IV	81	87	80	66	74
(4)	73	7						124	104
Mean	63	7	12	3.2	113	109	105	96	104
Median	64	8	12	III	114	111	96	96	106
Group B									
17B	128	12	12	III	120	128	148	127	145
22B	109	13	11	III	102	107	113	108	130
57G	109	13	16	III	99	126	139	132	130
61G	109	13	15	II	112	113	125	128	135
71G	113	12	19	VI	128	112	114	114	122
72G	110	12	8	IV	116	92	105	103	104
73G	105	8	9	III	125	111	129	110	131
87G	109	13	11	III	128	145	125	119	133
Mean	111	12	12.5	3.3	116	117	125	118	129
Median	109	12.5	11.5	III	117	112.5	125	117	130

development. A difference of 25 points in *IQ* has significance socially, educationally, and vocationally.

If reliance were to be placed on these data alone, the inference would be fairly clear. However, comparison of the actual situation in the homes leads to a different conclusion. As a group, the homes of Group (*b*) are superior to the homes of Group (*a*) on every count on which homes can be evaluated. The average income of Group (*b*) is easily double the average income of Group (*a*) families. Five of the eight had sent their children to private schools, nursery schools, or camps for more than one year, reflecting an intelligent interest in superior opportunities, financial stability, and social status. None of the families in Group (*a*) had been either interested or able to afford similar opportunities. All the children in Group (*b*) had had music, dancing, or art lessons, while only 5 of the 11 in Group (*a*) had such training. In the number of books, the extent of participation in church, civic, social, recreational, and cultural organizations, participation in Child Study and *PTA* groups, familiarity with and application of approved child rearing practices and attitudes, the number of toys, school equipment, typewriters, personal radios, the degree of freedom in spending allowances, deciding recreation, hours to be kept and other factors now believed to be essential for optimum social and emotional adjustment, the homes in Group (*b*) were definitely superior to the homes in Group (*a*). The one exception was 72G. This was the home in which the foster mother had been hospitalized for mental illness. The foster father, well educated in a foreign country, is a railroad section supervisor. Finances are limited, intellectual interests are non-existent. For several years this girl has competently managed a household. It is possible to speculate that under more favorable circumstances she too, might have attained higher test scores.

The general conclusions which may be drawn indicate that while in this study an increasing correlation between child *IQ* and true mother *IQ* is observed with increasing age, it cannot be attributed to genetic determinants alone. A more sensitive measure of foster parental competence in child development is necessary before small sample techniques of comparisons and analyses of differences can be fruitful. The present measures of education and occupation do not evaluate the crucial differences between outstanding, average, or less effective homes. The fact remains that the children are considerably superior to their mothers in mental development. There is a socially important difference between a group of people whose average *IQ* is 107-117, depending on the test selected, and another group whose *IQ* is 87.

Since the mean for the children is above the average for the population as a whole, it cannot be attributed to the phenomenon of regression alone.

2. *Education*

In addition to the intelligence test scores there was information on the education of 92 of the true mothers. Recognizing that it was an unreliable and questionably valid measure of ability, nevertheless, correlations between true mothers' education and child *IQ* were computed. Table 16 summarizes the results.

TABLE 16

Test I	.04±.09
Test II	.31±.07*
Test III	.37±.06*
Test IV (1916)	.31±.06*
Test IV (1937)	.32±.06*

*Reliable at the 1 per cent level of confidence (17, p. 212).

Here, too, there was an increase in correlations between the first and second tests, but the relationships then became stationary instead of showing a further increase with subsequent tests. Recalling the still lower correlations between child *IQ* and foster parent education, here again it is advisable to guard against an inclination to over value the significance of correlations of this size.

3. *Occupation*

Since both the true mothers and true fathers of the children originated primarily from the two lowest occupational classifications, attempts to identify a relationship between the mental development of the children and the occupational ranking of the parents were fruitless. The occupational status of the true fathers was occasionally considered in placement plans, but usually the information was not felt to be sufficiently reliable to influence the decision.

Goodenough (8), Terman (29) and others have found that children living with their own parents in the two lower occupational categories have mean *IQ*'s of approximately 95. In contrast, children living with their own parents in the professional and managerial occupations have a mean *IQ* of approximately 115. It is apparent that foster children in adoptive homes of all the occupational levels represented here compare favorably with own children in homes of the upper socio-economic level, rather than following the pattern found in the families from which they originated.

F. Conclusions

Perhaps the most important contribution this study can make to the planning of future research is to point out the inadequacies of easily available data, and the necessity of formulating more clearly the various criteria used in the selection and assessment of the foster homes and the children. It is clear that the objective data used here, education and occupation, do not represent the real basis for selection and are not closely related to the child's mental development. Judging from the trend of correlations between mother's and child's *IQ*'s, one might conclude that a relationship exists which became increasingly apparent with age. This is complicated by the evidence of selective placement, yet without a parallel relationship between foster parent education and child *IQ*. This one set of figures must not be permitted to overshadow the more significant finding that the children are consistently and unmistakably superior to their natural parents and in fact, follow and improve upon the pattern of mental development found among own children in families like the foster families. What may be the salient features in the foster homes which have produced this development of the children, is only suggested in this study. It is inferred that maximum security, an environment rich in intellectual stimulation, a well balanced emotional relationship, intellectual agility on the part of the foster parents— all these and other factors contributed to the growth of the child. Unfortunately, there is still no scale for the measurement of these dynamic aspects of the foster home situation. The futility of arguments based on correlations involving measures of education and occupation applies to both sides of the discussion.

The conclusions which may be drawn from the material presented here suggest that:

1. The above average mental development of the children adopted in infancy has been maintained into early adolescence. There has been no large scale decline in *IQ* either for the group or for large segments of it, although certain children have shown either wide fluctuation or a steady decline or rise as compared with the first test results.

2. The educational or occupational data available for foster or natural parents in the typical social history record are not sufficient to predict the course of mental development of the children. Other factors, primarily emotional and personal, and probably located in the foster home, appear to have more significant influence in determining the mental growth of the children in this group.

3. The intellectual level of the children has remained consistently higher

than would have been predicted from the intellectual, educational, or socio-economic level of the true parents, and is equal to or surpasses the mental level of own children in environments similar to those which have been provided by the foster parents.

The implications for placing agencies justify a policy of early placement in adoptive homes offering emotional warmth and security in an above average educational and social setting.

TABLE 16
APPENDIX

Case number	Foster father's education	Foster father's occupation	Foster mother's education	True father's education	True father's occupation	True mother's education	True mother's IQ
1B	12	Farmer	12	8	Unknown	8	Unknown
2B	16	Minister	10	9	R.R. Man	9	100
3B	7	Electrician	10	Unknown	Unknown	7	71
4B	12	Gas Sta. Owner	13	13	Student	12	Unknown
5B	14	Farmer	14	Unknown	Truck Driver	12	89
16B	7	Farmer	7	11	Farm Hand	8	73
7B	12	Jeweler	16	Unknown	Unknown	8	Unknown
8B	18	H. S. Princ.	14	9	Unknown	8	64
9B	13	Accountant	12	13	Student	Unknown	Unknown
10B	8	RR Conductor	8	13	RR Wkr.	11	64
11B	13	Linotype Op.	13	7	Machinist	8	104
12B	18	Dentist	16	Unknown	Unknown	9	76
13B	8	Farmer	10	12	Road Labor	10	81
14B	8	Main.-Foreman	8	Unknown	Laborer	7	78
15B	13	Co-own. Store	14	15	Accountant	13	79
16B	13	Wholesale Sale	12	12	Unknown	8	Unknown
17B	12	Ins. Salesman	12	Unknown	Salesman	12	128
18B	8	RR Swichman	9	Unknown	Unknown	8	65
19B	12	Farmer	12	5	Farm Hand	9	71
20B	10	RR Mail Car.	12	Unknown	Elec. Power Plant	7	Unknown
21B	16	Dis. Mgr, Oil Co.	17	Unknown	Policeman	11	75
22B	9	Garage Mec.	13	12	Student	13	109
23B	10	Dept. St. Mgr.	12	Unknown	Constr. Lab.	12	Unknown
24B	15	Drug Salesman	16	Unknown	Laborer	Unknown	Unknown
25B	11	Garage Mec.	7	Unknown	Unknown	Unknown	Unknown

TABLE 16 (continued)

Case number	Foster father's education	Foster father's occupation	Foster mother's education	True father's education	True father's occupation	True mother's education	True mother's IQ
26B	8	Trucker	11	8	Sk. Laborer	6	Unknown
27B	12	Farmer	14	12	Greenhouse Wkr.	8	88
28B	8	Farmer	7	10	Cobbler	8	Unknown
29B	10	Farmer	13	16	Teacher	14	Unknown
30B	20	Physician	16	Unknown	Store Mgr.	10	Unknown
31B	9	Stoker Tender	11	Unknown	Farmer	Unknown	Unknown
32B	8	Farmer	14	6	Laborer	7	90
33B	20	Physician	15	12	Farmer	12	96
34B	15	Own. Feed St.	9	10	RR Worker	10	95
35B	18	Supt. Schools	15	12	Creamery Wk.	10	80
36B	18	Mayor & Store	8	Unknown	Clerk	12	Unknown
37B	12	Garage Mgr.	12	Unknown	Merchant	8	Unknown
38B	17	Farmer	16	11	Farm Labor	14	Unknown
39B	13	Dis. Mgr. T & T	13	Unknown	Unknown	8	102
40B	10	Farmer	6	10	Farm Labor	8	92
41G	8	Farmer	12	8	Odd Jobs	9	88
42G	8	Farmer	12	Unknown	Day Labor	12	100
43G	20	Physician	16	Unknown	Farm Labor	Unknown	Unknown
44G	13	Executive	14	14	Carpenter Hlpr.	12	91
45G	13	Executive	14	7	Carpenter Hlpr.	9	70
46G	13	Farmer	15	8	Laborer	11	84
47G	15	Auto Salesman	13	8	Farm Labor	8	78
48G	15	Auto Salesman	13	8	Farm Labor	8	78
49G	16	Editor	16	Unknown	Unknown	Unknown	Unknown
50G	16	Editor	16	12	Usher	12	87.

TABLE 16 (continued)

Case number	Foster father's education	Foster father's occupation	Foster mother's education	True father's education	True father's occupation	True mother's education	True mother's IQ
51G	10	Butter Maker	10	7	Odd Jobs	7	Unknown
52G	13	Accountant	12	Unknown	Unknown	9	Unknown
53G	12	Grocer	15	Unknown	Unknown	8	63
54G	13	Service Mgr.	10	Unknown	Unknown	9	67
55G	13	Grocer	13	Unknown	Unknown	12	Unknown
56G	9	Engineer	15	5	Laborer	7	83
57G	16	OfficeClerk	16	Unknown	Unknown	13	109
58G	13	Produc. Clerk	13	8	Store Clerk	8	54
59G	8	Sander	12	12	Salesman	8	Unknown
60G	11	Syrup Maker	9	Unknown	Unknown	8	66
61G	16	Prop. Hatchery	13	12	Nursery Bus.	13	109
62G	8	Farmer	14	Unknown	Laborer	Unknown	Unknown
63G	15	Proprietor	12	Unknown	Unknown	12	88
64G	10	Window Trimmer	8	11	Unemployed	12	Unknown
65G	9	Garage Mec.	8	12	Farm Hand	12	95
66G	12	Farmer	13	6	Const. Gang	7	92
67G	8	Greenskeeper	15	Unknown	Unknown	6	65
68G	8	Ins. Salesman	12	14	Civil Eng.	12	Unknown
69G	12	Farmer	13	8	Foundry Wkr.	8	Unknown
70G	12	Ass't Emp. Mgr.	8	Unknown	Laborer	1	63
71G	18	Rl. Est. Broker	19	12	Laborer	12	113
72G	12	Section Foreman	4	8	Unknown	12	110
73G	8	Farmer	10	7	Unknown	8	105
74G	12	Office	16	Unknown	Farm Labor	12	96
75G	4	Farmer	12	Unknown	Unknown	8	78

TABLE 16 (*continued*)

Case number	Foster father's education	Foster father's occupation	Foster mother's education	True father's education	True father's occupation	True mother's education	True mother's IQ
76G	16	H. S. Teacher	14	8	Truck Driver	7	67
77G	13	Hardware	13	8	Farmer	13	Unknown
78G	16	Co. Engineer	16	11	Mechanic	9	80
79G	12	Farmer	16	12	Skilled Wkr.	11	Unknown
80G	16	H. S. Teacher	16	9	Unknown	11	Unknown
81G	8	Farmer	8	7	Truck Driver	11	Unknown
82G	11	Farmer	12	Unknown	Unknown	3	53
83G	8	Trucker	11	7	Laborer	11	Unknown
84G	12	Mailman	13	Unknown	Shoe Shop	8	74
85G	8	Cattle Trader	12	Unknown	Salesman	10	91
86G	13	Elec. Lineman	12	Unknown	Ins. Salesman	11	98
87G	9	Ret. Farmer	13	16	Eng. Student	13	109
88G	16	Veterinary	14	Unknown	Gas Station	12	92
89G	8	Poultry Sales	11	8	Laborer	10	91
90G	13	Auto Salesman	14	12	U. S. Navy	12	Unknown
91G	8	Road Grader	8	8	Auto Mechanic	8	Unknown
92G	17	Professional	16	11	Farmer	12	Unknown
93G	12	P. O. Clerk	11	12	R. Mail Carrier	12	88
94G	14	Executive	13	4	On relief	10	99
95G	8	R.R. Fireman	10	12	Truck Driver	11	90
96G	18	Supt. Schools	15	1f	Farm Hand	12	104
97G	8	Hdwe. Salesman	12	Unknown	Farm Hand	9	Unknown
98G	8	Farmer	8	Unknown	Farm Hand	12	88
99G	12	Farmer	15	Unknown	Unknown	Unknown	Unknown
100G	15	Farmer	14	11	Mechanic	12	76

TABLE 17
APPENDIX (*continued*)

Case number	Age at examinations				IQ on examinations				
	1	2	3	4	1	2	3	4	4L
1B	1- 3	4- 1	6- 3	13- 3	121	'114	115	105	115
2B	2- 5	4- 6	6- 5	13- 2	120	115	109	106	117
3B	1- 5	3- 8	6- 8	12- 7	131	109	113	95	106
4B	1- 7	4- 8	7-11	13-10	102	121	139	114	132
5B	1- 2	3- 4	6- 3	12- 3	126	115	113	90	99
6B	1- 4	3- 9	6- 2	13- 3	120	102	111	121	132
7B	1- 1	3- 8	6- 8	12-10	127	118	125	105	115
8B	1- 5	4- 5	6- 7	13- 8	126	125	114	96	106
9B	2- 5	4- 3	6- 9	13- 8	112	86	104	101	112
10B	2- 5	4- 9	7- 8	14- 1	125	109	96	87	100
11B	1- 6	4- 6	6- 7	13- 7	105	107	106	104	113
12B	0-11	2- 0	5- 3	11- 6	130	112	124	125	132
13B	1- 5	3- 4	6- 3	12- 5	107	120	109	115	118
14B	2- 5	4--0	6- 4	13- 5	104	108	125	124	141
15B	1- 7	3-10	5-10	12- 8	120	117	114	109	114
16B	5- 7	7- 1	10- 5	16- 4	125	134	126	110	129
17B	2-11	4- 2	6- 3	13- 2	120	128	148	127	145
18B	2- 1	4- 3	6- 8	13- 9	114	102	112	122	118
19B	1- 5	3- 8	6- 7	12-10	122	100	128	119	120
20B	1- 7	3-10	6- 0	13- 0	120	113	114	101	113
21B	3- 1	5- 7	10- 7	16- 2	119	101	102	97	106
22B	3- 7	5- 7	8-10	15- 0	102	107.	113	108	130
23B	3- 3	6- 4	8-10	15- 7	99	100	103	81	94
24B	3- 3	5- 2	8- 6	14- 5	118	113	122	109	123
25B	2- 6	4- 1	6- 6	13- 6	117	131	126	124	139
26B	1- 8	2- 8	5- 7	11- 7	134	130	115	100	111
27B	3- 6	5- 3	8- 3	14- 3	133	121	115	97	118
28B	1- 8	4- 4	6- 6	13- 6	103	87	103	110	121
29B	1- 7	3- 9	6- 8	12-10	105	116	125	118	122
30B	1- 1	4-11	6- 5	12- 5	141	95	105	98	106
31B	1-11	4- 9	8- 2	14- 1	99	95	92	88	104
32B	3- 2	5- 3	8- 2	14- 4	95	89	115	97	116
33B	2- 7	3-11	6-10	13- 9	82	106	105	105	109
34B	1- 7	4-11	7-10	13- 9	136	115	118	104	112
35B	3- 2	6- 1	8- 6	15- 6	104	107	107	96	113
36B	2- 0	4- 0	6- 3	13- 2	134	133	128	124	137
37B	1- 3	4- 7	6-10	13- 8	119	98	93	109	118
38B	2- 2	3- 9	6- 8	12-11	97	98	106	106	107
39B	1- 4	5- 8	8- 6	14- 5	119	103	101	86	101
40B	1- 7	3- 1	6- 0	12- 3	116	121	119	109	114
41G	4- 1	6- 9	9- 0	15- 9	90	94	95	77	90
42G	1- 4	4- 1	6- 3	13- 1	104	114	104	100	108
43G	2- 2	4- 2	7- 5	13- 2	125	124	116	127	134
44G	3- 0	4- 5	7- 8	13-10	99	102	128	126	142
45G	1- 4	2-10	6- 1	12- 3	135	112	118	118	124

TABLE 17 (*continued*)

Case number	Age at examinations				IQ on examinations				
	1	2	3	4	1	2	3	4	4L
46G	1- 3	2- 4	5- 2	11- 5	125	108	116	101	105
47G	1- 6	2- 6	6- 5	13- 5	102	90	99	73	78
48G	1- 6	2- 6	6- 5	13- 5	108	90	86	80	82
49G	3- 9	5-11	8-10	14- 9	116	115	130	116	138
50G	1- 3	3- 4	6- 3	12- 2	113	97	101	109	115
51G	2- 2	5- 1	8- 5	14- 5	115	108	112	89	99
52G	0-11	2- 8	5- 2	12- 1	135	113	97	107	102
53G	3- 5	5- 3	8- 6	14- 6	127	121	119	101	111
54G	1- 9	3-10	6- 8	12- 9	116	113	113	91	102
55G	2- 1	3- 9	6- 0	13- 0	135	142	142	123	131
56G	1- 6	4- 6	7- 9	13- 8	101	93	99	88	92
57G	1- 2	2- 7	5- 6	11- 8	99	126	139	132	130
58G	3-10	5-10	8- 0	14-11	117	114	119	98	113
59G	2- 5	4- 2	6- 8	13- 4	99	108	105	117	120
60G	1- 3	2- 3	5- 2	11- 4	105	109	90	105	115
61G	1- 3	2- 5	5- 4	11- 4	112	113	125	128	135
62G	6- 9	9- 4	12- 4	18- 6	112	106	101	110	133
63G	2- 4	4- 4	6- 4	13- 2	114	138	124	122	124
64G	2- 8	4- 7	6- 8	13- 5	120	120	120	123	129
65G	1- 3	3- 7	5-10	12- 9	140	130	126	118	125
66G	1- 1	2- 4	5- 3	11- 3	120	113	114	127	127
67G	3- 2	6- 2	9- 3	15- 0	110	111	114	95	103
68G	1-11	4- 0	6- 2	13- 2	151	146	132	141	152
69G	1- 6	4- 4	6- 5	13- 2	111	104	106	111	115
70G	4-10	7- 2	10- 2	16- 1	110	113	107	101	118
71G	1- 1	2- 4	5- 4	11- 4	128	112	114	114	122
72G	1- 6	4- 4	6- 6	13- 6	116	92	105	103	104
73G	2- 5	5-10	8- 9	14- 8	125	111	129	110	131
74G	1- 8	3-10	6- 1	13- 1	128	139	118	115	130
75G	2- 5	4- 5	6- 7	13- 7	138	125	139	116	123
76G	4- 2	7- 3	10- 6	16- 6	109	92	87	74	84
77G	1- 4	3- 1	6- 1	12- 3	136	130	141	121	130
78G	0-11	2- 0	5- 0	11- 3	109	112	127	131	139
79G	1- 6	4- 3	6- 1	13- 4	114	133	129	113	126
80G	2- 6	3-11	6- 4	13- 4	115	111	122	119	126
81G	2- 7	4- 3	6- 6	13- 6	89	94	95	79	80
82G	5- 7	7-10	10- 7	17- 2	81	87	80	66	74
83G	1-11	2-11	5-10	11-10	117	107	123	108	111
84G	2- 5	4- 2	6- 7	13- 8	121	132	132	113	120
85G	1- 6	3- 2	6- 3	12- 5	120	105	131	123	137
86G	1- 2	3- 1	6- 4	12- 6	142	135	147	123	137
87G	1- 3	3- 4	6- 3	12- 6	128	145	125	119	133
88G	2- 2	4- 7	7-11	14- 1	115	113	113	112	122
89G	1- 1	2- 8	4-11	11-10	105	130	115	111	123
90G	4- 9	7- 4	10- 3	16- 3	105	102	115	91	112

TABLE 17 (*continued*)

Case number	Age at examinations				IQ on examinations				
	1	2	3	4	1	2	3	4	4I.
91G	1- 4	3- 8	6- 8	12- 9	127	100	103	90	101
92G	2- 6	3- 5	6- 6	12- 3	126	117	110	107	106
93G	1- 4	3- 5	5- 7	12- 4	112	107	110	103	116
94G	1- 1	3- 5	6- 5	12- 4	117	112	109	101	111
95G	1- 4	2- 4	5- 2	11- 5	122	127	129	126	143
96G	1- 3	4- 2	6- 7	13- 7	108	124	116	113	121
97G	2- 0	5- 1	8- 1	14- 2	113	105	109	97	104
98G	1- 3	3- 7	6- 3	12-11	122	112	119	94	106
99G	1- 4	2- 4	4- 7	11-10	128	102	113	117	123
100G	1- 6	3- 9	6- 8	12- 7	122	107	128	101	111

REFERENCES

1. ANDERSON, C. L., & SKEELS, H. M. A follow-up study on a small sampling of the putative fathers in Skodak's study. Unpublished study. Iowa Child Welfare Research Station. State University of Iowa, December, 1941.

2. BRADWAY, K. P. IQ constancy on the revised Stanford-Binet from the preschool to the Junior High School level. *J. Genet. Psychol.*, 1944, **65**, 197-217.

3. ————. An experimental study of factors associated with Stanford-Binet IQ changes from the preschool to the Junior High School. *J. Genet. Psychol.*, 1945, **66**, 107-128.

4. CUNNINGHAM, B. V. Infant IQ ratings evaluated after an interval of seven years. *J. Exper. Educ.*, 1934, **3**, 84-87.

5. DEXTER, E. S. The relation between occupation of parent and intelligence of children. *Sch. & Soc.*, 1923, **17**, 612-614.

6. DRISCOLL, G. P. The developmental status of the preschool child as a prognosis of future development. Teach. Coll., Columbia Univ., *Child Devel. Monog.*, 1933, No. 13. Pp. 111.

7. EBERT, E. H. A comparison of the original and revised Stanford-Binet scales. *J. of Psychol.*, 1941, **11**, 47-61.

8. GOODENOUGH, F. The relation of the intelligence of preschool children to the occupation of their fathers. *Amer. J. Psychol.*, 1928, **40**, 284-302.

9. GOODENOUGH, F. L., & ANDERSON, J. E. Experimental child Study. New York: Century, 1931. Pp. xii+546.

10. HALLOWELL, D. K. Stability of mental test ratings for preschool children. *J. Genet. Psychol.*, 1932, **40**, 406-421.

11. ————. Validity of mental tests for young children. *J. Genet. Psychol.*, 1941, **58**, 265-288.

12. HARMS, I. E., & SKEELS, H. M. Reported education and verified education of mothers of infants committed to the Iowa Soldiers' Orphans' Home during 1940. Unpublished study. Iowa Child Welfare Research Station, State University of Iowa, September, 1941.

13. HIRT, Z. I. Another study of retests with the 1916 Stanford-Binet Scale. *J. Genet. Psychol.*, 1945, **66**, 83-105.

14. HOAKLEY, Z. P. A comparison of the results of the Stanford and Terman-Merrill revisions of the Binet. *J. Appl. Psychol.*, 1940, **24**, 75-81.

15. LAYMAN, J. W. *IQ* changes in older-age children placed for foster-home care. *J. Genet. Psychol.*, 1942, **60**, 61-70.

16. LEAHY, A. M. A study of certain selective factors influencing prediction of the mental status of adopted children in nature-nurture research. *J. Genet. Psychol.*, 1932, **41**, 294-329.

17. LINDQUIST, E. F. Statistical Analysis in Educational Research. New York: Houghton Mifflin, 1940. Pp. xii+266.

18. MERRILL, M. A. The significance of *IQ*'s on the Revised Stanford-Binet Scales. *J. Educ. Psychol.*, 1938, 641-651.

19. National Society for the Study of Education: The Twenty-Seventh Yearbook of the National Society for the Study of Education. Nature and Nurture. Part I. Their Influence Upon Intelligence. Part II. Their Influence Upon Achievement. Bloomington, Ill.: Public School Publishing, 1928. Pp. ix+465, xv+397.

20. National Society for the Study of Education: The Thirty-Ninth Yearbook of the National Society for the Study of Education. Intelligence: Its Nature and Nurture. Part I. Comparative and Critical Exposition. Part VII. Original Studies and Experiments. Bloomington, Ill.: Public School Publishing, 1940. Pp. xviii+471, xviii+409.

21. ROE, A., BURKS, B., & MITTELMANN, B. Adult adjustment of foster children of alcoholic and psychotic parentage and the influence of the foster home. *Quart. J. Stud. Alcohol*, 1945, No. 3. Pp. 164.

22. SATZMAN, S. The influence of social and economic background on Stanford-Binet performance. *J. Soc. Psychol.*, 1940, **12**, 71-81.

23. SCHMIDT, B. G. Changes in personal, social, and intellectual behavior of children originally classified as feebleminded. *Psychol. Monog.*, 1946, **60**, No. 5.

24. SKEELS, H. M. Mental development of children in foster homes. *J. Consult. Psychol.*, 1938, **2**, 33-43.

25. SKODAK, M. Children in Foster Homes. *Univ. Iowa Stud. Child Welf.*, 1939, **16**, No. 1. Pp. 156.

26. SKODAK, M., & SKEELS, H. A follow-up study of children in adoptive homes. *J. Genet. Psychol.*, 1945, **66**, 21-58.

27. SNYGG, D. The relation between the intelligence of mothers and of their children living in foster homes. *J. Genet. Psychol.*, 1938, **52**, 401-406.

28. SPEER, G. S. The intelligence of foster children. *J. Genet. Psychol.*, 1940, **57**, 49-55.

29. TERMAN, L. M., & MERRILL, M. A. Measuring Intelligence: A guide to the administration of the new revised Stanford-Binet tests of intelligence. Boston, Mass.: Houghton-Mifflin, 1937. Pp. xiv+461.

30. THEIS, S. VAN S. How foster children turn out. New York: New York State Charities Aid Assoc., 1924. Pp. 239.

31. WOODWORTH, R. S. Heredity and Environment. New York: Social Science Research Council Bulletin 47, 1941.

Personnel Counseling Service
Flint, Michigan

U. S. Public Health Service
San Francisco, California

CONSISTENCY AND VARIABILITY IN THE GROWTH OF INTELLIGENCE FROM BIRTH TO EIGHTEEN YEARS

Nancy Bayley

The Journal of Genetic Psychology, 1949, **75**, 165-196.

CONSISTENCY AND VARIABILITY IN THE GROWTH OF INTELLIGENCE FROM BIRTH TO EIGHTEEN YEARS*

Institute of Child Welfare, University of California

NANCY BAYLEY

A. THE PROBLEM AND THE SUBJECTS

Various explanations have been offered for the changes which occur in the *IQ*'s of many children as they grow older. Among these explanations it has been suggested previously that irregularities may be due, at least in part, to innate differences in the tempos of children's maturational processes (4). However, the extent to which this hypothesis is true, if at all, is obscured by certain characteristics of the testing instruments on which we rely.

If we use several different tests of intelligence, the resulting variations in scores will be in part a function of the methods of standardization; including such things as the nature of the standardization sample, and the method by which the scores are obtained. They will also be in part a function of the kinds of intellectual abilities tested. That is, some scales test primarily verbal abilities; others weigh more heavily mathematical, or spatial functions, and so on. Another variable factor is the relative freedom of the test items from cultural and educational influences (11). There is also, of course, the further difficulty of determining the various effects of environment in stimulating or retarding intellectual development.

It is not proposed here to deal with the environmental aspects of the problem, but rather to examine some of the trends of intellectual development as found in some currently used tests of intelligence when applied to a small but constant sample, from birth through 18 years of age.

Ideally, for purposes of measuring the rates of intellectual growth in individual children, we should be able to measure the same children from birth to maturity on a single test which is applicable over the entire age range. Such a test, furthermore, should be calibrated in absolute units, so that velocities of growth in individuals and over different segments of the span may be compared directly. However, in spite of repeated efforts to produce them there are no existing intelligence tests which meet either of these

*Accepted for publication by Harold E. Jones of the Editorial Board, and received in the Editorial Office on December 29, 1948.

criteria. It now seems unlikely, from the very nature of the growth of intellectual abilities, that such a test can ever be devised. The mental behaviors which are developing during the first year of life are very different from those developing in the three-year-old who has learned to talk fluently, and these in turn are very different from the complex mental functions of later ages. From an examination of the nature of the intellectual functions available for testing, the growth of intelligence would appear to be the maturing of a succession of partially overlapping functions which become increasingly complex as they approach adulthood (4, 5).

We cannot, then, expect to have a single test of intelligence which is applicable at all ages. Such a test, for example, as the Stanford-Binet, which extends from two years to adult levels, though called one test, is made up of a series of *different* items which change in nature as they become more difficult. The extent to which these items and similar items in other tests are measuring the same things can be judged more adequately after large numbers of normal representative children have been tested and retested at successive ages, and their test scores compared.

We are beginning to accumulate such series of tests on the same children. Most of the groups of children on whom longitudinal test data are available are not average samples but tend to be superior. Nevertheless, much valuable information about the nature of intellectual growth has come and will continue to come from such studies because they are concerned with the growth of individuals through time. We may hope eventually to fill in the gaps with growth records from more average and below-average population samplings, as well as from more adequate tests.

The Berkeley Growth Study children, as reported previously (9), come, for the most part, from socio-economically superior homes. What is more, their intelligence scores tend to be well above the average. There were originally 61 infants enrolled: 40 of them have continued in the study through most or all of their 18 years. The principal contribution which the Berkeley Growth Study records can make to our knowledge about the nature of mental growth is in the length of the age span for which test scores are available. Although the number of children observed is not large, these same children have been tested repeatedly, at regular intervals throughout their lives. The further facts that the children were tested at most ages by the same examiner,[1] and that all had a similar program of testing

---

[1] All tests were given by the author, with a few exceptions. Occasional infant tests were given by Dr. L. V. Wolff, the pediatrician who participated in the program of infants' tests and measurements; most of the two-year tests were given by Dr. Marjorie Pyles Honzik; and the eleven-year tests were given by Dr. Mary Shirley.

experience given under the same general situational conditions, contribute to the comparability of the test scores. These conditions make it possible to study both the growth trends of individual children and the relations of age and test to scores for a constant sample.

The schedule of the study includes mental tests at most or all of 38 ages for the 40 children. The tests considered in this paper, with the ages at which they were administered, are as follows: The California First-Year Mental Scale (7), given at one-month intervals through 15 months; the California Preschool Scale (23), given at three-month intervals through three years, and at six-month intervals through five years; the Stanford-Binet, 1916 Revision, at six and seven years (35); the 1937 Revision (37), Form L at 8, 9, 11, and 14 years, Form M at 10, 12, and 17 years; the Terman-McNemar Group Test (36), Form C at 13 years, and Form D at 15 years; and the Wechsler-Bellevue (39), Form I, at 16 and 18 years. The scoring procedures for these various tests are different, and they are standardized on samples which were selected by different criteria, with resultant norms which are not equivalent in difficulty. Comparisons on this sample are made in respect both to the standard norms, and to methods adopted for the study of intra-group relationships.

Several aspects of these children's mental-test scores have been reported in previous studies, for the earlier ages up to and including nine years (4, 5, 6, 8). As shown in these studies, there was little or no relation between their mental test scores before two years of age and their scores at later ages. Similar results from other studies have convinced most investigators that existing tests of infant intelligence are inadequate for predicting children's later intelligence. Two alternative explanations of this inconsistency in early test scores have been suggested: (a) It may be that although we have not yet found the right tests, further search will reveal some infant behaviors which are characteristic of underlying intellectual functions, whose nature is such that they can be used for purposes of predicting the quality of intelligence at later ages. Or (b) early intellectual growth may be variable (either inherently so, or through environmental influences), making it impossible to predict later intelligence from any aspects of early infant behavior.[2]

B. The Selection of More Predictive Test Items

In the search for items of infant and preschool child behavior which may prove of predictive value, L. D. Anderson (3), Bradway (10), and Maurer (28) have made studies in which the scores made at a later age were used

---

[2] Except in cases of extreme retardation.

as criteria for selecting items or groups of items from tests given the same children at younger ages. Anderson compared 5-year *IQ*'s with test scores earned between three and 18 months. Bradway retested 10 years later children from the two- to five-year standardization sample of the 1937 Stanford-Binet. Maurer retested at 15 years children who had been given the Minnesota Preschool Scale at 18 to 54 months. The results of these studies are interesting but have not so far given us any adequately predictive batteries of tests. Both Anderson and Bradway found language or verbal items to be in general most predictive. Maurer found that the most predictive items required attention and adaptation, but that language entered in only after it had acquired the status of a well-developed tool. All three authors selected items of the type which they felt should be assembled for tests which might prove more useful than current tests in predicting intellectual growth.

As yet no complete item-by-item analysis has been made on the Berkeley Growth Study children. But various aspects of intelligent behavior, such as vocabulary and form-board performance, were compared over a period of years, as well as several different combinations of mental-test items (5). Recently a preliminary analysis of items has been made by comparing the six brightest with the six dullest 16-to 17-year-olds. A selection was made of those items in the First-Year Scale which were passed (on the average) at least two months younger by the bright group than by the dull group. Thirty-one items met this criterion. Cumulative point scores composed of these 31 items still did not reliably differentiate the bright from the dull ones during the first year. For the 12 ages (months 3-14) at which scores were computed, only six of the 12 children made scores which were consistently in the same general direction (i.e., above or below the average for the 12 cases) as their 17-year scores. It seems unlikely that correlation coefficients for the entire group would be significantly above zero.

In all of the comparisons so far made on the Berkeley Growth Study children, little consistency in relative scores could be found during the first two to four years. After this age, however, intellectual progress became fairly stable.

C. The Means of Mental Age and *IQ* Scores from One Month Through 18 Years

The data for the first three years have heretofore been reported in the form of point scores and sigma scores. For purposes of comparison with other data, mental ages have been computed for the First-Year Mental

Scale. To do this the mean cumulative point score at each age tested was called the mental age for the corresponding chronological age. Then *MA*'s (in months and tenths of a month) were interpolated and assigned to each point score. *IQ*'s were computed by the usual *MA/CA* ratio. *IQ*'s were computed for the California Preschool Scale and subsequent tests according to the published directions for each scale.

The relative status of the Berkeley group may be seen from the curve of their mean mental ages in Table 1 and in Figure 1*a*. These children constituted the standardization sample for the First-Year Scale,[3] and composed a part of the sample for the Preschool Scale: therefore the mean mental

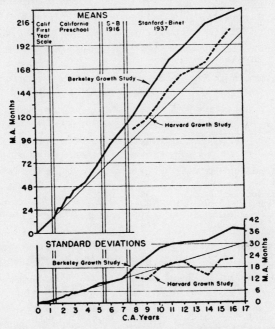

FIGURE 1

CURVES OF THE MEANS AND STANDARD DEVIATIONS OF MENTAL AGES FOR THE BERKELEY GROWTH STUDY CHILDREN FROM ONE MONTH THROUGH 17 YEARS, WITH COMPARABLE DATA FROM THE HARVARD GROWTH STUDY FOR YEARS EIGHT THROUGH 16

[3]No adjustment in these early mental ages was attempted. In view of the lack of correlation between earlier and later scores, we would not expect these children to show superior mental scores during the first year. The only other published data for the California First-Year Scale, those of Dubnoff, show the Russian infants she tested to be superior to our norms during the first nine months (13).

TABLE 1
MEANS AND *SD*'s OF MENTAL AGE AND *IQ*, BY AGE AND TEST
(Berkeley Growth Study)

	Age	Test	*N*	Mental age in months* Mean	SD	*IQ* Mean	SD
Mo.	1	Cal. First-Year	52	1.04	.195	103.8	19.5
	2	Cal. First-Year	58	1.998	.34	101.8	16.9
	3	Cal. First-Year	61	2.92	.41	97.5	13.6
	4	Cal. First-Year	58	4.01	.51	101.0	12.9
	5	Cal. First-Year	58	5.00	.60	100.3	12.3
	6	Cal. First-Year	57	5.96	.79	99.1	13.2
	7	Cal. First-Year	52	7.03	.705	100.7	10.2
	8	Cal. First-Year	53	8.08	.77	100.9	9.7
	9	Cal. First-Year	56	9.01	.77	100.1	8.5
	10	Cal. First-Year	56	10.13	.75	101.3	7.6
	11	Cal. First-Year	52	11.03	.78	100.9	7.5
	12	Cal. First-Year	53	12.06	.82	100.7	6.7
	13	Cal. First-Year	53	13.04	1.07	100.3	8.4
	14	Cal. First-Year	46	14.08	1.12	100.7	8.1
	15	Cal. First-Year	52	15.00	1.38	100.0	9.3
	18	Cal. Preschool I	49	18.38	2.20	102.4	12.0
	21	Cal. Preschool I	52	22.59	2.47	107.6	11.7
	24	Cal. Preschool I	47	26.29	3.09	109.5	13.3
	27	Cal. Preschool I	48	30.48	3.69	112.6	13.6
	30	Cal. Preschool I	46	33.96	4.11	113.1	13.6
	33	Cal. Preschool II	44	37.04	4.87	111.6	15.0
	36	Cal. Preschool I	47	42.83	5.20	118.8	14.4
	42	Cal. Preschool I	39	49.39	5.50	117.6	13.2
	48	Cal. Preschool I	44	52.28	6.64	109.4	14.1
	54	Cal. Preschool I	43	62.28	8.03	115.0	15.2
	60	Cal. Preschool I	46	70.60	9.90	117.8	16.9
Yr.	6	Stanford-Binet '16	48	88.71	11.01	123.4	15.6
	7	Stanford-Binet '16	46	103.65	12.64	123.0	15.1
	8	Stanford-Binet L	47	120.00	18.91	122.6	20.1
	9	Stanford-Binet L	45	139.40	23.56	129.0	22.2
	10	Stanford-Binet M	47	157.96	28.75	131.9	23.6
	11	Stanford-Binet L	45	174.51	30.22	132.5	22.1
	12	Stanford-Binet M	43	186.93	31.71	130.3	22.1
	13	Terman-McNemar C	36	——	——	115.6	21.4
	14	Stanford-Binet L	37	213.08	31.85	129.9	19.2
	15	Terman-McNemar D	37	——	——	121.7	19.1
	16	Wechsler-Bellevue	39	——	——	117.4	16.2
	17	Stanford-Binet M	40	231.55	36.08	129.1	19.9
	18	Wechsler-Bellevue	37	——	——	122.1	16.1

*Data ungrouped

ages and *IQ*'s for the first five years cannot be used for estimating the representativeness of the sample. For school ages, we see that the group is superior to the Harvard Growth Study cases as reported by Dearborn and Rothney (12), and included in Figure 1 for comparison. It is far superior to the test norms, as represented by the straight diagonal line. Some of this superiority we may attribute to practice effect and test sophistication.

The means of the *IQ*'s are presented in Table 1 and Figure 2. It is

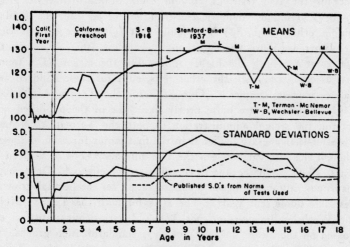

FIGURE 2

CURVES OF THE MEANS AND STANDARD DEVIATIONS OF *IQ*'S FOR THE BERKELEY GROWTH STUDY CHILDREN FROM ONE MONTH THROUGH 18 YEARS

obvious from their shifts, which range between 116 and 132 on the standard tests given after five years, that the norms used are not of equivalent difficulty at all ages. Stanford-Binet *IQ*'s average considerably higher than either the Terman-McNemar or the Wechsler.

Similar results are reported by other investigators. Sartain (33) for example, found that for 50 college freshmen, "*IQ*'s on the New Revised Stanford-Binet were significantly higher than those on the Bellevue Scale or the Otis Self-Administering Test of Mental Ability." He reported a Stanford-Binet *L* mean *IQ* of 129.48, *SD* 10.92, and a Wechsler-Bellevue Full Scale *IQ* mean of 117.48, *SD* 10.47.

The 1937 Revision yields higher scores for the Berkeley Growth Study than the 1916 Stanford-Binet. Ebert (14) has compared the 1916 and 1937 Stanford-Binets on a similarly selected superior group, and found consistently higher means on the 1937 Revision. But Ebert also found a consistent tendency for the means of this last revision to increase with age from six to 10 years, as our means do from eight to 10. Therefore a part of the change in our means from the 1916 to the 1937 revision would seem to be a function of the *ages* at which the tests were given. Another factor which is probably operating here is the general superiority in intelligence of this group. The distribution of scores in this sample might very well be different for the two tests (1916 and 1937 Stanford-Binet). Although McNemar (29) found symmetrical distributions of *IQ*'s for the standardization sample, others (e.g., 32) have found that *IQ*'s above 100 on the 1937 Stanford-Binet are more variable than those below 100. If this is true it might account for both the higher means and the larger *SD*'s found for this test, as compared with the other tests, both for these children and for other above-average samples. (Our *SD*'s for the Terman-McNemar and the Wechsler-Bellevue are more nearly like those of the published norms.)

Scores on the second administration of both the Terman-McNemar and the Wechsler-Bellevue are higher than the first scores for each of these tests, even though the interval between the two administrations of a given test is two years. This might be due to specific practice effects.[4] Or it may indicate inadequate allowance in the standardization for intellectual growth during these late adolescent years. The *IQ*'s for both the Terman-McNemar and the Wechsler-Bellevue are not *MA/CA* ratios, but statistical equivalents, based on the means and *SD*'s of their standardization groups. When cross-sectional samples are used for standardization it is often difficult to secure groups of comparable abilities for successive years, especially at these ages when many children are dropping out of school. Although most test norms are based on the assumption that adult intelligence is reached by 16 or 17 years, a number of studies (18, 24, 25) indicate that intellectual growth continues, on the average through 18 years, and even at least for some persons, to around 21 or 22 years.

D. VARIABILITY OF SCORES

1. *Mental Ages*

More significant than the means, it seems to me, is the trend of the standard deviations of mental ages from birth through 17 years (Table 1 and Figure 1*b*). It is plain that the *SD*'s do not increase at the constant rate

---

[4] All of these children are so accustomed to taking tests that we can attribute very little effect, at these ages, to any general learning experience in test-taking.

which is necessary if IQ's are to remain constant during growth. The SD's are too small during most of the first year and too large after seven years, and especially at 9, 10, and 11 years. These variations cannot be attributed to inequalities in the sampling of cases, as they are based on essentially the same cases throughout. But the Berkeley children are not alone in showing these age trends in variability. Although the Harvard Growth Study SD's are smaller for the same ages (see Figure 1b), they agree in indicating greater variability in scores from 9 to 11 years, in a sample which is also primarily "longitudinal" (12, p. 170).

2. IQ's

The SD's of the IQ's are given in Table 1 and shown graphically in Figure 2b. These standard deviations show strikingly why the IQ is a poor instrument to use in predicting later intelligence. When IQ's are used these children's scores are most variable at one month (when the SD is 20) and around 9 to 11 years (when it goes as high as 24); and least variable around one year (when it drops below seven IQ points). The variability tends to diminish again as maturity is approached.

The distributions of IQ's from six to 18 years are shown in Figure 3. Although statistical tests indicate that these distributions are within the limits of normal for samples of this size,[5] it is apparent that the high IQ's are limited at the later ages. The usual interpretation of such a curtailment of high scores is that the tests used do not have enough "top" for the brighter children. Another possible explanation is offered later in this paper.

E. Variability of Scores in a Strictly Constant Case Sample

Although the data presented thus far are on the same children for the most part, a glance at the N's in Table 1 shows that all 61 children were present at only one test age (three months). There is, thus, some fluctuation from age to age in the composition of the sample. It has been possible to select 21 ages, fairly well distributed over the 18-year span, at which the same 27 children were tested. The data on IQ's for this sub-sample, for all of whom there are scores at all 21 ages, are given in Table 2 and Figure 4. We have here sacrificed cases and testing ages to gain constancy of sample. The same age trends in means and SD's are found. This rules out the possibility that variations may be due to inconstant sampling of cases.

---

[5] Beta coefficients (30).

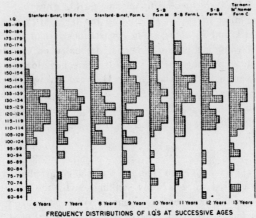

FREQUENCY DISTRIBUTIONS OF I.Q.'S AT SUCCESSIVE AGES

COMPARING SEVERAL DIFFERENT TESTS, AND THE SAME TESTS AT DIFFERENT AGES
BERKELEY GROWTH STUDY CASES

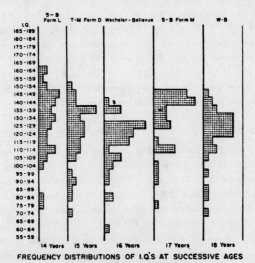

FREQUENCY DISTRIBUTIONS OF I.Q.'S AT SUCCESSIVE AGES

COMPARING SEVERAL DIFFERENT TESTS
AND THE SAME TESTS AT DIFFERENT AGES
BERKELEY GROWTH STUDY CASES

FIGURE 3

FREQUENCY DISTRIBUTIONS OF *IQ*'s AT SUCCESSIVE AGES (*a*) YEARS SIX THROUGH 13,
(*b*) YEARS 14 THROUGH 18

TABLE 2
MEANS AND *SD's** OF MENTAL AGES AND *IQ*'S OF 27 SELECTED CASES

CA		Mental age in months		IQ	
		Mean	SD	Mean	SD
Mo.	3	2.97	.46	99.07	15.35
	4	4.03	.45	100.59	11.02
	5	5.07	.62	101.78	12.15
	6	6.10	.74	101.56	12.28
	8	8.28	.67	103.48	8.40
	13	13.11	1.04	100.93	7.99
	15	15.08	1.32	100.56	8.64
	18	18.54	2.30	102.74	12.73
	21	22.56	2.05	107.19	9.73
	24	26.13	2.27	108.48	9.10
	27	29.59	3.15	109.48	11.88
	30	34.35	3.34	114.41	10.92
	36	41.84	4.52	116.19	12.68
	42	48.39	5.18	115.04	12.16
	48	51.07	5.35	106.74	11.28
Yr.	7	105.26	10.08	124.96	11.85
	9	143.63	21.09	132.81	19.52
	11	180.96	27.52	137.15	20.75
	14	217.33	28.92	132.59	17.70
	15			122.70	18.37
	16			120.52	12.12
	17	236.67	25.94	131.52	14.43
	18			124.44	12.28

*Data ungrouped.

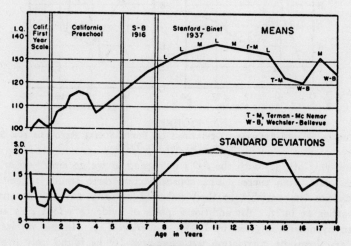

FIGURE 4
CURVES OF THE MEANS AND STANDARD DEVIATIONS FOR A STRICTLY CONSTANT SAMPLE OF
27 BERKELEY GROWTH STUDY CASES AT 21 TEST AGES

F. AGE CHANGES IN VARIABILITY FOR DIFFERENT TESTS

1. *Infant Tests*

The question arises whether changes in variability are due to the particular tests used. In Figures 5 and 6 some data are assembled on *SD*'s which have been published on tests of infants. The curves in *5a* are *SD*'s of point scores for two groups of infants—the Berkeley cases (4) and Russian babies tested by Dubnoff (13)—who were given the California First-Year Scale. In *5b* are *SD*'s of point scores reported by Fillmore for her Iowa Infant Scale (17) and by Nelson and Richards for the Gesell Schedules given to children in the Fels Foundation growth study (31). In Figure 6 are *SD*'s of *IQ*'s, for the Berkeley Growth Study, and *PE*'s of Kuhlman-Binet *IQ*'s as reported by Kuhlman[6] (26). For all tests and samples, and for different methods of scoring, there is decreased variability in scores at or

Point Scores

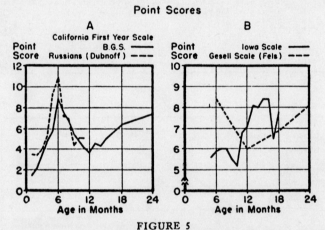

FIGURE 5

AGE CURVES OF THE STANDARD DEVIATIONS OF POINT SCORES REPORTED FOR SEVERAL DIFFERENT INFANT TESTS

near one year of age, with the *SD*'s increasing as we go either up or down the age scale from there. The consistency of these trends suggests that children are less variable in their behavior-maturity patterns at one year than earlier or later. An additional piece of evidence which may support such an hypothesis is given by L. D. Anderson (3). In his validation of infant test items by correlation with five-year *IQ* he found only five items (from a total of 97) at the one-year level which were "predictive." There were, by contrast, 16 items at six months and 18 items at 18 months.

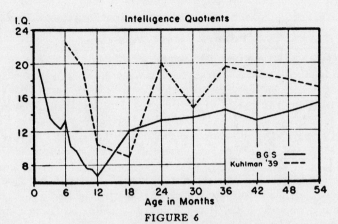

FIGURE 6

AGE CURVES OF THE STANDARD DEVIATIONS OF *IQ*'S: THE BERKELEY GROWTH STUDY
COMPARED WITH THE KUHLMAN-BINET

2. *Tests From Two to 18 Years*

There is, furthermore, evidence from other studies indicating changes in variability at other ages. Goodenough (19) has called attention to the trends in the 1937 Stanford-Binet norms. The *SD*'s of *IQ*'s in the standardization sample, as reported by Terman and Merrill (37), show trends which Goodenough suggests are inherent in the tests, and not due to chance variations in sampling as Terman and Merrill had assumed. These *SD*'s tend to decrease from two and one-half years to six years, when they are smallest, then to increase to a high level from 11 to 15 years, after which they drop again. McNemar (29) agrees that the changes in variability are probably not due to chance, and has set up a table for correcting *IQ*'s at the ages where the *SD*'s are smallest and largest.

We have made one check on the relation of case sampling to variability in the 1937 Stanford-Binet, for a part of its range, by comparing the 34 Berkeley Growth Study children who took the test at all seven ages from eight through 17 years. Form *L* was given at four ages, and *M* at three ages. The means and *SD*'s are given in Table 3. Whether we regard these as the same test, or two different tests, the trends are evident. The age changes in variability do appear to be characteristic of the test.

This characteristic trend, however, is not confined to the 1937 Stanford-Binet tests. Such other published material as the Harvard Growth Study

---

*The Kuhlman-Binet *PE*'s, as he uses them, are interquartile ranges (26). They are from his Table 28 and Figure 1.

TABLE 3
MEANS AND SD's STANFORD-BINET (1937 REVISION) MENTAL AGE AND *IQ* FOR 34
BERKELEY GROWTH STUDY CASES

C.A Years	Mental age, months		IQ	
	Mean	SD	Mean	SD
8.0	119.76	18.67	124.33	19.75
9.0	139.32	22.63	129.18	21.83
10.0	159.18	27.71	132.12	23.47
11.0	174.03	30.27	131.97	22.49
12.0	189.47	29.79	131.53	20.88
14.0	209.62	32.54	127.85	19.61
17.0	230.65	32.41	128.00	18.23

(See Figure 1) which adapts scores from several tests (12, 34), the studies of Freeman, *et al.*, of mental growth in Chicago children (1, 18), Ebert and Simmons' report on the Brush Foundation children of Cleveland (15), and data reported by Goodenough on Minnesota children (19, 20), all give greater *SD's* for mental test scores around 10 to 12 years of age than in the periods just before or after. The *PE's* (and hence the *SD's*) of Kuhlman-Binet *IQ's* tend to drop from two to six years, and to rise after six but become large and erratic after 13 years (26).

These studies include a variety of testing instruments, and both cross-sectional and longitudinal samples. The trends in variability are, of course, to some extent peculiar to the particular tests used. But there is enough concomitance in these trends to merit an investigation of the possibility that the tests may be reflecting underlying growth processes.

G. VARIABILITY: THEORETICAL CONSIDERATIONS

Although the age changes in variability[7] may be artifacts of current methods of selection and standardization of test items, they may equally well describe tendencies which are inherent in intellectual growth. It seems quite probable that both of the clear-cut periods of restricted variability in the Berkeley Growth study intelligence scores—toward the end of infancy and of adolescence—are due to the approach to maturity of the particular processes being measured. The mental processes which are developing during the first year are largely sensory-motor in character (2, 4). And although they form the basis for further intellectual development, precocity or retardation in them is not necessarily related to rates of development in the more complex processes which we call intelligence in school-age children

---

[7]The coefficient of variation, as used by Ellis (16) and Henmon and Livingstone (21) for example, seems inapplicable here. *V* only seems to minimize or obscure changes in variability which are of practical significance.

and adults. By one year of age most of the slow developers have caught up with those who were precocious in these simple coördinations. The *SD*'s thus become restricted to individual differences in mature functions.[8] In the same way the approach to mature intellectual status after 11 or 12 years could reduce the variability of performance as the children whose mental growth is more accelerated reach their own "ceilings."

On this interpretation the ceiling is a function (at least in part) of the child's changing growth rate, rather than of a scarcity of difficult items at the upper levels of the test. This is shown very clearly in the study of Freeman and Flory (18, pp. 38-41), who were concerned over the reduced *SD*'s on their *VACO* tests after 15 years. They attempted to increase the variability of scores on the upper levels of the Analogies test by adding top in the form of more difficult items. However, they did not succeed in changing the trend. An analysis of their Opposites test likewise indicated that its reduced variability at later ages was not due to a lack of differentiating items at the upper end of the scale.

It thus seems likely that the test scores are reflecting actual changes in variability which are inherent in the processes of development of any given function. During growth of a structure or function variability increases, in part because of increasing individual differences in capacity, and in part because of individual differences in the speed with which the maturing process takes place. These two factors are known to be operative in physical growth, and it seems reasonable to expect that they may be characteristic of many growth processes. During the stage of development when both factors operate freely, the variability of measures or scores will become greater with the general increments in the structure or function concerned. But as an increasing number of individuals stop growing, and the means level off to a constant value, the individual differences which remain become restricted to those of the achieved mature state. On this hypothesis, we should assume that in the present series of tests of mental growth we have scores on at least two types of function which develop successively, resulting in alternating periods of increasing and decreasing variability. These large general trends may well obscure similar tendencies, which are occurring more or less simultaneously, in more specific functions which develop in various parts of the growth span. The *VACO* tests are examples of this, as is seen in the varying trends of means and *SD*'s of the four tests in the Freeman and Flory Study (18). Thurstone (39) in testing five- and six-year-olds, found that

---

[8] This point has been discussed in detail in my monograph on Mental Growth during the First Three Years (4).

certain factors seemed to mature much earlier than others. Another example is found in the study of Jones and Conrad (24) for the subtests of the Army Alpha between the ages of 10 and 60 years. This last study indicates wide variations in rates of decline of different intellectual functions, as well as in their rates of growth. It is reasonable to expect that similar differences will be found in any broad sampling of mental functions.

II. CONSISTENCY OF GROWTH IN INTELLIGENCE

1. *Method of Scoring*

We have thus far discussed three different conditions which militate against a child's maintaining a "constant *IQ*" throughout his growth. First, differences in standardization from one test to another, with differences in relative difficulty, cause spurious changes in the *IQ*'s. This is shown in the considerable differences in mean *IQ*'s of the Berkeley Growth Study children for the different tests used. Second, we have found age changes in variability of the tested mental functions, so that if relative intellectual status is expressed either by scaled point scores[9] or by the ratio *MA/CA,* the scores of exceptional children are necessarily brought closer to the average during periods when variability is reduced. Third, it would appear that different functions are being measured on different segments of the mental growth span.

To eliminate, as far as possible, changes in the scores for our sample which may be due to either of the first two factors, we have transposed all of their mental test scores into Sigma Scores computed from the means and *SD*'s of the points earned by this group of children at each age tested.[10] Using these Sigma Scores, or Standard Scores, we can determine both for the group as a whole, and for the individual child, the extent to which the children maintain constant positions in a total group which has had similar testing experience.

2. *Relation to Age and Test-Retest Interval*

We have computed several series of correlation coefficients between tests given at successive ages, to determine the extent to which predictions can be made for the children in the group, for different ages and for different intervals between tests. Samples of these *r*'s are shown graphically in

---

[9]Freeman and Flory (18).
[10]Sigma Scores have for some purposes been transposed into their equivalent Standard Scores by multiplying by 10 and adding 50, thus eliminating all minus figures.

TABLE 4

CORRELATION COEFFICIENTS BETWEEN AGE-LEVEL STANDARD SCORES OF INTELLIGENCE*

Av.of months	4, 5, & 6	7, 8, & 9	10, 11, & 12	13, 14, & 15	18, 21, & 24	27, 30, & 36	42, 48, & 54	Years				
								5, 6, & 7	8, 9, & 10	11, 12, & 13	14, 15, & 16	17, 18
1, 2, & 3	.57	.42	.28	.10	-.04	-.09	-.21	-.13	-.03	.02	-.01	.05
4, 5, & 6		.72	.52	.50	.23	.10	-.16	-.07	-.06	-.08	-.04	-.01
7, 8, & 9			.81	.67	.39	.22	.02	.02	.07	.16	.006	.20
10, 11, & 12				.81	.60	.45	.27	.20	.19	.30	.23	.41
13, 14, & 15					.70	.54	.35	.30	.19	.19	.09	.23
18, 21, & 24						.80	.49	.50	.37	.43	.45	.55
27, 30, & 36							.72	.70	.58	.53	.46	.54
42, 48, & 54								.82	.71	.64	.70	.62
Years												
5, 6, & 7									.92	.85	.87	.86
8, 9, & 10										.94	.92	.89
11, 12, & 13											.96	.96
14, 15, & 16												.96

*These scores are the means of standard scores for three consecutive test-ages, e.g., months 1, 2, & 3; 4, 5, & 6, etc., and years 5, 6, & 7, etc. The last level is composed of only two test ages, 17 & 18 years. Each child's score is the average of all tests taken by him for the ages included in that level.

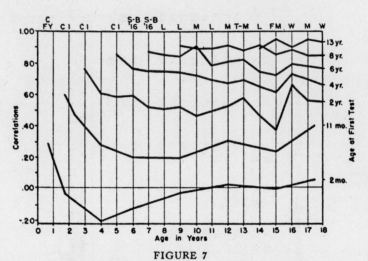

FIGURE 7

AGE CURVES OF CORRELATION COEFFICIENTS BETWEEN SCORES ON SELECTED INITIAL TESTS
AND SUBSEQUENT TESTS GIVEN AT YEARLY INTERVALS

Figure 7. Table 4 gives the r's for consistency of mental test scores for successive age levels in which each child's Sigma Scores for three successive test ages have been averaged. This particular set of r's, by the use of averages for three tests, eliminates most of the chance variations which occur in single test scores. Furthermore, the use of Sigma Scores eliminates the age changes in variability which would tend to alter the magnitude of the r's. For comparison, Table 5 gives the r's between single test IQ's for ages six through 18 years. Table 6 and Figure 8 give consistency correlations (single test point scores) for the 27 cases who make up a constant sample for a wide range of ages.

From these correlation coefficients we may see the extent to which the children's relative mental status remains constant. It has now become fairly well accepted that the size of a test-retest correlation for *young* children is a combined function of the age of the children and the length of the interval between tests.

The correlation coefficients, as we have pointed out in earlier publications (4, 5), indicate that these children's scores on the tests given before two years of age are quite unrelated to their test scores during school ages. They indicate, further, however, increasing stability of scores with increas-

TABLE 5

Correlations between Mental Test IQ's for Tests Given at Different Ages (6 Through 18 Years)

| Age at test | Stanford-Binet Form | | | | | | Terman-McNemar Form C | Stanford-Binet Form L | Terman-McNemar Form D | Wechsler-Bellevue | Stanford-Binet Form M | Wechsler-Bellevue |
	1916 7	L 8	L 9	M 10	L 11	M 12	13	14	15	16	17	18
6	.86	.85	.84	.90	.78	.81	.82	.74	.72	.79	.78	.77
7		.88	.83	.87	.82	.83	.88	.79	.75	.83	.83	.80
8			.91	.89	.89	.91	.88	.91	.85	.88	.84	.85
9				.88	.90	.82	.87	.86	.82	.87	.85	.87
10					.92	.90	.88	.92	.83	.88	.86	.86
11						.93	.91	.93	.89	.89	.92	.93
12							.87	.94	.85	.88	.90	.89
13								.89	.95	.90	.94	.93
14									.87	.92	.89	.89
15										.88	.89	.88
16											.89	.94
17												.90

TABLE 6
CONSISTENCY CORRELATIONS BETWEEN MENTAL TEST POINT SCORES AT INDICATED AGES FOR 27 SELECTED CASES

Age at test	Months						Years					
	6	13	18	24	36	48	7	9	11	15	17	18
Mo.												
3	.35	.02	—.05	—.13	.05	—.03	—.15	.08	.08	—.04	.12	—.03
6		.63	.35	.08	.13	.09	—.12	.04	—.07	—.26	—.04	—.24
13			.60	.47	.41	.23	.13	.13	.02	—.18	.002	—.14
18				.50	.54	.41	.33	.14	.11	—.02	.20	.03
24					.74	.47	.60	.43	.43	.27	.41	.39
36						.64	.53	.55	.48	.33	.56	.40
48							.71	.76	.69	.54	.71	.52
Yr.												
7								.79	.74	.71	.79	.68
9									.90	.77	.84	.80
11										.89	.92	.87
15											.88	.84
17												.79

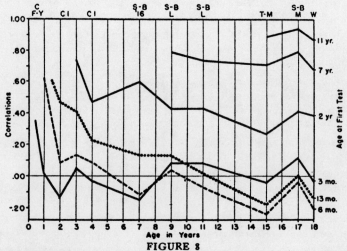

FIGURE 8
AGE CURVES OF CORRELATION COEFFICIENTS FOR A CONSTANT SAMPLE OF 27 CASES

ing age.[11] By two years the r's with tests at later ages hold up fairly well, rarely dropping below .50. The school-age correlations drop off only slightly as the interval between tests is increased for higher age levels. Studies on other children such as those of Honzik (22), Goodenough and Maurer (20), Ebert and Simmons (15), and Anderson (2) show very similar correlational trends.

3. Correlations between Scores on Different Tests

It has been suggested (2) that the consistency of the test scores will be affected by the use of different tests at different ages. In very few studies has the same test been given to the same children at all ages. One reason for this is that no test has been standardized for the entire age span. Furthermore, even if something had been named the same test, it would necessarily be comprised of very different items at the different age levels. Especially do the infant and preschool tests differ from the later ones. Perhaps the closest approach to this desirable condition of similar functions in a single testing instrument given to the same children over a wide age range, is to be found in the study of Freeman and Flory, in which the *VACO* tests were used from six through 18 years (a period of relative stability). This study shows individual variations in growth which are similar to our data, even though in the Berkeley Growth Study we do not have this constancy of testing instrument. Three forms of the Stanford-Binet, the Terman-McNemar Group test, and the Wechsler-Bellevue were given at various ages during this same age span.

The effect of changing tests on the Berkeley Growth Study group's relative status may be seen from Table 7. In this table the r's are grouped according to the tests involved. For 12 comparisons between repeats of the same test, the mean of the r's is .89.[12] For 26 comparisons between different forms of the Stanford-Binet the mean of the r's is .87. For 40 comparisons between unrelated tests the mean of the r's is also .87. The lowest r in this last group is .72 between the 1916 Stanford-Binet at six years and the Terman-McNemar at 15 years. It is likely that the age at first testing and

---

[11]Honzik's (22) findings that "the magnitude of a correlation between tests varies directly with the age ratio $\dfrac{CA \text{ at first test}}{CA \text{ at second test}}$ holds up fairly well to about five years. After this age, however, there is much greater constancy than the ratio would predict. See Figures 7 and 8.

[12]Computed by the formula $\dfrac{(N-3)xZ's \text{ for } r's}{\Sigma(N-3)}$, see Lindquist (27, pp. 218-219).

TABLE 7
INTERCORRELATIONS BETWEEN TEST SCORES ACCORDING TO THE TESTS COMPARED (SIX THROUGH EIGHTEEN YEARS)

Intercorrelations When the Same Test is Repeated (Mean of 12 r's = .89)

S-B, 1916 CA	N	r	S-B, L x L CA	N	r	S-B, M x M CA	N	r	TMG, C x D CA	N	r
6x 7	44	.87	8x 9	45	.91	10x12	41	.90	13x15	33	.95
			8x11	44	.89	10x17	39	.86			
			8x14	36	.91	12x17	37	.90			
			9x11	43	.90				W-B x W-B CA	N	r
			9x14	35	.86				16x18	36	.94
			11x14	37	.93						

Intercorrelations between Different Forms of the Stanford-Binet (Mean of 26 r's = .87)

1916 x L CA	N	r	1916 x M CA	N	r	L x M CA	N	r	L x M con't CA	N	r
6x 8	45	.84	6x10	46	.90	8x10	45	.89	14x10	36	.92
6x 9	44	.84	6x12	42	.81	8x12	42	.91	14x12	35	.94
6x11	44	.78	6x17	39	.78	8x17	39	.84	14x17	36	.89
6x14	36	.74	7x10	45	.87	9x10	44	.88	11x10	43	.92
7x 8	44	.85	7x12	41	.83	9x12	40	.92	11x12	41	.93
7x 9	44	.81	7x17	40	.83	9x17	38	.85	11x17	39	.92
7x11	44	.82									
7x14	37	.79									

Intercorrelations between Unrelated Tests (Mean of 40 r's = .87)

S-B, L x TMG CA	N	r	S-B, L x W-B CA	N	r	S-B, M x TMG CA	N	r	S-B, M x W-B CA	N	r
8x13	37	.88	8x16	40	.88	10x13	36	.88	10x16	40	.88
8x15	38	.85	9x16	39	.87	10x15	38	.83	12x16	36	.88
9x13	36	.87	11x16	40	.89	12x13	34	.87	17x16	40	.89
9x15	37	.82	14x16	36	.92	12x15	36	.85	10x18	36	.86
11x13	37	.91	8x18	36	.85	13x17	33	.94	12x18	34	.89
11x15	38	.89	9x18	34	.87	15x17	37	.89	17x18	36	.90
14x13	33	.89	11x18	35	.93						
14x15	36	.87	14x18	33	.89						

S-B 1916 x TMG CA	N	r	TMG x W-B CA	N	r	S-B 1916 x W-B CA	N	r
6x13	36	.82	13x16	32	.90	6x16	40	.79
7x13	36	.88	15x16	35	.88	7x16	41	.83
6x15	38	.72	13x18	31	.93	6x18	36	.77
7x15	39	.75	15x18	33	.88	7x18	36	.31

*See footnote 12.

the length of the interval between tests is at least as significant in causing this low r as the fact that they are two different tests. It would appear that for this group of children the consistency of their intellectual status relative to each other is very little influenced by the use of these different tests. This is true, even though the IQ's as computed according to the several test norms, are often quite variable.

I. The Growth of Intelligence in Individuals

Individual age-curves of intelligence scores, as represented by Sigma Scores (or Stanford Scores) are very informative. In a previous study (5) the Sigma Score curves were presented for all 48 children who had completed the first nine years of the study. From inspection of the curves it was concluded that only a fifth of the group had maintained approximately the same relative status throughout the nine years. The others showed varying types of shifts in status, often consistent in their trends over long periods. While some grew more slowly and others more rapidly than the average, still others had successive periods of rapid and slow growth.

Examples of individual trends for the entire 18 years are shown in Figures 9 to 12, which present the mental scores of four different children in the study. For the purpose of comparing the IQ with the Sigma Score, which represents more accurately the interrelations of the children in this study, each child's scores are plotted in two ways. The broken line gives the IQ's derived from the published norms for the tests used. (These charts are drawn to the scale of one SD to 15 IQ points, which approximates the average, for all the ages, of the SD's of IQ's in this group.) The solid line represents the Sigma Scores, which show the children's status in the Berkeley Growth Study group[13]

Inspection of the curves gives the impression of great instability of scores during the first year or two, regardless of the method of scoring. Usually the IQ's are more variable, but sometimes, especially near one year of age, the Sigma Scores are more deviant. During the ages when the variability of the IQ is greatly restricted it is much more difficult to earn deviant IQ's, even though relative to the group a child's score might be outstanding. Case 14 F (Figure 9) is an example: at 12 months she was the most precocious child in the study, earning a score three SD's above the group mean (i.e., a Sigma Score of 3.00). Her IQ, however, was only 124, which would ordinarily be interpreted as about $1\frac{1}{2}$ SD above average. When she was three years old, on the other hand, her Sigma Score had dropped to .80 while her IQ had risen to 132. Another case, 5 M (Figure 10), shows much greater variability in his Sigma Scores before five years, and in his IQ's after this age. Although both of his curves indicate rapid growth and an upward trend in scores between 18 months and two years, the early retardation was much more marked in the Sigma Scores, and the later acceleration was by far greater in the IQ's.

---

[13]The IQ's are all higher than the Sigma Scores after the first few years. This is to be expected as the former are computed from the test norms, while the latter are computed from the means of MA's or point scores for this superior group.

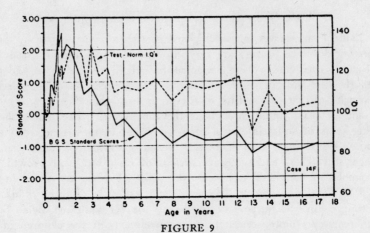

FIGURE 9

CURVES OF THE INTELLIGENCE SCORES OF CASE 14 F: THE SOLID LINE REPRESENTS HER
RELATIVE POSITION (STANDARD SCORE) IN THE BERKELEY GROWTH STUDY;
THE BROKEN LINE GIVES *IQ*'s COMPUTED ACCORDING TO THE
DIRECTIONS FOR THE TESTS USED

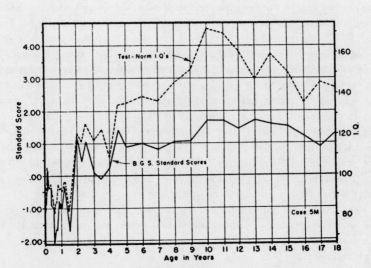

FIGURE 10

STANDARD SCORE AND *IQ* CURVES FOR CASE 5 *M*

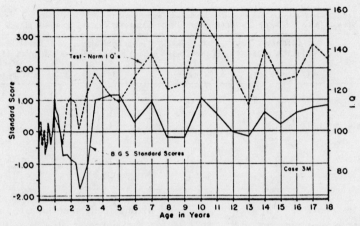

FIGURE 11
STANDARD SCORE AND *IQ* CURVES FOR CASE 3 *M*

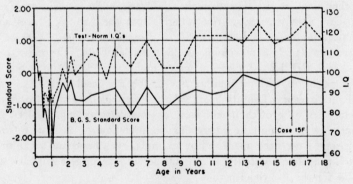

FIGURE 12
STANDARD SCORE AND *IQ* CURVES FOR CASE 15 *F*

Further examination and comparisons of the individual Sigma Scores reveals the normal variations in individual mental growth. We have quantified the individual differences in "constancy" by assigning "Intelligence Lability Scores" to all of the Berkeley Growth Study children. This was done by computing, for each child, the mean and *SD* of his Standard Scores earned over given age-intervals. A child's standard deviation from his own mean is his *Lability Score*. A high score, or large *SD*, signifies greater lability or variation from the child's own central tendency. Data on these .scores are

TABLE 8
MEANS AND *SD*'s OF INTELLIGENCE TEST LABILITY SCORES FOR 40 CASES

	Infancy Months 1-21 I (17 test ages)	Preschool Years 2-5 II (8 ages)	School-age Years 6-18 III (13 ages)	Total Span 1 Mo. to 18 Yrs. IV (38 ages)
Means				
Boys	6.78	4.32	3.39	5.46
Girls	6.78	4.19	3.31	5.41
Total	6.78	4.25	3.35	5.44
SD's				
Boys	2.00	1.61	1.14	1.36
Girls	1.73	1.55	.99	1.05
Total	1.87	1.58	1.08	1.22

given in Table 8. For the 17-test period of one to 21 months, the Infant Lability Scores averaged 6.8, *SD* 1.9; for the eight-test Preschool period of two to five years, the mean Lability Score is 4.3, *SD* 1.6; and for the 13-test School-age period of six to 18 years, the mean is 3.4, *SD* 1.1. This is another way of showing that the children maintain their own relative status more closely as they grow older. Both the Lability Scores and the individual differences in Lability (*SD's*) decrease with age. For the entire 18-year span (with a maximum of 38 tests per child) the mean Lability Score is 5.4, *SD* 1.2. Individual scores range from 12.23 for a boy in the Infancy period to 1.21 for another boy in the Preschool period.

Whether or not a Lability Score such as this will have value in describing characteristics of growth in children, or in differentiating children in any significant way, should be interesting to investigate. A few preliminary comparisons have been made. For example, we found no sex differences in Intelligence-Test Lability at any age-period, the largest critical ratio being 0.24 for the Preschool period.

Intelligence Test Lability has been correlated with level of intelligence at the several age-periods (see Table 9). The *r*'s are all practically zero,

TABLE 9
CORRELATIONS SHOWING THE RELATION OF INTELLIGENCE TEST LEVEL TO LABILITY SCORES FOR 40 CASES

Age at lability score	*r* with Intelligence Level at same age	*r* with mature Intelligence Level*
Months 1-21	—.02	—.005
Years 2-5	—.08	—.14
Years 6-18	.12	.18

*Mean Standard Score for years 16, 17, and 18.

the largest being that of mature intelligence with School-age Lability. This *r* of .18 is not significant but it is in line with McNemar's (29) finding of small significant relations between the magnitude of the *IQ* and test-retest differences. For the School-age period, the upper Quartile (10 cases) in intelligence has a mean Lability Score of 3.9, *SD, .84*; the middle 50 per cent is intermediate in Lability with a mean of 3.3, *SD, 1.2*; while the lowest intelligence quartile has a mean Lability of 3.0, *SD, .85*. The critical ratio between the means of the first and fourth quartile is 1.16. On Mc-Nemar's interpretation, this slight difference is inherent in the methods of test construction, and does not indicate that the brighter children are any less stable in their abilities over a period of time than those whose intelligence is mediocre or inferior. It does mean, however, that in interpreting the scores we should allow for some greater variability of *scores* at the higher levels of intelligence.

There appears to be little tendency for a given child to have a characteristic Lability pattern at all ages. Intercorrelations between the scores earned for the three age-periods are: Infancy with Preschool, .26; Infancy with School-age, .19; Preschool with School-age, —.29. As may be seen from the *r*'s in Table 10, the score for the total 18-year span is determined almost

TABLE 10
CORRELATIONS SHOWING THE CONSISTENCY OF INTELLIGENCE TEST LABILITY SCORES FOR 40 CASES

Periods compared	*r*
Infancy with Preschool	.26
Infancy with School-Age	.19
Infancy with Total Span	.97
Preschool with School-Age	—.29
Preschool with Total Span	.38
School-Age with Total Span	.28

entirely by the Infancy scores, where the lability is so much greater than at the later ages.

Another approach is to select for study those children who are characteristically *labile* or *stable*. For this purpose we have called *labile* the 10 children (25 per cent) with the largest Lability Scores, and *stable* the 10 with the smallest scores, for any given period. Of the 40 children in the study there were four (two boys and two girls) who were *labile* for the total 18-year span and also for two of the three shorter periods. Similarly, there were two boys and two girls who were *stable* by the same criterion. Thirteen children (seven boys and six girls) were both *labile* and *stable* at different periods. For example, a child would be very stable (in the lower Lability quartile) in his intelligence scores for several years, yet at another time he would become labile, with considerable change from test to test (i.e., in the upper Lability quartile). Only six (five of them girls) maintained moderate scores (i.e., in the middle 50 per cent) for all three periods as well as for the total 18-year span.

Whether the four children who can be characterized as generally labile are significantly different in any other respects from the four stable children, or whether these eight in turn are different from the six moderately labile, will have to await a more complete analysis of cases. The differences are not related to adult intelligence level: only one of the four labile children falls in the upper quartile of intelligence; the other three, as well as the four stable children are in the middle 50 per cent. It would appear, from inspection of the individual curves, that a high Lability Score is often the result of a consistent shift in relative mental status during the period covered by the score. Possibly a more fruitful measure of lability would be one which rules out consistent shifts in intelligence level by measuring the deviations of scores from a smoothed curve. As for the present method of measuring lability, it shows that not only are there wide individual differences among these children with respect to the lability of their intelligence test scores, but also that the degree of lability at one stage is no indicator of lability at another stage in the mental growth process.

The impression gained from inspection of the individual Sigma Score curves is corroborated by the Lability Scores. The relatively great lability of scores during the first two years is also evidenced in the correlation coefficients. However, even at the later ages, when the r's between tests are high, some individuals are more steady than others in their mental progress. What is more, a child who had been labile may steady down to consistent intelligence test scores, while another child whose progress had been stable may speed up or slow down, thus increasing his Lability Score.

J. SUMMARY

It has been the purpose of this report to present the growth trends in intelligence for a group of 40 children who had been tested at most or all of 38 testing ages from one month through 18 years of age. Attention has been focused primarily on age changes in variability of intelligence test scores and on individual consistency in relative scores.

Some evidence has been found which indicates that the distributions of intelligence test scores do not exhibit consistent trends in variability during growth. There appear to be periods in which the abilities of children are relatively homogeneous, and others in which there are much greater individual differences. These periods are found in the scores obtained from a number of different tests and investigations, and thus seem to be inherent in the processes of mental development.

It is postulated that greatest homogeneity in scores occurs for a function when it is just starting to develop; that scores are most dispersed when that function is still growing rapidly but when those who are growing most rapidly in the function are not yet mature; and that as the slower-growing individuals reach maturity in the function the differences again become somewhat restricted. Consequently, if the tests are adequate measures of the abilities under consideration, fluctuations in the standard deviations of scores would be caused by the successive (and at times partially concurrent) developing and maturing of different types of intellectual ability.

If these postulates are valid, it would seem well worth while to direct studies, not only toward isolating, but also toward discovering the onset and course of development, of the different functions, or "factors," of intelligence. Furthermore, the tools with which we measure general intelligence should be fashioned with these considerations in mind.

Statistically, in order to increase the constancy of relative mental test scores (and to compare abilities in the same children through periods of time), it is important to use scores which do not fluctuate with the SD's. It is also necessary to rule out differences due to the use of different tests with unequal standardizations. These sources of irregularity have been controlled for the Berkeley Growth Study by computing Sigma Scores (and Standard Scores) from the means and SD's of the point scores or mental ages earned by these children.

The consistency of the mental test Sigma Scores is then studied by means of test-retest correlations, of individual age-curves, and of Lability Scores. The latter measure the extent to which each child fluctuates from his own intelligence level, in tests taken during a given age-span.

By all three methods of comparing, it is seen that children's scores are very labile during infancy, and become gradually more stable. By school age the prediction of the general level of intelligence is fairly stable. However, there are considerable individual differences in lability at all ages. This is true for our Sigma Scores, but when the test-norm IQ's are used there is much wider fluctuation, especially for those children with the more deviant scores. Such deviant IQ's should, in practice, be interpreted with great caution. These data point to the desirability of using some form of Standard Score (or *IQ*'s derived from Standard Scores) instead of the ratio *IQ*.

The high *r*'s between scores on the Stanford-Binet, Wechsler-Bellevue, and Terman-McNemar Group tests indicate that these three tests measure much more nearly the same abilities than would be expected from the children's differences in *IQ*'s. Equivalent scores for these tests, based on comparable case samples would be useful in practice.

Boys and girls were found to be equally labile in their test scores. Children with high levels of intelligence were not significantly more labile than those with less intelligence, in this group.

For the school-age period which is definitely more stable than for younger ages, the children's Lability Scores averaged about one-third of a standard deviation, or roughly five or six *IQ* points. This figure is very similar to those given for earlier studies which emphasized the "constancy of the *IQ*." It must be kept in mind, however, that our Lability Scores are *SD*'s based on 10 to 13 tests per child (for the school-age period), and do not represent the extremes, but the central tendencies for a number of tests. Although many children maintain fairly constant levels of intelligence after six years of age, in some there are wide shifts in mental level. These shifts may occur at any age, and over a wide range of intellectual ability.

REFERENCES

1. ABERNETHY, E. M. Relationships between mental and physical growth. *Monog. Soc. Res. Child Devel.*, 1936, **1**, No. 7.
2. ANDERSON, J. E. The limitations of infant and preschool tests in the measurement of intelligence. *J. of Psychol.*, 1939, **8**, 351-379.
3. ANDERSON, L. D. The predictive value of infancy tests in relation to intelligence at five years. *Child Devel.*, 1939, **10**, 203-212.
4. BAYLEY, N. Mental growth during the first three years: A developmental study of sixty-one children by repeated tests. *Genet. Psychol. Monog.*, 1933, **14**, No. 1.
5. ————. Mental growth in young children. *Yearb. Nat. Soc. Stud. Educ.*, 1940, **39**, 11-47.
6. ————. Factors influencing the growth of intelligence in young children. *Yearb. Nat. Soc. Stud. Educ.*, 1940, **39**, 49-79.
7. ————. The California First-Year Mental Scale. Berkeley: Univ. California Press, 1933.
8. BAYLEY, N., & JONES, H. E. Environmental correlates of mental and motor development; a cumulative study from infancy to six years. *Child Devel.*, 1937, **8**, 329-341.
9. ————. The Berkeley growth study. *Child Devel.*, 1941, **12**, 167-173.
10. BRADWAY, K. P. Predictive value of Stanford-Binet preschool items. *J. Educ. Psychol.*, 1945, **36**, 1-16.

11. DAVIS, W. A., & HAVIGHURST, R. J. The measurement of mental systems (can intelligence be measured?). *Sci. Mo.*, 1948, **66**, 301-316.

12. DEARBORN, W. F., & ROTHNEY, J. W. M. Predicting the Child's Development. Cambridge: Sci-Art Publishers, 1941.

13. DUBNOFF, B. A comparative study of mental development in infancy. *J. Genet. Psychol.*, 1938, **53**, 67-73.

14. EBERT, E. H. A comparison of the original and revised Stanford-Binet scales. *J. of Psychol.*, 1941, **11**, 47-61.

15. EBERT, E., & SIMMONS, K. The Brush foundation study of child growth and development: I. Psychometric tests. *Monog. Soc. Res. Child Devel.*, 1943, **8**, No. 2.

16. ELLIS, R. S. The "laws" of relative variability of mental traits. *Psychol. Bull.*, 1947, **44**, 1-33.

17. FILLMORE, E. Iowa tests for young children. *Stud. Child Welf.*, 1936, **11**, No. 4.

18. FREEMAN, F. N., & FLORY, C. D. Growth in intellectual ability as measured by repeated tests. *Soc. Res. Child Devel.*, 1937, **2**, No. 2.

19. GOODENOUGH, F. L. Studies of the 1937 revision of the Stanford-Binet scale: I. Variability of the *IQ* at successive age-levels. *J. Educ. Psychol.*, 1942, **33**, 241-251.

20. GOODENOUGH, F. L., & MAURER, K. M. The Mental Growth of Children from Two to Fourteen Years. Minneapolis: Univ. Minnesota Press, 1942.

21. HENMON, V. A. C., & LIVINGSTONE, W. F. Comparative variability at different ages. *J. Educ. Psychol.*, 1922, **13**, 17-29

22. HONZIK, M. P. The constancy of mental test performance during the preschool period. *J. Genet. Psychol.*, 1938, **52**, 285-302.

23. JAFFA, A. S. The California Preschool Mental Scale: Form *A*. Berkeley: Univ. California Press, 1934.

24. JONES, H. E., & CONRAD, H. S. The growth and decline of intelligence: A study of a homogeneous group between the ages of ten and sixty. *Genet. Psychol. Monog.*, 1933, **13**, 223-294.

25. KNEZEVICH, S. The constancy of the *IQ* of the secondary school pupil. *J. Educ. Res.*, 1946, **39**, 506-516.

26. KUHLMANN, F. Tests of Mental Development. Minneapolis: Educational Test Bureau, 1939.

27. LINDQUIST, E. F. Statistical Analysis in Educational Research. Boston: Houghton Mifflin, 1940.

28. MAURER, K. M. Intellectual Status at Maturity as a Criterion for Selecting Items in Preschool Tests. Minneapolis: Univ. Minnesota Press, 1946.

29. McNEMAR, Q. The Revision of the Stanford-Binet Scale: An Analysis of the Standardization Data. Boston: Houghton Mifflin, 1942.

30. MILLS, F. C. Statistical Methods Applied to Economics and Business. (Rev. Ed.) New York: Holt, 1948.

31. NELSON, V., & RICHARDS, T. W. Fels mental age values for Gesell schedules. *Child Devel.*, 1940, **11**, 153-157.

32. PARKYN, G. W. The clinical significance of *IQ*'s on the revised Stanford-Binet scale. *J. Educ. Psychol.*, 1945, **36**, 114-118.

33. SARTAIN, A. Q. A comparison of the new revised Stanford-Binet, the Bellevue scale, and certain group tests of intelligence. *J. Soc. Psychol.*, 1946, **23**, 237-239.

34. SHUTTLEWORTH, F. K. The physical and mental growth of girls and boys age six to nineteen in relation to age at maximum growth. *Monog. Soc. Res. Child Devel.*, 1939, **4**, No. 3.

35. TERMAN, L. M.   The Measurement of Intelligence.   Boston: Houghton Mifflin, 1916.
36. TERMAN, L. M., & McNEMAR, Q.   Terman-McNemar Test of Mental Ability. Yonkers-on-Hudson: World Book, 1941.
37. TERMAN, L. M., & MERRILL, M. A.   Measuring Intelligence: A Guide to the Administration of the New Revised Stanford-Binet Tests of Intelligence. Boston: Houghton Mifflin, 1937.
38. THURSTONE, L.   Theories of intelligence.   *Sci. Mo.*, 1946, **62**, 101-112.
39. WECHSLER, D.   The Measurement of Adult Intelligence.   Baltimore: Williams & Wilkins, 1944.

Institute of Child Welfare
University of California
Berkeley 4, California

ENVIRONMENTAL INFLUENCES ON MENTAL DEVELOPMENT

Harold E. Jones

CHAPTER 11

ENVIRONMENTAL INFLUENCES ON MENTAL DEVELOPMENT [1]
HAROLD E. JONES

The Nature of Mental Ability

The studies reported in this chapter are based primarily upon results from the use of standard intelligence tests. The influence of environment on mental ability will therefore, in the first instance, be observed only through its effect upon mental test scores. The validity or general significance of such scores rests upon the extent to which they serve as indicators of a wider range of adaptive behavior (that is, of mental capacities or potentialities). No test is as valid as we would like to have it, but the significance of scores is particularly open to question in the case of subjects who have had special practice, or who are outside the cultural or educational range of the sample on which the test was standardized. If these or other conditions have

[1] The subject of this chapter has been covered in comprehensive reviews in two *Yearbooks of the National Society for the Study of Education*, prepared respectively by Terman *et al.* (1928) and Stoddard *et al.* (1940); in three issues of the *Review of Educational Research*, edited by Stoddard (1933, 1936) and Jones (1939); in *Heredity and Environment* by Schwesinger (1933) and *The Dynamics of Population* by Lorimer and Osborn (1934); and also in numerous textbook treatments. With our knowledge still inconclusive at many points, the rapid growth of research in this field testifies to its continuing vitality and also to the continued need for critical summaries and appraisals. The present treatment deals with research through the year 1941.

Acknowledgments are due to Miss Jane Loevinger for assistance in connection with this chapter, and also to Doctor Herbert S. Conrad for reading the manuscript and for numerous suggestions.

disturbed the appropriateness of the test in question for the individuals in question, the effect of the environment can, of course, be interpreted only with reference to a narrow range of test functions, and not with regard to a broader concept of intelligence.

Individual differences in mental ability have been discussed by E. L. Thorndike (1927) as involving three principal aspects, *level, range,* and *speed*. The level of ability which a person reaches is defined by the difficulty of mental tasks which he can perform; the range or breadth of ability is defined by the number of different tasks which he can perform at various levels. If the items of an intelligence test are classified from "easy" to "hard," two individuals may be able to solve problems at the same level of difficulty, but one may achieve a higher total score than the other because he solves a greater variety of problems at that or at preceding levels. Speed, or rate of work, is also a factor in mental efficiency, although regarded as of less direct importance than the other aspects of ability.

A useful line of inquiry would be the study of the effects of environment upon specific aspects of intelligence, as represented for example in level, range, or speed scores, or even more specifically in test items, groups of items, or component scores derived from factor analysis. In this field, however, few attempts have been made to deal analytically with constituent factors; the principal studies are limited chiefly to general measures of mental function. These general measures, concerned with the capacity to utilize symbols and to acquire *intellective* adaptations, are ordinarily expressed in terms of a composite score, such as the IQ.

It is readily seen that, in our present state of theory, intelligent behavior can be designated more readily by illustration than by abstract definition. This implies, of course, an empirical and functional point of view concerning the nature of intelligence. The reader who wishes a fuller statement as to current emphases in the theory of intelligence is referred to a discussion of this problem by Freeman (1940).

The Nature of Environmental Influences

The individual organism comes into being and develops in a maternal environment which supplies nourishment and other biological needs and also provides both protective shielding and some opportunity for functional stimulation. These environmental supports are essential if the organism is to grow, or even to survive. In this connection, no one asks the question, "Which is more important, nature or nurture?" for both are obviously indispensable. Structural and, ultimately, functional development is an outcome of (1) the interaction of genes with their intracellular environment, (2) the interaction of cells in the intraorganic environment, and (3) the interaction of the organism with its extraorganic surroundings. The hereditary "determiners" or genes cannot function unless the various aspects of the environment play their necessary rôles. On the other hand, the influence of environmental factors is subject to very definite limitations, for (to cite one example) no normal environmental force can change an individual with chromosomes of one species into an individual with the characteristics of a different species. Developmental differences large enough to distinguish species are thus hereditary effects which extrinsic factors cannot (in any given individual) wholly simulate or counteract.

The problem of environmental influences becomes less a matter of general principles, and more a matter for specific analysis, when we turn our attention from the growth of the single individual to the consideration of factors which affect individual differences. In this area we may with reason ask, "Which is more important, nature or nurture?" If, however, we attempt to reply to the question (as applied to mental abilities) with an over-all generalization, we shall immediately find ourselves in logical difficulties. Suppose that we address ourselves to the task of determining the causes of illiteracy. Haldane (1938) has pointed out that, among adults in England under forty years of age, illiteracy is probably most often due either to mental deficiency or to blindness. But among adults in Elizabethan England, or in India today, illiteracy may be attributed primarily to the lack of educational opportunity.

Thus we are led to say that hereditary and environmental influences on intelligence do not constitute a single problem for which a single quantitative answer can be found, but a family of problems, each with its own relatively complicated answer.

Quantitative Approaches

Hogben (1933), in a book rich with illuminating examples of the interaction of heredity and environment, points out that statistical methods are useful in detecting the *presence* of either sort of influence, but he questions the meaningfulness of attempts to *quantify* the relative influence of genetic and nongenetic causes of variations.

"No statement about a genetic difference has any scientific meaning unless it includes or implies a specification of the environment in which it manifests itself in a particular manner" (p. 14). Haldane (1938) has similarly made the point: "The question of the relative importance of nature and nurture has no general answer, but . . . a very large number of particular answers" (p. 36). The analysis by Whipple (1928) and by Schwesinger (1933) of the heredity-environment problem is also relevant to the present discussion. In a cogent statement as to the relation of specific conditions to the effects of training, Whipple has urged that results should be formulated in detailed terms of the approximate percentages of a given group which can be expected to show improvements of various amounts.

One of the earliest and most widely criticized quantitative statements was Burt's (1921) regression equation for predicting Binet mental age from schooling, "reasoning ability," and chronological age. Both Holzinger and Freeman (1925) and Burks (1928a) have demonstrated the error in direct inference from regression coefficients to proportional contributions.

Fisher (1918) has developed methods by means of which, granted the applicability of certain assumptions, "it is possible to calculate the numerical influence not only of dominance, but of the total genetic and nongenetic causes of variability" (p. 433). These methods have been used by Conrad and Jones (1940) to test hypotheses concerning the nature of hereditary transmission of intelligence but not for the purpose of calculating the numerical influence of nature and nurture.

Methods for determining the proportional influence of causal factors have been applied to studies of foster children by Burks (1928b), Wright (1931), Leahy (1935), and Wallis (1936), and to studies of twins by Newman, Freeman, and Holzinger (1937). Leahy's computations gave the home environment the very meager credit of determining not more than 4 per cent of the variation in mental ability (stated in terms of variance, or the square of the standard deviation). A more liberal estimate by Burks was 17 per cent. Wright (1931) and Shuttleworth (1935) have reworked the data of these investigators, applying statistical corrections which give results differing somewhat from each other and from the original studies.

We need not at this point be greatly concerned about reconciling these statements or interpreting the highly mathematical criticisms which various members of the quantitative school of thought have leveled at each other's techniques. For all these statements, it is important to understand that: (1) The proportional contribution of heredity and environment does not refer to the make-up of individual IQ's nor to the general level of intelligence, but either to average effects upon *individual differences* or to differences between groups. (2) Existing studies are based on fallible and incomplete measures both of intelligence and of the environment; this fact should be remembered when the data are being manipulated to yield an apparently highly exact result. (3) Even if it is logically feasible to seek a single value for the effect of environment, this particular value may not apply in samples involving (*a*) a different environmental level, (*b*) a different hereditary selection, (*c*) a change in variability of either of the above factors, or (*d*) a change in any special conditions which may affect the interaction of these factors.

The remainder of this discussion will be concerned with results from several different types of approach. Each of these contributes in its own way to our understanding of what environment can and cannot do; each provides some clue as to the relative importance of environmental factors under specified circumstances. For the time being, however, we must think of these results as rough approximations rather than as precise and final statements.

Mental Growth Curves

One approach to the analysis of environmental influences is based on the study of mental growth curves. If the intelligence of children (relative to age) were generally found to be constant throughout childhood, few questions would be raised about the rôle of differential environmental factors, except perhaps as these may be assumed to operate in the prenatal period or in early infancy.

If, on the other hand, mental development of individuals is marked by variable or systematic changes (that is, by fluctuations or age trends, relative to the group), the nature and extent of possible environmental influence become an issue of some interest. Such changes, if they occur, are not necessarily due to the environment or subject to educational controls. They may be attributable to errors of measurement; to normative defects of the test; or to changes in the composition of the test, or of intelligence, at different levels. They may be due to variations in the temporary state of the subject, dependent upon physical condition, rapport, and motivation. Or they may express a neurophysiological growth pattern differing in rate of evolution for different children; such maturational changes are well established in the patterns of physical growth for various organs, and for the body as a whole. Any of these factors, in any combination, may conceivably operate to alter the apparent or actual course of mental development. One of our first problems, therefore, is to ascertain the facts as to the regularity of

growth, and then to attempt an assessment of the various agencies which may be responsible for irregular or unpredicted variations.

Growth in Terms of Averages. An implicit belief in the lawfulness and uniformity of mental development has at times accompanied the acceptance of IQ and mental age as indices of intelligence most convenient for general use. For any group of children with an average IQ of 100 at age 10, the average will remain substantially the same at 11 and at 12 years if we allow for slight practice effects which tend to increase the IQ, and slight standardization errors which in our present instruments usually tend to decrease it. This constancy, however, is the necessary outcome of a scale conceived in terms of mental age,[1] In such a scale, a gain of one year in mental age is that increment which occurs (on the average) in one chronological year, and the average rate of development during childhood must appear to be constant since it is expressed in terms of constant and equal increments of mental age. It is, of course, now generally understood that such a picture of growth is merely a convenient artifact—convenient largely because of its adaptability for use in connection with an educational grade system based on chronological age.

A theory of environmental influence should be able to deal with the fact that in terms of units other than mental age the growth of intelligence may not be

[1] Heinis (1926) has derived a logarithmic formula for mental growth and proposed the use of a "Personal Constant," based on the logarithmic equation, to avoid alleged arbitrary features of the mental age scale. This proposal has been analyzed in a definitive discussion by Bradway and Hoffeditz (1937). Gesell (1928), in plotting developmental age, has also used a logarithmic method to express the relative rate of what is "arithmetically implicit" in an age scale.

linear, but with increasing age may show a decreasing rate of change. This is illustrated in Table 1, adapted from Freeman

TABLE 1

MEANS AND STANDARD DEVIATIONS, BY AGE, FOR THE *VACO* GROUP INTELLIGENCE TEST

Age	Mean Score	SD	Annual Gain	Gain SD
8	82.3	....	....	....
9	106.1	24.4	23.8	0.98
10	127.7	28.8	21.6	0.75
11	150.0	31.5	22.3	0.71
12	172.2	31.6	22.2	0.64

and Flory (1937). The intelligence scale used in this study consisted of vocabulary items, analogies, a completion test, and an opposites test. In terms of point scores, it can be seen that the annual gains are quite constant or linear within this age range. Annual gains, however, decrease sharply when expressed as a fraction of the SD; this is a more rational way of indicating age changes than merely in terms of raw scores or of mental age.

Rate changes in mental growth can also be estimated in terms of the overlapping of distributions of scores at successive ages. In a somewhat selected group, Bayley (1933) has shown that in early childhood overlapping is very small even when retests are given at short intervals. Thus, at 5 months no cases in her sample equal or exceed the average mental score attained at 6 months. At 5 years, on the other hand, evidence of age changes can hardly be seen within a period so short as a month. The distributions for tests given at month intervals overlap to such an extent that they are almost identical.[1]

[1] Individual development involves a multiplication of environmental contacts, and also an increasing scope of response to the environment. This might reasonably be expected to produce an orderly *increase* in the rate of mental growth during early childhood and adolescence, if envi-

IQ Constancy. Another source of evidence concerning variability in growth is based on the study of changes in individual scores. Although average IQ's maintain approximate constancy by force of standardization, individual IQ's are under no such requirement. The common finding that the probable error of an IQ (Stanford-Binet) is approximately 5 points appears reassuring from the point of view of those who wish to classify children on the basis of a single test, but, when we consider this statement, we should also bear in mind the fact that with a probable error of 5 points (if differences are normally distributed) one child in five may deviate as much as 10 points in a retest.[2] Such a difference is of sufficient practical importance to justify an inquiry into its possible causes.

Predictive Correlations. IQ differences on retests may be influenced not merely by changes within the group but also by upward or downward trends of the group as a whole; such trends could be due to practice effects, to errors in standardization, or to other factors which will be discussed in a later section. If our interest is primarily in the constancy with which individuals maintain their relative rate of mental growth, the most straightforward index is the coefficient of correlation between mental status on two different occasions.

ronment is of predominant importance in mental growth. Current research, however, has shown that basic mental test abilities decrease in their rate of growth, that they reach a peak in the late teens or early twenties, and that they decline in later maturity; these facts suggest the presence of innate or organic limitations in the individual's response to his environment.

[2] The reader may consult Hildreth (1926) for empirical evidence on this point. However, the probable error of the IQ is not a fixed value, but may vary according to the age, intelligence level, and test experience of the subject. In the Terman and Merrill (1937) standardization, the average difference between IQ's on Form M an L was 5.9 for cases with IQ of 130 or above, decreasing to 2.5 for cases with IQ below 70.

Various reviews [1] have shown that retest correlations are rarely as high as .95, and most commonly fall between .80 and .90. Reports on this subject, however, are often difficult to interpret, since they have usually included cases at many different age levels and with different test intervals. R. L. Thorndike (1933) has shown that on an immediate retest the most probable correlation is .89. This value falls to .87 at 10 months; .81 at 30 months; .70 at 60 months. It is recognized, however, that age as well as test interval may influence the results. If the first test is given as late as at 10 years of age, prediction may be better than Thorndike's estimate; thus, in a study by Byrns and Hennon (1935), 250 college students were located who had been tested 8 to 10 years previously. For this selected group the initial IQ (National Intelligence Test) correlated .81 with a group test score obtained in college. On the other hand, if the initial test is given in infancy, correlations with later status may fall close to zero.

During the first year of life, adequately reliable measurements can be obtained of mental functions on the basis of various types of items involving problem solving, imitation, memory, and other forms of adaptive reaction. Such measurements are of possible importance in adapting a régime to a child's developmental level at any given time. Moreover, individual differences in these mental functions are reasonably consistent over periods of several months. Bayley (1940a) has obtained mental scores with a reliability of .94 by averaging scores obtained at 7, 8, and 9 months. These correlate .81 with scores

3 months later, but only .39 with scores at around 21 months; .22 with scores at around 30 months, and practically zero with all later measurements, to 6 years and beyond. Although other studies have not covered this age range, similar results have in general been reported between mental tests given at 1 year and 3 to 4 years later.[2]

From such results, it might be expected that in the case of mental scores obtained still earlier in infancy, the correlations with later status would also vary around zero. It is interesting to note, however, that Furfey and Muehlenbein (1932), L. D. Anderson (1939), and Bayley (1940a) all report negative correlations between test scores obtained at 6 months or earlier and test scores obtained at 4 years or later. Although the prediction indices found in these studies are not statistically significant, they are sufficiently consistent to suggest that early status and later growth rates may be negatively related. Speculation on this point may well be re-

[1] The best of these are by R. L. Thorndike (1933, 1940). Earlier reviews have been published by Foran (1926, 1929) and by Nemzek (1933). Useful summaries are also given by Pintner (1931) and by Hirsch (1930a), the latter adding further evidence from a cumulative study of a large sample.

[2] For 91 cases, L. D. Anderson (1939) reported a correlation of .06 between Gesell scores at 1 year and the Stanford-Binet at 5 years. Furfey and Muehlenbein (1932) found a correlation of −.20 between mental scores at 12 months, on the Linfert-Hierholzer scale, and Stanford-Binet IQ's given at an average age of 4.8 years.

With the feeble-minded and in cases involving a definite pathology, such as mongolian idiocy and some birth injury cases, it would be expected that a fairly consistent picture of retardation would be observable from infancy. Case records reported by Gesell, Castner, Thompson, and Amatruda (1939) give convincing evidence on this point. In a representative sampling, however, such cases are either absent or too few to produce much effect upon the retest coefficients.

A number of writers have been optimistic as to the possibility of obtaining improved prediction through the selection and differential weighting of items in the infant tests. The practical possibilities of this procedure remain to be demonstrated, although current studies by Nelson and Richards (1938, 1939) and Richards and Nelson (1939) have yielded promising preliminary results.

served until the findings are confirmed by other studies. Of possible relevance is the investigation by Dubnoff (1938), who tested 489 infants in Kazan, U.S.S.R., by the California First Year Mental Scale. Approximately one-third of the group was of Tatar extraction; one-half was tested in homes, and one-half (factory workers' children) in crèches or factory nurseries. Scale scores during the first year favor the Kazan group; in terms of the variability of the Kazan group, the difference is about 2 SD at one month. From the fourth to the eighth month the difference drops to about 1 SD and by the tenth month the averages become approximately equal in the two groups. It could be contended that the relative gain of the California group from 1 to 10 months is due in part to a more favorable environment with regard to medical care, diet, sunlight, and to a more intelligent régime of care by the mother. Dubnoff comments:

> Due to the cold winters, the Kazan child is heavily clothed, and often wrapped in blankets which prevent freedom of movement. Except for about two months of the year he is never exposed to sunlight. Rickets is prevalent. . . . The level of education of the parents is very markedly lower than that of the California sample (p. 70).

Environmental factors, however, cannot be adduced to explain the initial superiority of the Kazan infants. Dubnoff's work, together with other related studies, may lead to the speculative suggestion that between natio-racial groups, as within a given group, a slight tendency exists for early precocity to be associated with a slower mental growth at later ages, and perhaps with a lower average intelligence level at maturity. A parallel situation may be noted when we compare different animal species; among the primates, for example, the maturity of performance at a given age in infancy can be used *inversely* to predict the general level of adaptive ability that will be attained at adolescence.

To summarize the foregoing, we have noted an apparent slight tendency for mental scores in early infancy to be negatively correlated with mental scores at 4 years or later. At 12 months of age the correlation is close to zero. Beyond that point, however, a positive relationship emerges. Figure 1 shows the correlations of scores at 10 years with scores at each preceding year for the sample of cases previously reported on by Bayley (1933, 1940a) and by Bayley and Jones (1937). The index of forecasting efficiency $(1 - \sqrt{1 - r^2})$ is also shown. It is apparent that as early as 2 years of age individual differences are beginning to appear which carry forward to some extent into later childhood.[1] The increase in predictive power is somewhat more rapid in the preschool period than later.

The Age Ratio. J. E. Anderson (1940) has pointed out that as we go up the age scale the prediction of later from earlier status involves an increasing proportion of similar elements. The 10-year tests are in content more similar to the 9- than to the 8-year tests. Moreover, the cumulative composites of performance which are represented in test scores are more similar between adjacent than between separated age levels. They become increasingly similar for adjacent levels as we approach maturity, since the increment from one year to another will have a proportionately smaller effect upon total scores.

Figure 1 represents correlations based upon actual scores (point scores or mental ages). The scores for each individual change each year as a result of successive increments of growth. What would happen if we were to set up an artificial

[1] See also reports by Honzik (1938) and L. D. Anderson (1939).

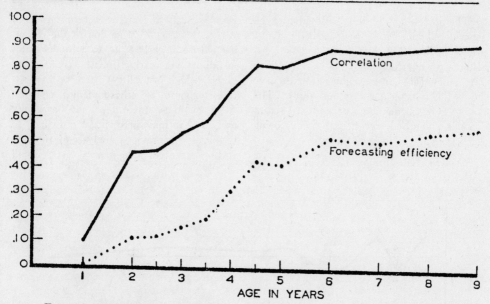

FIGURE 1. Mental scores at 10 years as related to scores in each preceding year.

series in which the increments for each year were cumulated at random? Thus, at 3 years individual A would be given an arbitrary score consisting of his own score at 2 years plus B's increment from 2 to 3 years. The resulting 3-year score could then be added to C's actual increment from 3 to 4 years, in order to obtain an arbitrary 4-year score for A. Such a series (as Anderson has shown by cumulating random numbers) would necessarily result in a correlation curve very similar to that actually obtained in Figure 1. Several factors might operate to produce differences in the two curves. For example, if actual mental growth involves greater annual increments for those who already have higher status, then the correlation curve for actual scores, other things being equal, will be higher than that based on arbitrary cumulations. But in any event we must expect that the predictive power of our tests will be proportionate to the age of testing. It will also be inversely propor-

tionate to the length of the interval over which prediction is attempted. Honzik (1938) has proposed the concept of the Age Ratio $\left(\dfrac{\text{CA at Test 1}}{\text{CA at Test 2}}\right)$ to express both these factors. The Age Ratio shows a high positive correlation with retest coefficients during the first ten years.

Two consequences of this may now be pointed out. If hereditary components in mental ability are more fully manifested at maturity than at earlier ages, children whose eventual status is to be either high or low will tend to fall nearer the mean in earlier tests, and in later tests will gradually approximate their final position.[1]

[1] This appears to be illustrated in a study by P. Cattell (1937), who made ability classifications of children on the basis of an average of initial tests and retests (thus eliminating changes within extreme groups due to regression). Children of superior average ability tended to increase in IQ on the retest. Among mental defectives, Roberts, Norman, and Griffiths (1938) have reported an average downward shift of about 2 IQ points per year in the age range

The foregoing argument should also be considered in relation to statements about the "plasticity" of early childhood (susceptibility to environmental influences). Figure 2 illustrates an individual growth curve of a fairly typical or normal form. The curve is based on sigma or standard scores and is smoothed, the actual points being also shown. It may be noted that this is a relative, not an absolute, growth curve.

years. Such a growth pattern has been variously interpreted as due to the changing nature of early tests, to a fundamental instability in early growth (related to physiological instability), and to a sensitive response to environmental changes. Although these factors cannot be wholly excluded, it may be pointed out that, in terms of the previous analysis of the Age Ratio, curves of this general type would

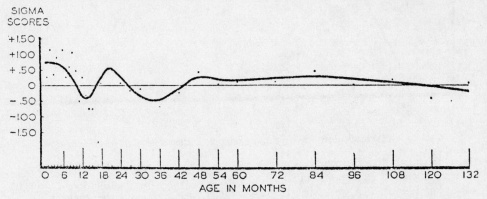

FIGURE 2.   An individual mental growth curve, based on sigma scores.

A horizontal line indicates that the child is maintaining his position in the group; an ascending or descending line indicates that he is growing faster or slower than the group average. The mental growth[1] of the individual represented in Figure 2 is marked by some irregularities during the first four years. At 4, however, he achieves a fairly even, stable position which is maintained with only very minor changes to 10

be expected to be fairly common even in a constant environment, or in a function insensitive to differential environmental factors. We should be cautious in attributing greater retest changes in early childhood to some inherent factor of modifiability if it is possible that they are chiefly due to a statistical factor, namely, to a relatively small proportion of similar elements in successive tests.

A Classification of Factors Influencing Changes in Test Scores

In order to assess the importance of environmental influences on mental growth, we should attempt to gain some conception of the range and magnitude of other influences which affect test scores. These were

from 10 to 14 years. It is, of course, possible that this latter finding is associated with an earlier limit of growth in the feeble-minded.

[1] Sigma score curves indicate changes in status, relative to the group, from one measurement to another. They do not provide a direct measure of growth, and, since they are usually based on unanalyzed composite scores, they do not permit inferences as to the composition or dynamics of growth. From this point of view, it may be sounder to regard them as "status curves" than as growth curves.

briefly indicated on page 585 and are here discussed in greater detail.

Changes in Test Composition. Changes due to the measurement of different abilities cannot be attributed to "chance" factors and yet are not true variations in the growth rate of any one function. For example, consider two children, one possessing unusual motor aptitudes but poor at verbal tasks, the other showing an opposite pattern of abilities. Prior to two years of age, the first child is likely to stand relatively high, but these positions will be reversed at later ages when intelligence tests become more verbal in content. Marked shifts in status due to such factors are probably not very common, since, in general, mental test abilities are intercorrelated positively.

Administrative Factors. "Error" factors other than a shift in the ability stressed are of many sorts, including differences in the test situation, errors in administering or scoring tests, and differences in the "personal equation" of different examiners. This latter was apparently a negligible factor in studies by Goodenough (1928b) and Kawin (1934), but has been emphasized by P. Cattell (1937) in connection with the interpretation of mental test data from the Harvard Growth Study.

Negativism. An important aspect of the relation between subject and examiner, especially in preschool years, arises from the tendency of young children toward negativistic responses, which reduce test scores.[1] Of several studies on this subject, Mayer's (1935) report on negativism encountered in the normative group of the Revised Stanford-Binet is probably most comparable with the ordinary test situation, since the effort was primarily toward getting the best possible response, with the study of negativistic responses only a secondary aim. Under good testing conditions and with highly trained examiners, the average number of negativistic responses per child ranged between 4 and 7, at ages 2½ to 4½ years. About 75 per cent of the cases in that age range gave at least one negativistic response in one of the two testing periods. At 2 years of age less than 25 per cent of the total negativism could be overcome by adroit management, but at 5½ years 90 per cent was overcome. This latter would be true, however, only with skilled examiners, and it is possible that at these ages slight differences in examining technique may be of critical importance to test scores.

Practice Effects. Practice and special training on the part of the subject may introduce spurious changes in mental test scores. According to Terman and Merrill (1937), the *average* gain from a first to a second test is, at different age levels, 2 to 4 IQ points. Successive additional tests may produce smaller gains, but in a longitudinal study the cumulative effect may be so great that results cannot be appropriately stated in terms of IQ, but must be transformed into percentile or scale scores based on cases receiving equivalent amounts of practice. Analyzing results from several group tests, Adkins (1937), following Thorndike, has suggested that the improvement of scores on retest with the same examination may be largely a matter of increased speed on tasks previously solved. The implication is that work-limit tests are of greater value than time-limit tests for longitudinal studies. The reader interested in recent work on practice effects and other conditions of testing will find a list of such

[1] Whereas error factors are frequently susceptible to environmental changes, and thus operate to reduce constancy coefficients, it may be noted that retest correlations may be spuriously raised if an error factor occurs systematically; for example, if children negativistic on one occasion tend also to be negativistic on succeeding tests, with similar effects upon scores.

studies in a review by R. L. Thorndike (1940).

Coaching. One special case of practice effect which deserves separate mention is the effect of coaching or specialized training.[1] Although our present studies in this field point to no very clear-cut conclusion, they suggest, as might be expected, that training is most effective when devoted to material similar to that in the test, and that the effects of training are, characteristically, to produce a temporary but not permanent rise in IQ. The application of these findings is greatest at the preschool level, since the test materials at those levels are more like everyday playthings than at later ages. Although it has not been demonstrated that children of preschool age are particularly susceptible to the effects of special coaching, it is highly probable that nursery schools differ more than grade schools with respect to the similarity of school "curricula" to the testing situation. Earlier reports on the effects of coaching have been reviewed by Burks (1928c).

Intrinsic and Extrinsic Factors. All the factors discussed above may be regarded as involving errors in measurement. In addition to these error factors, mental growth may be conceived as involving actual changes, which have an origin in either intrinsic or extrinsic factors. Intrinsic alterations may arise from specific or general changes in the rate of growth. Relevant factors are the form of the growth curve, with reference to possible cyclical changes, and the age of completion of growth; a neurophysiological basis is implied.

Extrinsic influences on mental growth are roughly of two sorts, social and personal. The social factors include general environ-

[1] The studies of Greene (1928) and Casey, Davidson, and Harter (1928), reported in the *Twenty-seventh Yearbook of the National Society for the Study of Education,* are particularly relevant to this problem.

mental conditions,[1] such as socioeconomic factors in the home and neighborhood and specific educational régimes. What are here called personal factors are those nonability aspects of a person's make-up which actually affect the course of growth in ability rather than merely modify the score at a particular test period. The personal factors, if traumatic, such as physical diseases or extreme emotional episodes, may affect mental growth fairly directly. The more permanent aspects of physical and mental constitution may influence mental development by virtue of the fact that they comprise part of the equipment through which the individual assimilates the environment.

The main problem of this chapter is the evaluation of the extent and nature of *extrinsic influences* on mental development. We are concerned with *error factors* mainly to discount them in considering irregularities in obtained growth curves. The maturational factor leading to intrinsic differences in growth rates can only be mentioned; as yet there is no evidence to separate its effects from those of other factors. Among the extrinsic influences, the reviewer's emphasis will reflect the status of the present literature and will not attempt a systematic evaluation of the relative importance of these factors.

One of the first facts with which we are confronted is that in the preschool period the prediction of later intelligence can be improved by taking into account a measure of the home environment. The varying interpretations of this finding will be discussed in the ensuing section.

Relationships to Cultural-Economic Factors

Education of the Parents. Figure 3, from Bayley's data, shows, at successive ages, the correlation between mental scores of children and the education of their parents (in terms of the average years of schooling of father and mother). This is an admittedly imperfect index of the cultural status of the parents and an even less perfect index of the extent to which cultural factors actually enter into the child's environment. Nevertheless, if we compare

For such findings the most obvious interpretation is that better-educated parents provide environments more stimulating to mental growth and that in general children tend to acquire the intellectual status characteristic of the environment to which they are exposed. Equally logical,

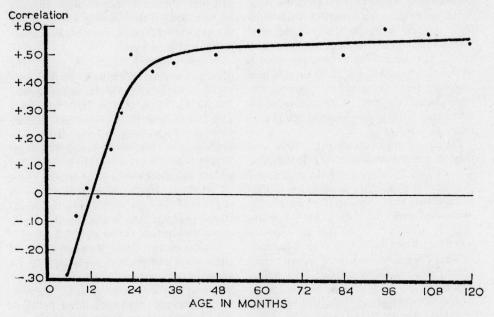

FIGURE 3.   Children's mental scores at successive ages as related to parents' education.

Figures 3 and 1, we can see that the parents' education (obtained prior to the birth of the child) yields a better prediction of the child's intelligence at 10 years than does the child's own test score at ages prior to 2 years.

The relation of parents' education to the child's test score is negative in infancy (a fact consonant with the discussion on page 587). It increases sharply during the period of one to two years, and thereafter shows only minor changes. Somewhat similar correlation curves have been reported by Bayley and Jones (1937) for other measures of social and economic factors.[1]

however, is an interpretation based on the maturing of hereditary potentialities. As a corollary to the discussion of the Age Ratio, the argument has been advanced

[1] Correlations with social status are usually lower than with measures of parent education. Stroud (1928) reported an r of .25 between IQ and tax assessments; Chapman and Wiggins (1925), an r of .32 between IQ and the Chapman-Sims Scale of Socio-economic Status. These studies were based on large samples. When cultural items are included in a home rating or an environmental scale, Burks (1928b) found a correlation of .42 and Leahy (1935) one of .53 with intelligence measures. In interpreting correlational data in this field, attention must be given to the characteristics of the socio-economic measures, particularly with regard to skewness of the distributions.

that, as children approach their eventual intelligence level, they manifest the degree of relationship to parents' intelligence (or to other factors correlated with parents' intelligence) that would be expected on the basis of the inheritance of abilities. The correlation curve as given in Figure 3 presents us with hypotheses rather than with definitive evidence of causal relationship. Each of these hypotheses may serve as a partial explanation of the facts as obtained, but their relative cogency cannot be estimated unless we turn to evidence involving some form of experimental design. Such evidence will be presented in connection with a discussion of studies of foster children.

Perhaps the most elaborate study employing correlational methods is by Van Alstyne (1929), who examined the relationship between children's intelligence (Kuhlmann-Binet) and various factors in the home environment. The sample, consisting of seventy-five 3-year-old children, was drawn from very diverse environments in New York City, and the obtained correlations are probably somewhat higher than would be found in a more representative group. Table 2 presents illustrative results from this study. Van Alstyne pointed out

TABLE 2

THE MENTAL AGE OF CHILDREN AS RELATED
TO ENVIRONMENTAL FACTORS

(From Van Alstyne [1929].)

Child's MA by:	r
Mother's education	.60 ± .05
Father's education	.51 ± .06
"Opportunity for use of constructive play materials"	.50 ± .06
"Number of hours adults spend daily with child"	.32 ± .07
"Number of playmates in home"	.16 ± .08
"Number of hours father reads to child"	.06 ± .08
Nutrition index	−.03 ± .08

that these correlations do not permit any conclusion as to causal factors. It is of interest that several positive correlations emerged in the case of variables which could have little conceivable direct effect upon intelligence: thus, a biserial r of .54 ± .08 was found between the child's MA and whether or not he slept alone in his own bed. This is merely one aspect of the general relation between socioeconomic status and intelligence.

Occupation and "Social Class." The principal sources of material on the relationship of intelligence to socioeconomic factors include a volume by Schwesinger (1933) and one by Lorimer and Osborn (1934). Subsequent reviews have been published by Neff (1938) and Loevinger (1940). Neff pointed out that in various studies of school children a range of about 20 points in IQ has been found between children of the highest and lowest socioeconomic groups. This is also found for preschool children, as shown in Table 3.

Similar occupational differences are found when other criteria are employed. If, for example, we examine the percentage distribution of the parents of gifted children, or the parents of persons listed in *Who's Who in America*, we find a very disproportionate number in the higher occupational brackets. On the other hand, parents of children admitted to feeble-minded institutions tend to cluster in the lower brackets. The assertion has been made by Neff that the occupational hierarchy in IQ can be accounted for entirely in environmental terms. This would also seem to be implied in Pieter's (1939) suggestion of a "coefficient of innate intelligence," to be obtained through dividing the IQ by an environmental index. Conceding that a difference in IQ may have a somewhat different significance when children are compared within the same occupational class and in sharply separated classes, it still appears

TABLE 3

MEAN IQ'S OF PRESCHOOL CHILDREN, CLASSI-
FIED BY FATHER'S OCCUPATION *

Father's Occupation	Goode-nough (1928b)	Terman and Merrill (1937)
I. Professional	116	116
II. Semiprofessional and managerial	112	112
III. Clerical and skilled trades	108	108
IV. Semiskilled and minor clerical	105	104
V. Slightly skilled	104	95
VI. Unskilled	96	94

* Goodenough's sample consisted of 380 Minneapolis children between the ages of 18 and 54 months; the Kuhlmann-Binet was given twice to each child, the means reported in Table 3 being based on the initial test only. The Terman and Merrill sample consisted of 831 children, ages 2 and 5½ years, in the standardization groups for Forms L and M of the revised Stanford-Binet. In this latter sample, an additional classification of "rural owner" was included, with a mean IQ of 99.

unwarranted to explain group differences wholly in terms of extrinsic factors.

The hypothesis that the intelligence differential between the social classes is to some extent an hereditary sampling difference follows from two assumptions: (1) individual variations in intelligence are, in part, genetic in origin; and (2) differences in the selection of occupations and in occupational success are, in part, determined by intelligence. At the present time probably the majority of psychologists regard these assumptions as plausible. Current efforts are directed not toward proof or disproof, but rather toward assessing the approximate importance of different factors under specified conditions.

Special interest attaches to the fact that the social differential in intelligence is well

established as early as 2 or 3 years of age, and relatively constant in later childhood. If due chiefly to environmental effects acting directly, one would expect it to be small at 2 years but to increase gradually with age. Another line of evidence, contrary to the environmental hypothesis, has been supplied by Lawrence (1931), who showed a relationship between children's IQ and the occupational status of their parents, even where environmental differentials were ruled out (in the case of children removed from their homes in infancy and brought up in an institution). D. C. Jones and Carr-Saunders (1927) have added a further relevant finding in comparing the intelligence of children of different social origins who have lived in an orphanage for varying lengths of time. Continued residence in this less differential environment apparently had little or no effect in reducing or "leveling" the original social differential in intelligence.

A study by Outhit (1933) provides an interesting comparison between the intelligence of children and their parents. Fifty-one families were represented, with four or more children in each family. The Army Alpha was used with adults and with children above 12, scores being transformed into IQ's for comparison with the Stanford-Binet IQ's of the younger children. Figure 4 indicates a tendency toward greater occupational differences among parents than among children or, in other words, a tendency for children of either superior or inferior parents to regress toward the mean of the total group. This result would be predicted on the basis of genetic factors, but, so far as home environments are concerned, it is not entirely clear that environmental theory would lead to the same expectation.

Asher (1935) and others have with some justice argued that tests standardized on one social group may give misleading re-

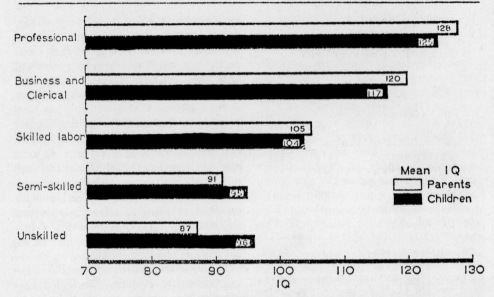

FIGURE 4. Parents' and children's intelligence, in different occupational classes. (After Outhit.)

sults when applied to other groups. This is a special case of the general principle that the validity of items varies according to the experience or cultural background of subjects taking the tests. Another example can be found in the case of experience dependent upon age, as in the study by Jones (1931) of juveniles and adults who had the same mental ages but who performed very differently on different types of test items. Although such studies are illuminating with regard to the specific composition of group differences, little attention has been given to comparative item analyses in connection with occupational groups. The technique has, however, been employed in several studies of rural and urban children.

Rural-Urban Studies. That rural children in the United States attain lower average IQ's than urban children has been confirmed in a number of investigations summarized by Shimberg (1929) and Pintner (1931). It has sometimes been suggested that this is an artifact of the tests used. Tests are usually devised by city dwellers and validated on city children; it is reasonable to expect that their content and perhaps also their time limitations will tend to handicap rural children. Peterson (1928) has emphasized the rôle of test experience and of competitive exercises in school in producing a "set" for efficient performance. Relevant attitudes and incentives may be stimulated in varying degrees by different school systems, and rural children in general probably receive less practice than urban children in working at high pressure under speed and accuracy requirements.

The ever-present problem of test content has been considered by Shimberg (1929), who demonstrated that the urban superiority on an information test could be reversed if the test were originally scaled from items supplied by rural teachers and standardized on a rural group. A similar experiment has not been attempted with other types of material; it is probable that a distinctive "urban" and "rural" content is more apparent in an information test than in other tests. Several investigations have reported not merely a low IQ for rural children, but also an IQ diminishing with age: (1) the well-known study by Gordon (1923) of English gypsies and canal boat children, showing marked negative correlations between age and IQ; (2) Asher's (1935) study of children in the east Kentucky mountains (in this group the median IQ dropped steadily from 84 at 7 years to 60 at 15 years); (3) a report by Edwards and Jones (1938) on school children in the mountains of north Georgia (IQ's dropped from around 100 at ages 7 to 9 years to 76 at age 14, and 70 for those older); (4) Jordan's (1933) study of the children of mill workers in a North Carolina town (IQ's decreased from 100 at the age of 6 to 85 at 13 years); (5) studies of Iowa children by Baldwin, Fillmore, and Hadley (1930) and by Skeels and Fillmore (1937). In the last report, children from underprivileged homes (either rural or urban) were examined at the time of entrance to an orphanage; the mean IQ diminished from 93 at age 4 to 80 at age 14.[1]

These findings have been variously interpreted as due to (1) "the retarding effect of poor homes on mental development" (Skeels and Fillmore, p. 438); (2) the ef-

[1] Speer (1940a, 1940b) and a number of other investigators have utilized similar material from children referred to institutions because of conditions in their own homes. Older children, who have lived longer in homes characterized by poverty and frequently by other undesirable factors, have lower average IQ's than younger children from similar environments. It must be noted, however, that these test scores are not based on cumulative records or on sibling comparisons, but on different samples which may have been subjected to different selective factors. Thus it seems likely that among the older children in very inferior environments some of the brighter ones have already been removed by relatives or other agencies.

fect on the Stanford-Binet of "continued existence at a critically low level of social and cultural status" (Neff, 1938, p. 739); or (3) the effect of using tests which at higher age levels become increasingly inappropriate for the groups to which they are applied (Asher).

The first of these interpretations, in line with other Iowa studies, proposes an actual psychological handicap resulting from a poor environment. The second and third interpretations are more purely psychometric, although the second seems to imply some actual cumulative handicap in mental test abilities, whereas the third is concerned primarily with an age differential in the tests which lowers their validity.

It would be permissible to hold all these interpretations simultaneously, but they would still fail to give an adequate picture of the complex situation involved in the comparison of different cultural groups. Terman and Merrill (1937) have called attention to the fact that in their standardization sample the mean IQ for rural children was 99.2, for urban children 105.7. The urban group was defined as including all subjects from areas having a population density of 1000 or more per square mile, and the rural group as all others. A slight tendency was noted for the rural group to show a decreasing IQ at the beginning of the school period, whereas children of slightly skilled and unskilled laborers show an increase at this period. The authors comment:

These trends are too small to be very reliable and should be regarded merely as suggestive. Even if the trend were reliable it would require an extensive research, carefully planned for that purpose, to determine whether the lowered IQ of rural children can be ascribed to the relatively poorer educational facilities in rural communities, and whether the gain for children from the lower economic strata can be attributed to an assumed enrichment of intellectual environment that school attendance bestows (p. 49).

In the attempt to study the possibility of differential environmental handicap on different test items, Jones, Conrad, and Blanchard (1932) made an item analysis of test results for 351 New England rural children, aged 4 to 14, as compared with 905 cases in the 1916 Stanford-Binet standardization, and also with 212 cases from a relatively homogeneous urban sampling, highly superior in socioeconomic status. The three groups had mean IQ's of 92, 101, and 117, respectively. When the individual items were scaled, marked differences were found in the relative difficulty of the items in the three samples, leading to the conclusion that even when an attempt is made to attain "equal units" on a psychological scale these are strictly relative to the sample. A test scaled on one group may show marked inequalities when applied to other groups. Several tests were identified as showing a sharp differentiation between the three groups, with a tendency for the differences to increase with age. These were all verbal items. In a common environment, the acquisition of verbal skill may, by and large, be regarded as a good index of intelligence; but in widely differing environments it may become predominantly a good index of the environment, and the resulting intelligence quotients will then require reinterpretation.

In this particular study, the authors estimated that social and educational factors could on the average account for about half the mean difference of 10 points in IQ between the rural and the normal urban group. These environmental handicaps, however, appeared to be specific to certain test items, rather than general. As would be expected if the rural-urban difference is in part due to a difference in

hereditary capacities, certain types of tests were found with a marked difference which could not readily be explained in terms of differential opportunities for special training, or differential interest or motivation.[1] On the basis of this item-and-age analysis, the conclusion was offered that the rural group (although representative for the communities studied) presented an inherently poorer selection than the urban comparison groups.

The study of selective rural migration (selective drainage into urban centers and urban occupations) may in the future result in a fuller understanding of rural-urban differences. It is interesting that both in the study discussed above and in an English study by Thomson (1921) fewer high IQ's were found in rural communities accessible to city districts than in comparable communities more remotely located. Areas supplied by good transportation and near a growing urban center are probably in some regions more subject to selective drainage. Similar interpretations may apply to results obtained by Bickersteth (1919) in the Yorkshire dales and by Macmeeken (1939) in isolated rural and coastal sections of northern and western Scotland. It is hard to see how the children in these remote localities could have acquired relatively high average IQ's on the basis of superior cultural opportunities. Economic factors are important in determining the nature of selective migration. Lorimer and Osborn (1934) have cited a number of surveys indicating that in relatively prosperous rural areas the cities attract from both the upper and lower extremes of social status. In depressed rural areas, on the

[1] These included the ball-and-field test, memory for designs, digit memory, picture description, and comprehension.

Results which are in general similar to these of this study have been obtained by Bruce (1940) in a Virginia survey of rural white and Negro children.

other hand, a survey by Gee and Corson (1929) indicated that the less intelligent are more frequently "bound to the land," whereas those of higher social, educational, and intellectual status tend, in greater proportions, to migrate to urban centers. This is supported by Mauldin (1940) and Sanford (1940), on the basis of data from small southern communities.[1]

In concluding this section, the interpretation of rural handicap as due to lack of cultural privilege is seen to provide only a partial explanation. Commenting on the lack of schooling of southern mountain children,[2] Goodenough (1940a) points out that our pioneering New England ancestors did not find schools ready made in the wilderness.

They made schools, and it did not require two centuries of residence for them to do so. Accordingly, I find it hard to accept the idea that the low IQ's of the mountain children are to be explained solely on the basis of educational deprivation. One is forced to ask: Why were they so deprived? (p. 329).

The principal outcome of the socioeconomic and rural-urban studies is to emphasize the fact that, among groups as among individuals, differences cannot be explained in terms of a fixed structure of relationship. With changes in any of the related factors (test composition, hereditary selection, or environment) group or individual differences will represent chang-

[1] For other studies of rural groups, see Clark and Gist (1938), who reported the occurrence of selective migration in Kansas, and Klineberg (1938), who reported its occurrence in a study in southern Germany, but found no evidence for it in a parallel investigation in New Jersey. Conflicting evidence in this field is not an indication of inadequacy in the studies involved, but rather of the varying balance of the complex factors influencing selection.

[2] See Sherman and Key (1932) and Sherman and Henry (1933).

ing degrees of hereditary or environmental influence.

Racio-Cultural Comparisons. According to the bias or special interest of different investigators, comparative studies of Negroes and whites have been quoted as providing evidence of (1) hereditary racial differences or (2) environmental effects.[3] It is well established that in the same communities white children tend to show higher average IQ's than Negro children, with an increasing difference manifested during the school period. Several studies have also indicated, among mixed bloods, a relationship between intelligence and the degree of white admixture; this has not always been confirmed in studies controlling the factor of social status. Until further more crucial evidence is supplied, we must remain in some doubt as to the bearing of Negro-white investigations upon the nature-nurture problem.

In the case of other natio-racial differences, such as have been reported in studies of migrant groups in the United States, the problem is even more complicated by questions of intragroup selection (selective migration) as well as questions bearing on environmental handicaps and the appropriateness of tests. On the basis of tests ordinarily accepted for measuring intelligence, the weight of evidence points to the probability of a difference, in terms of averages, between United States native whites and Negroes, and between American citizens of North European and South European descent. It is possible, but not certain, that this difference would wholly disappear if a correction were made for social status and educational differences. The effect of such a correction can hardly be predicted at the present time, for no one as yet has conducted an experiment in which

[3] For research summaries with contrasting interpretations, see Pintner (1931) and Anastasi (1937).

controlled selections of children varying as to racial background have been reared under similar environmental conditions. This would be entirely feasible either in an appropriately planned institution or in foster homes where precautions are taken to insure comparable physical and social environments.

Another approach which has given suggestive results is represented in the work of Klineberg (1935), who studied the intelligence of Negro migrants from the South in relation to their length of residence in New York City. Children newly arrived had an average IQ of 81.4 (Stanford-Binet), as compared with 84.5 for those who had been in New York two to three years, and 87.4 for those in residence longer than four years. It is reasonable to interpret this as an environmental effect, provided that similar selections of migrants arrived in successive years, and provided also that no selective factors have operated with regard to continued residence in New York. Could an educationally improved environment, exerting its effects early enough and long enough, bring the average IQ of these children not merely to 87 but to the norm of 100 or even higher? Such a conclusion has sometimes been offered, but would seem to involve a premature "extrapolation" from the facts now available.

Mental and Physical Relationships

A slight positive relation has frequently been reported between intelligence and various measures of physique and physical condition. The best-known treatise in the field is Paterson's *Physique and Intellect* (1930). Jones (1933b, 1936, 1939), in a series of reviews, has summarized approximately three hundred studies, and reviews by Shock (1939a, 1939b), Carmichael (1940), and Shock and Jones (1941) cover recent research on physiological relationships.

Physical Measures. It is well known that in certain types of dwarfism (cretins) the arrest of physical growth is accompanied by mental retardation. A similar relationship also holds, in some degree, within normal samples. One of the more competent studies in this field is by Abernethy (1936), who found positive correlations between intelligence and various physical measures at all ages from 8 to 17 years; in the case of height the average r was .26 for boys and .16 for girls. These results are supplemented at the lower ages by Bayley (1940b), who reported an average correlation (between intelligence and height) of .20 for boys and .22 for girls in the age range of 2 to 8 years.[1]

The relevance of this topic to the present problem is in part indicated by B. S. Sanders' (1934) discussion of differential physical growth:

Evidence of differential growth, or its end result—differential size—shows that everywhere children with a superior socio-economic environment are on the average heavier and taller than their age-mates exposed to a less favorable environment. . . . The study does not dispute the fact that in all probability there are inherent differences between the various socio-economic classes. Its one and only contention is that the role of environment cannot be overlooked. . . . And, if environmental differences are important enough to affect physical growth, it is most probable that they affect psycho-social adaptations and behavior as well (p. 299).

[1] More recently, Katz (1940) has reported correlations approaching .40 between median IQ of five tests and height at successive ages from 3 to 5 years. Such atypically high coefficients are less surprising than the fact that for boys the corresponding r's are close to zero. Over one hundred cases are included for each sex. These results have not been confirmed by other investigators.

The hypothesis implied in the foregoing was subjected to a test by Honzik and Jones (1937), who examined the relationship of height to intelligence in a group of approximately 200 children representative of Berkeley, California. Correlations close to zero were found at each age from 21 months to 7 years, but the uniformly positive coefficients for both boys and girls suggested the presence of a genuine, even if meager, relationship; there was, moreover, a slight tendency for growth rates in height or weight to be correlated with increments in mental scores. As in other samples, mental test scores showed an increasing relation to social status [1] (.04 at 21 months, rising to .42 at 7 years). Height also showed a positive but not an increasing relation to social status (.20 at 21 months, and also at 7 years).

In the study of this problem, correlational procedures, dealing with average relationships in a total group, may be less effective than the comparative study of individual growth curves. Honzik and Jones have presented such curves for height, weight, and intelligence, with raw measurements transformed into sigma scores to permit direct comparison as to changes in status in the group. Although some cases showed independent or even diverging curves, a number exhibited a striking concomitance in trend. The suggestion has been made that mental-physical relationships are due to a common influence of the social environment, acting upon intelligence through social example and education, and upon physical factors through nutrition and hygiene. In this study, however, the relationship between height and intelligence was found to be independent, or nearly so, of the measured factors in the environment, since the partialing out of social status (as measured) had little ap-

[1] A socioeconomic index based on parent education, occupation, income, and social ratings.

preciable effect upon the correlations. For the sample in question it seems probable that genetic factors, and the association of traits in assortative mating, are more important than cultural-economic factors in determining the fact that brighter children tend to be taller and heavier than children of below-average intelligence.

Health and Physical Defects. If physical condition exerts a direct effect upon mental functioning, it may perhaps be expected that intelligence will show a closer relation to measures of health than to measures of physical growth. Our concern here is with studies of general health, nutritional status, or minor physical defects, and not with neurological or endocrine disorders, or psychopathologies. In one of the earliest studies in this field, Ayres (1909) computed the incidence of physical defects in three groups of children classified as dull, normal, and bright on the basis of progress in school. Three thousand three hundred and four cases were included. The percentage of each type of defect is given in Table 4.

TABLE 4

PERCENTAGE INCIDENCE OF PHYSICAL DEFECTS IN THREE GROUPS

	Bright	Normal	Dull
Defective teeth	34	40	42
Adenoids	6	10	15
Enlarged tonsils	12	19	26
Enlarged glands	6	13	20
Defective breathing	9	11	15
Defective vision	29	25	24
Other defects	11	11	21
Average number of defects per child	1.07	1.30	1.65

Similar findings have been reported by Sandwick (1920) and Kempf and Collins (1929). Where correlations have been computed, these are approximately of the same order as for other physical traits such as height or weight. Among the highest r's reported are those found by Dayton (1928–1929) for approximately 14,000 retarded school children in Massachusetts ($-.29 \pm .01$ for boys, $-.25 \pm .01$ for girls, IQ by physical defects). These correlations, similar to those found for other physical-mental relationships, serve merely to describe the fact that physical and mental handicaps are associated in the same samples. We cannot conclude that one type of handicap has caused the other, although to a very small degree such causal relationships may be present.[1]

In such defects as infected tonsils, a quasi-experimental approach is possible through studying the mental test performance of children before and after surgical removal of the infection. It has not been possible to show that such focal infections progressively impair mental ability, or that their removal has a beneficial effect upon intelligence (see reports by Rogers, 1922; Lowe, 1923; and Richey, 1934). In a few studies, evidence is available concerning the effect of an improved physical régime upon mental functions. Westenberger (1927) selected the poorest 10 per cent, with regard to physical defects, from a sample of approximately four hundred school children in Wisconsin. Medical and surgical treatment was provided over a nine-month pe-

---

[1] In a study of fifth-grade children in New York City schools, Maller (1933) determined the correlation between the average IQ for each school and the percentage in each school having a given defect. The coefficients were $-.50$ for defective teeth, $-.40$ for visual defect, $-.28$ for malnutrition. These relatively high correlations are due to the use of averages, and can be used for predictions about neighborhoods rather than about individuals. It is clear that districts with better health records tend to have higher average IQ's; these districts also have superior socioeconomic status, as shown by a correlation of .50 between average IQ and average rentals. Although Maller's results are of unusual interest in describing important aspects of urban social structure, they of course give no indication as to the source of the relationships.

riod, but without observable effects upon mental development. The investigator concluded: "The influence of defects upon academic performance and intelligence has been somewhat exaggerated in the past." Similar negative results were obtained by Kohnky (1913) in connection with a program of dental treatment and instruction in dental hygiene, and by Hoefer and Hardy (1928) in a carefully planned three-year study of the effect of health education.

Effects of changes in physical condition are more likely to be noted in school achievement than in measures of intelligence. Thus, in later reports Hardy (1936) and Hardy and Hoefer (1936) have shown that children participating in a health instruction program improved in their school work to a greater degree than members of a control group. Even these gains, however, are not entirely attributable to changes in health régime, since the special attention given to the experimental cases may have had not merely indirect psychological effects, but also more direct effects, through changes in motivation.

Nutrition. Fritz (1935) and Jones (1939) have summarized a number of studies dealing with the effects of nutritional factors upon mental abilities. It is of course to be expected that small positive coefficients will be obtained when measures of nutritional status are correlated with IQ. These correlations arise from the same causes that determine a positive relationship between socioeconomic status and IQ (see pp. 592 ff.) and tend to disappear if nutritional variations are examined within a single social group. An exception to the latter statement may be found in cases close to a subsistence margin. Thus, among 293 children from slum areas, O'Hanlon (1940) found a significant correlation ($.18 \pm .04$) between nutritional condition and IQ.

A more satisfactory approach to this

problem is through an experimental procedure, as illustrated in the following two examples. Twenty-five children selected by Smith and Field (1926) as markedly underweight were given school lunches over a 6-month period, together with health lessons and various motivational devices designed to bring about physical improvement. As compared with normal controls, striking gains were shown in weight, but mental development appeared to be unaffected. A similar experiment was conducted by Seymour and Whitaker (1938) in a group of 25 underprivileged children (6½ years old) matched with a control from a similar social selection. The experimental group was given daily breakfasts in school, adequate as to variety and amount, whereas the control group received their usual inadequate breakfast of bread and tea at home. Differences between the two groups began to appear on standardized tests (such as cancellation) by the tenth day, but the superiority of the experimental group diminished after the breakfasts were discontinued. Neither of these two experiments points to any actual change in mental growth as a result of nutritional gains.

Among mental defectives Poull (1938) has reported that when malnourished children receive an improved régime IQ gains are greater than in a control group. This was particularly true of children below 5 years of age, leading to the question as to whether persistent malnutrition, beyond 5 years, might do "irreparable" harm in mental development. The cases, however, are too few for definite conclusions. It has frequently been noted that the relationship of mental and physical traits is more readily demonstrated among the feeble-minded than among normals. This may be due in part at least to a larger proportion of the feeble-minded who suffer, in various degrees, from the effects of organic handicaps

expressed both in physical structures and in mental function. Stout (1937) has summarized a study of 10-year-old children by the statement: "The fact that a child is normal in intelligence gives little or no clue as to what his health or physical condition may be." On the other hand, among the 2 per cent at the lowest extreme in intelligence it is clear that we have a disproportionate incidence of many different types of physical defects.

More specific aspects of nutrition (such as the effects of vitamin B_1 or vitamin C administration) have been considered in a number of studies of young children, but in regard to psychological relationships the work in this field is still very preliminary.

Seasonal Factors. An interesting subsidiary problem has been raised by a number of investigations showing a relationship between IQ and month of birth. These studies, principally by Pintner and his associates (Pintner and Forlano, 1934, 1939; Pintner and Maller, 1937; Mills, 1941), but supported by other investigators, purport to show that both in the northern and southern hemispheres children born in the late spring, summer, or fall have slightly higher average IQ's than children born in the winter months. These differences are related to health statistics for the warmer as compared with the colder months. In the case of children of exceptionally high intelligence the most favorable month of birth appears to be slightly different than for the total population. For children with IQ's above 130, and also for individuals of distinction listed in the *Dictionary of American Biography,* Huntington (1938) has reported a high rate of births in the late winter or early spring months. In conformity with his theories of climatic influence, he has argued that children born from February to April have a maximum developmental advantage due to the fact that the early months of the pregnancy fall in the preceding late spring and summer. It is these months, he believes, that provide the most favorable extrinsic conditions for promoting physical vigor and general development. Huntington has been criticized to the effect that he has failed to account for the complex operation of cultural factors influencing conceptions and abortions. "The various seasonal trends in births cannot be denied, but their explanation in terms of meteorological and resulting physical factors must be subject to doubt until more direct evidence is obtainable" (Jones, 1939, p. 99).

More recently, Goodenough (1940c) has shown for a sample of over three thousand cases that seasonal differences in the *frequency* of births occur in the higher but not in the lower occupational groups. Since children at the higher socioeconomic levels also average higher in IQ (see p. 595), the birth month factor in intelligence can apparently be fully accounted for on the basis of selective planning or other conditions related to cultural status. This argument is supported by the fact that in samples presenting a restricted socioeconomic range, as in studies of college students (E. L. Clark, 1939; Held, 1940; Forlano and Ehrlich, 1941), intelligence differences related to birth month are either reduced or eliminated.

A different aspect of seasonal variation is considered in studies which have dealt with IQ changes in young children in relation to the month of testing. Wellman (1934) has reported that children in the University of Iowa Nursery School tend to show higher IQ's in the spring than in the fall. She attributed this to the effect of nursery school attendance. Lodge (1938), however, and Jones (1941) obtained similar results among children not in nursery school. In the latter study, data for 1798 tests, given to children between the ages of 2 and 5 years, were examined with reference to the month of testing. The cases were balanced in such a way as to eliminate the influence of age and of test practice. The highest average IQ's were found in November, December, and January; the lowest in May, June, and July. Several alternative interpretations were offered for these results, in terms of (1) the influence of climatic factors (such as periodic storms) upon mental performance, (2) the influence of climatic factors upon basic rates of mental growth, and (3) seasonal variations in play activities which have a positive transfer in mental test performance. Further studies are needed in different geographic areas in order to confirm these findings and, if they are confirmed, to provide an adequate explanation of the results.

Physiological Maturing. Chronological age is not always a good index of the *physiological time* through which a child has lived. In a group of the same age, wide individual differences will occur in the level of maturity assessed by physiological methods. These developmental indications include dentition, pubescence, the age of menarche, skeletal age assessed from X-rays, and anatomical age assessed from physical growth patterns. It has been suggested that a child's IQ at any given time should be computed by referring mental age to physiological rather than chronological age $\left(IQ = \dfrac{MA}{PA} \text{ rather than } \dfrac{MA}{CA} \right)$.

This is illustrated in Figure 5. Case 9M presents a mental growth curve, in terms of raw scores, consistently superior to the average of the total group. He is, however, somewhat retarded in physiological maturing, and if allowance is made for this we find that his growth curve (plotted against skeletal age) is even further above the group average. Case 25M has a mental growth curve which agrees very closely with the average, but in skeletal development he is markedly accelerated. In terms of the number of *physiological years* he has lived, we note that his mental development lags considerably behind expectation. When data are treated in this way,

(at a given level of chronological age) are usually too low to command special interest.[1] In one of the most comprehensive studies yet reported, Gates (1924) obtained a measure of skeletal age as well as height and some other physical measurements; the multiple r of these with men-

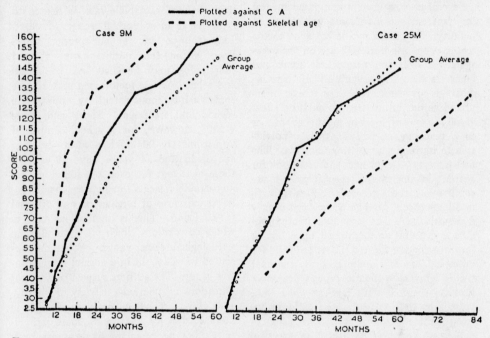

FIGURE 5. Individual mental growth curves, based on chronological age and on skeletal age. (After Bayley.)

it is possible that clues will sometimes be uncovered which will be useful in interpreting deviate mental growth curves or even in improving the prediction as to subsequent growth.

Unfortunately, however, the concept of physiological age is still somewhat vague. The various measures of physiological maturity agree with each other very imperfectly, and a satisfactory composite measure has not yet been achieved. When we correlate a single index, such as skeletal maturity, with mental age, the coefficients

tal age was only .21. In the same sample, mental age predicted educational achievement to the extent of a correlation of .60; when the physical measures were added, this correlation was increased only to .63.

Zuck (1936) and Todd (1938) have sponsored the belief that environmental influences acting through illness or nutri-

1 Abernethy (1936) and Bayley (1940b) have reported correlations which at most ages are positive but close to zero. Higher correlations were obtained by Severson (1920–1921) and by West (1936), although in the latter case the coefficients dropped with increasing age.

tional disturbance have a direct effect upon mental development, and also that a prior effect is frequently manifested in the X-rays of the skeleton. Individual cases can no doubt be found to support this view, but the general importance of such relationships remains to be demonstrated.

Several studies have investigated mental test performance in relation to the age at puberty. In general, these have led to the tentative finding that IQ's are on the average lower in late-maturing individuals and higher in the early-maturing.[1] If these indications are confirmed, they can be interpreted as due either to a stimulating effect of sexual maturing upon mental growth or to a tendency of early-maturing individuals to represent a superior selection. The first interpretation would lead us to look for a spurt in the rate of mental growth accompanying the increased physical growth in adolescence; this has never been clearly demonstrated.[2] The second and more probable interpretation might rest upon one or several selective factors. It is possible, for example, that (for quite different reasons) the lower socioeconomic groups are more heavily weighted with late-maturing individuals as well as with those of lower intelligence (see p. 595).

A readily measured aspect of physical condition is basal metabolism. At the pathological extremes, with which we are not here directly concerned, striking evi-

dence of correlated physical and mental effects can be found in such conditions as cretinism and myxedema, with equally striking evidence as to the mental improvement following thyroid treatment in certain cases. It is reasonable to inquire as to whether thyroid function, measured through basal metabolic rate, is related to intelligence in a normal range of cases. This is important for our present topic, since within this normal range thyroid functioning may be disturbed by illness and other extrinsic factors and may also be controlled to some extent by appropriate régime and treatment. Shock and Jones (1940), however, for a school sample of approximately 90 children at an average age of 12 and 14 years, have at each of these ages and for each sex found no demonstrable relationship between highly reliable measures of intelligence and of basal metabolism.[3] This is another instance in which correlations which are quite clear in pathological cases vanish or become obscured when sought in a normal representative group. The authors suggest that "slight variations in functional activity of the thyroid gland are not reflected in changes in mental capacity because in most individuals other adaptive mechanisms are present which may compensate for this thyroid deficiency" (p. 374). To carry over this conception to the general problem of environmental influence, it is a reasonable hypothesis that intelligence itself involves an adaptive mechanism which can to some degree compensate for variations in the environment, at least within an ordinary range of social and physical conditions.

[1] A review by Shock (1939a) has summarized a number of investigations (Baldwin, Terman, Lutz, Stone and Barker, Freeman and Flory, Abernethy) in which positive results were obtained. Negative results (as by Reymert, 1940) have occasionally been reported. It is of course well known that at the pathological extreme exceptionally early maturity (pubertas praecox) occurs without corresponding precocity in mental functions (Keene and Stone, 1937).

[2] The Harvard Growth Study, summarized by Dearborn and Rothney (1941), contains a large body of material pertinent to this hypothesis. No relation was found between the physical growth cycle and performance on intelligence or achievement tests.

[3] Similar results have been obtained in other investigations reviewed by these writers, with the exception of two reports by Hinton (1936, 1939), asserting correlations ranging from .80 at age 6 to .53 at age 15 between IQ and basal metabolic rate. The study is difficult to evaluate because complete data are not furnished.

Environmental Factors in the Family Constellation

Birth Order. The hypothesis has been advanced that children who are the first-born in their families suffer, on the average, a handicap in mental development due to both physical and social disadvantages. The fact of physical disadvantage is well established. Many studies have shown that the first-born are on the average smaller and lighter at birth than later-born in the same families. They include more prematures, and more cases of abnormal confinement. Jones and Hsiao (1933), in a study of 310 pairs of pregnancies, found among the first-born a greater proportion of instrumental delivery and of cases marked by poor physical condition after birth. A smaller proportion of the first-born receive normal breast-feeding (Schlesinger, 1923). Studies of later health and physical development[1] have not yielded consistent results; there is, however, a tendency to report a higher incidence of tuberculosis among the first-born.

The educational and social handicaps of the first-born are a matter of speculation rather than of direct proof. It is argued that first-born have the disadvantage of less experienced nurture by the parents, of less social stimulation (from older sibs), and frequently also of a less well-established economic security. However great or little these environmental differences may be, it is apparent that even in combination with a certain degree of physical handicap the average effects upon mental development are negligible.

It is unfortunate that investigators of this problem have been deceived by a number of errors of interpretation, the most important of which arises from the relation between birth rate and social status. Since families of higher social status

[1] Summarized by Hsiao (1931).

tend to have fewer but, on the average, more intelligent children, in a mixed population the first- or second-born, for example, will have higher average IQ's than third or fourth children. This, of course, is not actually a consequence of order of birth but is due merely to the fact that the earlier birth orders are weighted with children from small families, who constitute a superior selection. If we attempt to remedy this difficulty by limiting our comparisons to children of the same family, a new difficulty arises from the fact that many intelligence tests are so standardized that the IQ tends to drop slightly with age. This artifact produces a lower average IQ among children of the earlier birth orders (since they are, on the average, older when tested). Another factor to be considered is the unfavorable weighting of late birth orders due to maternal age. It has been clearly shown that the offspring of mothers near the end of the childbearing period are marked by a slightly greater incidence of certain types of mental defect, including mongolism.

In an earlier critique (Jones, 1933a) of research in this field evidence has been given that when these and other methodological difficulties are properly controlled no birth order differences in intelligence occur in normal samples. So far as this problem is concerned, we must then dismiss the environmental arguments as having little net weight. Atypical results, however, have been encountered in certain highly selected samples. Studies of gifted children by Terman (1925) and of eminent men by Ellis (1926), Cattell (1927), and Huntington (1938) have shown a distribution of birth orders differing from chance expectation, and strongly favoring the first-born (see Figure 6). No satisfactory explanation of this finding has been given. It is possible that the first-born more often become eminent because of greater incentive, but one would hesitate to apply this interpretation to the Terman material. An explanation in terms of differential educational opportunity would have even greater difficulty in including Terman's results with children. At least for this latter study, which is the only one dealing directly with intelligence test data, it is

sampling or of tests deficient in reliability or validity.[1]

In one of the earliest studies in this field Pearson (1903) found that family resemblances in mental traits were of the same degree as those in physical traits such as height, eye color, span, and head measurements. From this he concluded,

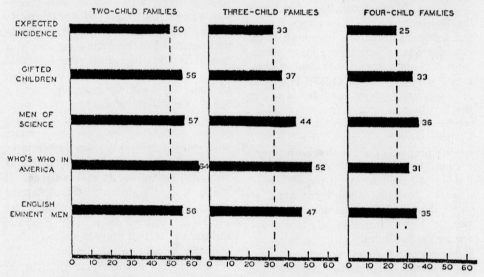

FIGURE 6. Percentage incidence of first-born, according to size of family.

rectly with intelligence test data, it is likely (as suggested by Terman) that the true explanation will involve some selective factor, such as the greater tendency to locate older than younger members of incomplete families in a restricted age range.

Sibling Resemblance. The significance of a correlation of .50 is sometimes described as "that degree of resemblance which is ordinarily found among brothers and sisters living in the same family." This order of relationship is now so well established that a study reporting a markedly lower sibling correlation in intelligence would be immediately suspected of an inadequate

"We are forced . . . to the conclusion that the physical and psychical characters in man are inherited within broad lines in the same manner and with the same intensity" (p. 204). Two considerations, however, must lead us to a more cautious interpretation of the evidence. First, our present knowledge of genetic mechanisms suggests that if intelligence has an hereditary basis it is genetically more complex than a trait such as eye color; differences in genetic composition might well be expected to produce differences in family resemblance coefficients. Second, a given degree of re-

1 See Schwesinger (1933) for a summary of earlier investigations.

semblance may (theoretically) be attained not only through the influence of a common heredity but also through the effects of living in a common environment.

Still another consideration involves the degree of selective mating in the population. Pearson, in his theoretical calculations, assumed that the correlation between husband and wife in intelligence was close to zero, but more recent studies show that the husband-wife coefficient tends to be as high as, if not higher than, the sibling coefficient.[1] Differences in selective mating with respect to different traits would be expected to have important effects upon family resemblances in these traits. We must conclude, then, that from a given degree of sibling resemblance no *immediate* inferences can be drawn as to causal factors. The pattern of sibling correlations, however, may prove significant when considered in relation to certain hypotheses of environmental influence. These hypotheses are:

I. Siblings of the same sex share, on the average, a more common social environment than siblings of opposite sex. Hence on an environmental basis higher correlations could be predicted for brothers or for sisters than for brothers-and-sisters.

II. Siblings close together in chronological age share a more similar environment than children widely separated as to age. Changes in social and economic status of the family, in home and neighborhood, and in the age and personal characteristics of the parents, as well as differences in schools and teachers, might be expected to have some average effect in lowering correlations for siblings with a wide natal interval, that is, separated by several years in age.

III. Older siblings have lived together longer than younger siblings, and hence share a greater accumulation of environmental influences. It may also be assumed that as

[1] Reviewed by Jones (1929) and H. M. Richardson (1939).

children grow older they become responsive to a wider range of environmental factors; in these factors families are more diverse than in factors to which younger children are sensitive. The effect of a greater variability in family environments should (on an environmental hypothesis) be to increase sibling correlations.

Each of these hypotheses may, at certain points, be questioned on theoretical grounds, but they have a sufficient common sense basis to justify an empirical test. Table 5 gives data relevant to the

TABLE 5

SIBLING CORRELATIONS

| | Like-Sex Siblings | | Opposite-Sex Siblings | |
	Pairs	r	Pairs	r
Group A	159	.47	153	.55
Group B	178	.40	144	.55
Group C	158	.44	169	.46

first of these hypotheses, from a study by Conrad and Jones (1940). A representative sample of 777 pairs of children in New England rural communities was divided into three groups, on the basis of the tests used (Stanford-Binet, Army Alpha, or Stanford-Binet and Alpha).

The correlations tend to vary around .50, with no tendency for like-sex siblings to show higher r's. As a matter of fact (although the differences are not reliable), the higher r's are attained by the opposite-sex pairs.[2] The authors comment:

[2] Studies by Willoughby (1927) and S. K. Richardson (1936) also report no reliable differences in the coefficients for like-sex and opposite-sex siblings.

It is possible that the family constellation involved factors of interstimulation, rivalry or identification, that are somewhat different for same-sex than for opposite-sex siblings, and these may be reflected in the correlations.

Such factors, if they are conceived as influencing the development of basic mental abilities, may tend to balance out other factors associated with the more common environment of children of the same sex. On the present evidence, however, it is apparent that a defense of Hypothesis I will require ambitious ventures into speculation.

Data relevant to Hypothesis II have been supplied by Conrad (1931) for a sample of 778 pairs of siblings. Correlations were calculated for three different age groups and for siblings who were (1) less than three years apart in age and (2) more than three years apart. The coefficients varied around .50, and no comparisons yielded significant differences. The natal interval problem may be approached also by correlating the score difference (IQ, or sigma score) of each sib pair with the age difference (natal interval) of the pair. A positive correlation would be expected if a greater age separation of siblings is accompanied by a greater difference in IQ. For large samples, Conrad in the above-mentioned study and Finch (1933) found all correlations unreliably different from zero. The temporal factor has been examined by S. K. Richardson (1936) in a different way by determining correlations for siblings tested at similar ages (on the average, six months apart in age) and at separated ages (on the average, three and a half years apart). For 101 cases in each group, identical coefficients (.49) were obtained. It is evident that the environmental influences associated with age differences of siblings are (on the average) without perceptible effect.

With regard to Hypothesis III, Figure 7 presents evidence as to increase of sibling correlation with age. This material, from unpublished data of Jones and Conrad, is based on a sample of 225 pairs of rural children tested with the Stanford-Binet, and 210 pairs tested with the Army Alpha. For each subgroup, the maximum age interval between each pair of siblings is five years. In each test, the correlations show a definite tendency to increase with age. Although this is consonant with the hypothesis of increasing or cumulative environmental influence, it is unfortunately impossible to eliminate other factors which may also contribute to the age trend.

One might inquire why the correlation drops so sharply when we shift, at around ten years, from the Stanford-Binet to the Army Alpha. The Stanford-Binet is not more reliable than the Alpha at this age, but it is probably more valid. The difference between these two tests at the same age may be due to much the same validity factors that operate to produce a difference within a given test at different ages. In other words, although the results indicated in Figure 7 can be plausibly attributed to environmental factors, it is equally plausible to account for them in terms of an increasingly valid measurement of basic abilities involving, with increasing age, the more complete expression of hereditary potentialities. It is interesting to note that in the case of the Alpha the highest sibling r (.54) is obtained in an age range extending into maturity, with many of the sibling pairs no longer living in the same homes. Environmental separation has apparently not tended to reduce measures of resemblance. Comparable results have been reported by Hildreth (1925), who found a correlation of .49 for 78 pairs of siblings

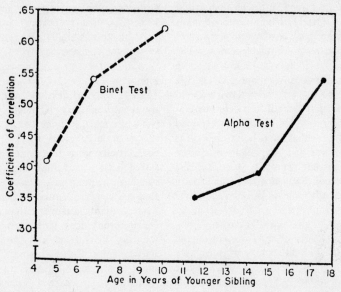

FIGURE 7.   Sibling correlations, according to age of the younger sibling.

separated, on the average, from four to five years.[1]

Before leaving this topic, reference should be made to one other type of sibling study which is of considerable interest for the present problem. This involves the measurement of resemblance among siblings reared in an institutional environment. If the similarity of brothers and sisters is due in part to the fact that they are reared in the same homes, the correlations would be expected to drop not merely when they are separated in different homes, but also when they are brought together into the relatively homogeneous physical and social conditions of an orphanage. The best-known evidence on this topic is from a study of 216 pairs of siblings in California orphanages; the reported correlation (.53) shows no evidence of an effect of institutional life.[2] For siblings in a Hebrew orphan asylum in New York, Hildreth (1925) obtained a lower correlation, but, on the other hand, found no evidence of a reduced variability such as would be expected if a common environment is influential. Similar results as to variability

[1] In the well-known Chicago study by Freeman, Holzinger, and Mitchell (1928) incidental data were reported for 130 pairs of siblings who had been separated for at least four years in different foster homes. The sibling correlation was .25, a diminished resemblance which may have been due to the reduced similarity in their environments. Burks (1928b, p. 321), however, has shown that this correlation rises toward the customary value if cases are omitted below 5 and above 14 years of age, eliminating individuals who are less adequately measured by the Stanford-Binet scale. In future studies, it will be desirable to know the sibling correlation before as well as after separation. If adoptive children are for any reason selected members of their families, and if the families themselves are a selected group, initial as well as the final correlations may be low because of reduced variability.

[2] Originally reported by K. Gordon (1918–1920, 1919), the data were reanalyzed by Pearson (1918–1919) and Elderton (1923) in order to control age factors and also to render the correlation tables symmetrical. In correlations of siblings and of twins, the recommended procedure is to plot each pair of cases twice, transposing the axes (Fisher, 1930, pp. 178 ff.).

changes were obtained in an English study by Lawrence (1931), who compared institution children with a control group of children living in their own homes. The evidence suggests that when children move to a more uniform environment their IQ's do not become similarly standardized.

In a small number of studies, correlations have been reported between *unrelated* siblings living in the same homes. This is a promising method for examining the effect of the environment provided the original placement has not been made with reference to any social factor related to intelligence. Perhaps the best evidence on this problem is given by Freeman, Holzinger, and Mitchell (1928), who measured the intelligence of 112 pairs of unrelated children living in the same homes. On a genetic basis alone, the correlation would be expected to be zero, whereas the coefficient actually obtained was .25. Although significantly lower than for true siblings, it suggests that a common environment tends to produce some degree of resemblance among individuals living together. However, a part of this relationship must be assigned to a selective rather than to an environmental factor, since the evidence concerning foster child studies (see p. 621) indicates that placement agencies tend to locate children with some regard to the social and educational status of their true parents.

Twins. Studies of twins offer unusual advantages in the assessment of environmental influence, but up to the present few "crucial" results can be reported from investigations in this field. The following types of comparisons have been employed:

1. *Fraternal twins versus ordinary siblings.* On a genetic basis, fraternal twin correlations should be of the same order as coefficients for sibling resemblance (approximately .50). In fact, however, they tend to range slightly above this figure,

occasionally being reported as high as .70. This difference in correlation, if genuine,[1] may be attributable to the more common environment shared by twins. In line with this interpretation are the results from an ingenious study by S. K. Richardson (1936), who artificially "twinned" siblings by recording their IQ's for tests given at the same ages. Under these conditions (as noted in a previous section), the sibling correlations were the same as when computed with the ordinary age intervals (.49 in each computation). On the other hand, true twin correlations tended to diminish when control measurements were employed for different ages (for example, one twin recorded at 8 years and the other at 10). Richardson concluded that "the environment of twins from birth is so similar that it tends to increase their natural resemblance" (p. 197). The twin correlation in this case was .73 for 92 pairs; the correlation for twins as of different ages was .57 for 45 pairs. This difference is not fully significant, and would, moreover, be considerably diminished if Richardson had corrected for variability differences. The procedure is nevertheless a promising one and should be applied in further study with a larger number of cases.

2. *Younger versus older twins.* In the earliest twin study using mental test data, E. L. Thorndike (1905) found that in various traits twins 12 to 14 years of age exhibited correlations no higher than those of twins 9 to 11 years of age. He argued that, if twin resemblance is due to environment, correlations ought to increase with age. We have here a possibility of a more sensitive test of the hypothesis discussed on page 610, but still with difficulties in

---

1 Twin correlations are subject to spurious inflation because of defects in test standardization, producing slightly lower average IQ's at higher ages. Some investigators have not understood the necessity of partialling out CA in order to control this factor.

interpretation. Thorndike's negative results (supported, in general, by later studies) have suggested to some writers that small environmental factors may be acting in opposite directions. The effect of longer residence in the same home may make for greater resemblance; but, on the other hand, with increasing age twins may become more independent in their choice of activities.[1]

3. *Fraternal versus identical twins.* More definitive results have been expected in this than in the preceding types of analysis, since we have a comparison in which environmental factors have been assumed to operate in a similar manner while genetic factors vary. The genetic difference consists in the fact that identical twins share the same gene determinants, whereas fraternal twins share a similar heredity only to the extent of ordinary brothers and sisters. Investigations have agreed that identical twins are on the average much more similar in intelligence than fraternal twins. Table 6 shows the twin correlations obtained in two representative studies.

Newman, Freeman, and Holzinger found a mean IQ difference of 9.8 for pairs of siblings, of 9.9 for pairs of fraternal twins, and of 5.9 for pairs of identical twins. This latter difference, it will be noted, is similar to that reported on page 586 in connection with studies of the constancy of the IQ.[2]

Such results would be expected if twin

[1] This can also be expressed by saying that interfamilial variations (differences among families) may tend to produce correlated changes in twins, with an increasing degree of resemblance, whereas intrafamilial variations may lead to uncorrelated or even negatively correlated changes.

[2] Assuming that in representative samples identical twins correlate .90 in intelligence, ordinary siblings .50, and random pairs .00, Page (1941) has applied a formula predicting that the average intrapair IQ difference will be approximately 6 points for identical twins, 13 for siblings, and 19 for unrelated pairs, in terms of the 1916 Stanford-Binet.

TABLE 6

RESEMBLANCE OF IDENTICAL AND FRATERNAL TWINS IN INTELLIGENCE

(Stanford-Binet IQ, corrected for age.)

Investigator	Fraternal Twins		Identical Twins	
	N	r	N	r.
Stocks and Karn (1933)	119	.65	68	.84
Newman, Freeman, and Holzinger (1937)	52	.63	50	.88

similarities were primarily genetic, but we must also take into account the fact of a greater degree of environmental similarity. Several studies have shown that identical twins spend more time together, enjoy more similar reputations, are more likely to be in the same classrooms, have more similar health records, and in many other respects share a more common physical and social environment than that ordinarily experienced by fraternal twins (Stocks, 1930–1931; Jones and Wilson, 1932–1933; Wilson, 1934; Lehtovaara, 1938).

Comparisons of twin populations are sometimes made not in terms of resemblance coefficients but more coarsely in terms of intrapair "concordance" or "discordance" as to specified traits. Thus Rosanoff, Hardy, and Plesset (1937) found that among identical twins in whom one member of the pair had been identified as mentally deficient 91 per cent of the co-twins were also classed as deficients. Among fraternal twins this measure of concordance dropped to 47 per cent.

4. *Twin resemblance in contrasted abilities.* Here we are concerned with the comparison of (a) abilities subject to training and (b) traits usually thought to be relatively independent of training. In E. L. Thorndike's (1905) study it was found that the degree of twin resemblance in various traits bore little or no relationship to the susceptibility of traits to training. Hence it could be argued that for both kinds of traits twin resemblance is primarily an expression of genetic factors. Lauterbach (1925) and Wingfield (1928) have also used this method in demonstrating, to their own satisfaction, the relatively minor importance of environmental factors. For identical and fraternal twins combined, Wingfield found twin correlations of .75 for IQ, .76 for educational quotient, .78 for arithmetic scores, and .85 for spelling scores, with no fully reliable differences. The problem is, however, one of great complexity, and many factors affecting (a) the incidence of training and (b) the genetic constitution of the trait in question may operate to produce results which make direct comparisons difficult between different traits.

5. *The method of co-twin control.* Technically superior to the preceding method is a procedure limited to identical twins, in which one member of a twin pair receives specific training while the other is reserved as a control. During the experimental period both twins undergo mental growth owing to intrinsic maturation and to general functioning, and any residual difference between the twins must be attributed to the experimental factor in the environment. First introduced by Gesell in the study of motor traits, the application of this method by Strayer (1930) in studying language development, and by Hilgard (1933) in connection with memory tests, has led to conclusions emphasizing the importance of intrinsic factors. A co-twin study covering a limited age period can, however, yield no general statement as to the comparative rôle of training and maturation. Its results will apply *only* to that particular age level and to the *specific functions* which are experimentally trained.

During the past decade a number of investigators in the U.S.S.R. have employed the co-twin method, with reference to various traits including intelligence (reviewed by Levit, 1935). Although we must regard this as a potentially powerful tool in the study of factors influencing development, in this country at any rate we have not yet been able to apply it to a sufficient number of cases (usually, only to a single pair of twins) or over a sufficiently long period of time to throw much light on our present problem.

6. *The comparison of identical twins reared apart.* In the absence of opportunities for the experimental separation of twins, the next best thing is to make use of separations which have occurred as a result of adoption in different homes. Here also reports have usually dealt with a single pair of twins, but in the well-known volume by Newman, Freeman, and Holzinger (1937) results have been assembled for a total of 19 pairs. The sample is, of course, a heterogeneous one, consisting of twins separated at ages ranging from 2 weeks to 6 years; at the time they were studied, their ages ranged from 12 to 60 years.

Ratings of the differences in the educational environments of the twins were made by five judges, three of whom knew only the case histories and two of whom also knew the twins. For all except six pairs of twins, the differences in ability were of about the same size as are found among identical twins reared together. Twelve pairs had small or negligible differences both in ability and in educational environment; for one pair there was no marked difference in ability even though a large difference in formal schooling had occurred. One pair with similar formal schooling showed a marked difference in ability corresponding to other differences in cultural opportunity; the remaining five pairs had experienced large or fairly large differences in education and showed corresponding differences in ability. Correlations for the nineteen pairs were below the usual coefficient for identical twins, but higher than the usual coefficients for siblings reared together (.67 for the Stanford-Binet IQ; .73 for the Otis IQ). Conclusions from this research, emphasizing environmental factors more strongly than in most twin studies, have been challenged in a number of reviews.[1] The method remains, however, a most important one, and, following the lead of Newman, Freeman, and Holzinger, we may expect significant results from a gradual accumulation of further cases of twins reared apart.

7. *Longitudinal studies of twins.* Psychological case studies of twins have been exemplified not only in the work of Freeman and his associates, but also in an interesting report by Koch (1927) on a pair of Siamese twins, and in several studies by Carter (1934) on mature identical twins. These have been based on cross-section and retrospective records rather than on cumulative data. Detailed studies are greatly needed in which the year-to-year development of twins is examined with reference to the relationship of developmental and environmental changes, the consistency

of small differences, and the interrelationship of differences. With cumulative observations it is possible to examine the rôle of factors which are usually inaccessible to experimental techniques (illness, accidents, and various "crises" of development).

More complete reviews of twin research have been made by several investigators.[2] Although frequently exploited in journalistic treatments, it is clear that twin studies are not merely a scientific "stunt," but deserve continued serious attention as a basic approach to nature-nurture problems. Certain safeguards, however, must be maintained with regard to the following difficulties in twin research:

1. *Number of cases.* Plural births occur only in the proportion of about 11 per 1000.[3] A large population must be covered in order to establish an adequate sample. Thus, in locating approximately 500 pairs of twins, Wilson and Jones (1931) found it necessary to survey a school enrollment of over 75,000 pupils.

2. *Sampling methods.* The best method of locating twins is through birth records, or by a questionnaire placed in the hands of all members of the group that is to be sampled. If reliance is placed on a census of twins by teachers, this method may lead to reporting all fraternal twins who are

1 Burks (1938a), McNemar (1938), Woodworth (1941). Woodworth has emphasized the fact that when twins of identical heredity are subjected to environments differing about as much as those of the children in an ordinary community, the twins nevertheless remain much more similar than random pairs of children in such a community. This would suggest that interfamilial and general educational differences are not of primary importance in determining variations in IQ in the general population.

2 Some of the best-known treatments are by Dahlberg (1926), Hirsch (1930b), Gesell (1931), Levit (1935), Newman, Freeman, and Holzinger (1937), Carter (1940), and Newman (1940). Especially valuable is an analysis of twin and foster-child studies by Woodworth (1941).

3 Triplet births occur in the proportion of approximately 1 per 8000, and other forms of plural birth are so rare as not to provide dependable scientific material. Considerable interest, however, is commanded by the recent volume by Blatz, Chant, Charles, *et al.* (1937) on the quintuplets, and by several publications dealing with small samples of triplets. The best known of these is by Anderson and Scheidemann (1933).

sufficiently similar to be in the same class-rooms, but may fail to place on record the fraternal twins who, being less similar, are located in different grades or different schools. Such a factor would spuriously increase coefficients of twin resemblance among fraternals, and may be responsible for unexpectedly high correlations reported by some investigators. A representative sample of twins may ordinarily be expected to include about one-quarter identicals and three-quarters fraternals.

3. *The classification of twins.* In classifying twins as fraternals or identicals, various methods have been used, including reference to obstetric data on fetal membranes; physical measurements; skeletal X-rays; finger prints and palm prints; hair color, form, and distribution; eye color and the pattern of iris pigmentation; microscopic capillary examination; blood agglutination grouping; and also more subjective methods based on the impression of similarity in general appearance. No one of these methods provides an infallible means of diagnosing identical twins, but with the application of a variety of methods a very high degree of agreement can be obtained in independent assessments by different investigators. In studying a given trait, such as intelligence, it is unsafe to use this trait as a part of the basis for diagnosis. Thus Hirsch (1930b) selected identicals in terms of criteria which included mental similarity, a procedure which may have had the effect of exaggerating differences in correlations between the two types of twins. In general, however, errors in diagnosis will spuriously *reduce* the difference between identical and fraternal twin correlations. It is sometimes a wise policy to exclude a small percentage of cases as "undetermined," if these cases show a conflict in the objective criteria employed for classification.

4. *General selective factors.* Twins are subject to a heavier infant mortality than are the single-born. The effect of this upon the selection of surviving twins is not fully known. One would expect it to improve the selection slightly; but, if this is so, then the prenatal or circumnatal factors affecting the development of twins must impose a decided handicap, for those surviving into school age are on the average slightly inferior to single-born in terms of a number of physical and mental criteria. This factor may also operate to eliminate divergent members of twin pairs, with the effect of increasing our measures of resemblance for those that survive.

An additional factor to be considered in interpreting research findings is that twins live in a very special social environment. Except in the case of twins reared apart, general conclusions from twin studies may not be immediately applicable to other selections of cases or other types of environment.

Parent-Child Resemblance. Chiefly because of the difficulty of obtaining intelligence test data for adults, relatively few studies of parent-child resemblance have been reported. In an early investigation, Pearson (1910) obtained a correlation of .49 between father and son, using ratings of mental ability. Subsequent studies employing intelligence tests have in general supported his finding that the resemblance of parents and children is of the same order as that of brothers and sisters.[1] This is not unexpected on the basis of hypotheses of genetic causation, but on an environmental hypothesis one would expect

[1] Somewhat lower coefficients have been reported by Willoughby (1927) and Freeman, Holzinger, and Mitchell (1928), but Pearson's results agree closely with those of Burks (1928b), Jones (1928), Banker (1928), Outhit (1933), Leahy (1935), and Conrad and Jones (1940). A review of earlier studies may be found in Carter (1932).

the sibling correlation to be higher, since the conditions under which brothers and sisters are reared, in a given family, are more similar than the conditions under which the members of two different generations are reared. It is a matter of unusual interest that these markedly differential factors in childhood environments seem unable to exert any distinguishable effect upon the family coefficients.

The suggestion has sometimes been made that, since the mother spends more time with her children during early childhood and has more direct supervision over their activities, a greater resemblance might be expected between mother and child than between father and child. So far as mental abilities are concerned, this does not appear to be the case. With the largest sample reported to date, Conrad and Jones (1940) found no differences in parent correlations. In this study the parents and children over 14 years of age were tested with the Army Alpha; between 10 and 14 either the Alpha or Stanford-Binet was used; and below 10 the Stanford-Binet was used exclusively. Table 7 summarizes the results.

TABLE 7

PARENT-CHILD CORRELATIONS

	Stanford-Tested Offspring		Alpha-Tested Offspring	
	N	r	N	r
Father	232	.49	196	.49
Mother	269	.49	245	.48

The striking uniformity in these results would of course be predicted on a genetic basis, since on the average the two parents play an equal rôle in transmission of hereditary characters. The greater rôle of the mother in the intimate determination of the child's early environment appears to have no differentiating effect with regard to intelligence. An alternative interpretation, however, might be that such an effect, if present, is balanced out by some other environmental factor.

As in the case of the sibling coefficients, a tendency exists for parent-child correlations to increase with age, especially if we compare results for preschool children and for adolescents. But again, as in the case of the sibling coefficients, the results are difficult to interpret, since an age change could be expected on the basis of both environmental and hereditary hypotheses, and also as a result of any increase in validity of the tests.

We have seen that studies of family resemblance have frequently led to ambiguous results as to the relative importance of environmental factors in mental development. In general, however, they have emphasized interfamilial differences in heredity as equally or more potent than differences in family environments, for a normal range of subjects. These studies not only have their own implications, but they are also of value in providing a normative background for the interpretation of results from a quasi-experimental type of investigation, in which "true" family resemblance is compared with the degree of resemblance achieved in foster relationships (see the section on children in foster homes, p. 621).

The Effects of Schooling

The theory of intelligence or capacity measurement implies a curvilinear relationship between education and test scores (for children of a given age). Children of school age with no education will make low scores, regardless of their natural talents or "educability." But it is assumed that, beyond a certain level of educational advance, and within a normal range of school opportunities, increments in training will not be accompanied by corresponding increments in mental test score. To assume otherwise would be to regard intelligence tests merely as tests of schooling. We know, however, that in groups relatively homogeneous as to education wide differences occur in test performance and that these differences persist even after extended exposure to a similar educational environment.

If it is maintained that mental growth can be controlled within narrow limits by educational factors, the burden of proof rests with those making this claim. It would appear to be a simple matter to set up an experiment in which an adequately large group is given experimental training of a type regarded as basically stimulating to mental development, and to compare the subsequent mental test records of this group with records obtained from a carefully matched control. In such an experiment, however, numerous precautions need to be taken. It is unfortunately true that in previous work these precautions have rarely been observed in their entirety:

1. The experimental and the control group should consist of matched pairs from the same population, one member of each pair being assigned at random to the experimental or the control procedure. It usually happens that the experimental group is already "given" to the experimenter, in the membership of a specific school sample. He must then make a search for suitable controls. Unless he is fully conversant with the factors which have determined the selection of the experimental sample, it is unlikely that he will succeed in matching this selection completely. Thus, if exceptional intelligence of the parents is a factor determining the

placement of children in nursery schools, a matching on the basis of children's IQ will be unsatisfactory, since the children in the experimental group will show differential gains merely as a result of increasing approximation to the level of ability characteristic of their families.

2. In the selection of cases, homogeneous groups are needed. In the nursery school, for example, it is possible that educational experiences provided in the school exert differing effects according to the age and cultural background of the children concerned. The mixture of cases of various ages and various social groups (as usually occurs) may yield results extremely difficult to interpret. An additional factor to consider in selection is the much-discussed phenomenon of statistical *regression to the mean*. If, for example, a group of children of below-average ability is selected for special educational attention, retests will probably show a movement toward the mean not necessarily because of true changes but because of compensation for errors of measurement which influenced the original selection. These difficulties, as well as other ambiguities, can be reduced by increasing the reliability of our measurements, as, for example, by the procedure of basing all scores on the average of two tests on successive days.

3. The criteria for matching the experimental and control pairs should include chronological age, initial IQ, and physical status of the children, intelligence (or, at any rate, education) of the parents, and a socioeconomic index for the home. It is important to obtain the initial IQ's under comparable conditions. Thus, if the nursery school children are tested in the stress of their first attendance at school and the control children are tested under familiar conditions at home, the experimental group may show larger gains on a second test, owing chiefly to gains in rapport. With

THE EFFECTS OF SCHOOLING

young children, attention should be given to assessments of effort, cooperation, freedom from inhibition, response to success or failure, and other motivational factors considered with reference to possible effects upon test performance. It would, of course, be desirable to establish controls on the basis not merely of a single period, but of a series of tests representing a segment of the growth curve prior to the beginning of the experiment. Children are sometimes given superior educational opportunities because their mental growth appears to be temporarily restricted. This apparent restriction, however, may be due to any of the intrinsic or extrinsic factors discussed on page 592. Later gains, giving the impression of an improved rate of growth, may represent changes in these factors rather than the effects of the nursery school experience.

4. The experimental situation should be analyzed and described in detail. Investigations which give a vague report of positive effects from undefined "school experience" can neither be interpreted nor repeated unless the specific basis of these effects is made known. Such information is also necessary in order to determine whether the effects are (a) merely specific transfers to certain kinds of test items, (b) the result of attitude changes or increased incentive, or (c) a more generalized change in mental efficiency.

5. Subsequent test comparisons of the experimental-control pairs must involve equal amounts of test practice, comparable tests, and comparable conditions in testing. If retests are made by persons who are strangers to the control group, but (as teachers or staff members) are well known to the children in the school, differential apparent gains may occur as a result of this factor.[1] These considerations lead to

a further requirement; namely that, when a test is given, the examiner should not be familiar with the results of previous tests and should not know whether the child is in the experimental or in the control group. Subjective factors in the administration and scoring of such a test as the Stanford-Binet may lead to a conscious or unconscious biasing of the results by examiners who think they know how the results "ought" to turn out. Krugman (1939) and Goodenough (1940b) have discussed the possible rôle of these subjective factors in determining basal and final ages and in reaching decisions as to the scoring of marginal successes or failures.

6. The test program should be continued for several years, in order to determine whether possible effects are temporary (and specific to certain test items at certain ages) or whether they are expressed in more lasting effects upon mental development.

7. Finally, since any obtained effects are likely to be small in magnitude, a substantial number of cases is needed in order to reach a well-founded decision as to the significance of differences.

The reports on the effects of nursery school training should be examined in the light of the foregoing experimental criteria.

gains were also those regarded by the teacher as showing the greatest improvement in personality traits. Krugman (1939), in difficult clinical cases, attributed the largest changes in test performance to changes in rapport or cooperation. The following comment by Black (1939) is also illuminating:

"In our experience at the Harriet Johnson Nursery School we have found resistance and shyness to be far less characteristic of the nursery school than of the non-nursery school child, regardless of age. The school situation itself tends to produce rapport between examiner and child before the examination begins. Freedom, a feeling of security in the school situation, and in increasing sense of the friendliness and trustworthiness of adults recognized as belonging to the school make the test situation relatively easy for the child and the examiner" (p. 164).

[1] In the report by Barrett and Koch (1930) the nursery school cases making the greatest IQ

An early study by Woolley (1925), with inadequate controls, reported an apparent effect of preschool education upon mental development. Similar results were obtained a few years later by Barrett and Koch (1930) in an orphan asylum group. Because of the small number of cases and the lack of adequately defined experimental conditions, and also because of negative evidence in two other studies (Hildreth, 1928; Goodenough, 1928a), the majority of workers in this field turned from the problem as presenting little hope of further reward. It is to the credit of the Iowa group of investigators that they maintained a persistent interest in the possible effects of nursery school education and formulated an extensive and versatile program of research. In general, this research has been interpreted by Wellman and her associates as indicating potency of the preschool environment in generating marked and persistent changes in mental growth. The *Thirty-ninth Yearbook of the National Society for the Study of Education* (Stoddard *et al.*, 1940) contains a summary of the Iowa studies, together with reports on nine other preschool investigations, the majority of which were stimulated (in 1938 and 1939) by the strikingly positive findings reported from Iowa.

It may be noted that for the most part the various studies show a negligible relation between IQ change and length of attendance in nursery school. With a few exceptions they agree in showing a slight difference in favor of nursery school groups when these are compared with control groups. Although in nearly every case the difference is statistically unreliable, the findings are sufficiently consistent to be of interest.[1] At the present time disagree-

ment exists as to the extent to which errors of measurement, of experimental procedure, and of statistical treatment may be responsible for results which have been so enthusiastically advocated as evidence that mental growth responds promptly and permanently to educational influences in the nursery school. In our discussion of IQ constancy and the mental growth curve it was shown that with many children the preschool period is marked by a considerable degree of irregularity or variation in mental growth. It is tempting to the educator to believe that these variations are readily subject to his management and control, but as yet we cannot regard the evidence in this field as satisfactory. No one doubts, however, that the nursery school presents opportunities for promoting development in traits more directly amenable to environmental influence, and perhaps more essential for adjustment at this age level. In commenting on the Iowa studies, Burks (1939) has stressed the importance of such factors:

The preschool ages constitute the period *par excellence* not only for developing constructive attitudes toward tasks, but for integrating these with a sense of personal value and with feelings of security in social relationships. To accomplish this integration, however, would not necessarily mean that maximal mental growth during the preschool years was necessary or even desirable for all children. Rather, it would seem that the growth of adaptive behavior should be stimulated and guided—often in special instead of in all areas—so as to achieve an harmonious balance with the

---

[1] Of the nine studies referred to above, one (Starweather and Roberts, 1940) tends to support the Iowa conclusions, but unfortunately does not include a control group. The remaining eight investigations, all published in 1940 (L. D. Anderson, Bird, Frandsen and Barlow, Goodenough and Maurer, Jones and Jorgensen, Lamson, Olson and Hughes, and Voas), point to essentially negative conclusions.

The highly controversial literature on this topic includes discussions by McNemar (1940), Goodenough (1940a), R. L. Thorndike (1940), Stoddard and Wellman (1940), and Wellman, Skeels, and Skodak (1940).

expanding personality needs of each particular child (p. 555).

It seems probable that such gains in IQ as have been reported are not too large to be accounted for in terms of the effect of personality improvement upon mental functioning.

The effect of environmental factors in later schooling will not be considered here in detail. The evidence in this area is even less satisfactory than in the nursery school studies, chiefly because of the lack of data from comparison groups in definitely contrasting educational situations. Goodenough (1940a) has summarized relevant studies in this field through the year 1939, concluding that "the attempts to demonstrate the differential effects of different kinds of school practice upon child achievement have been disappointingly meager when suitable controls have been employed," and that differential effects upon intelligence are even harder to demonstrate by methods used up to this time (p. 330). This should not be taken to imply that the problem has already been answered in the negative, but rather that our present need is for more definitive research.

Children in Foster Homes

Only a limited view of the possible effects of environmental influence can be given through the experimental control of the school environment. Unfortunately, no studies have been made of a representative sample of children observed under conditions involving an experimental, and parallel, modification of factors both in the home and in the school. Such a study would require the random separation of pairs of siblings (or, preferably, identical twins) and their rearing in homes and schools possessing certain specified differences. We do, however, have a number of investigations of children placed in foster homes. These, though limited in a number of respects, provide us with some of our most penetrating evidence concerning the nature-nurture problem.

Studies of foster children have been discussed in reviews by Goodenough (1940a) and Loevinger (1940), and need not be presented here in detail. The two researches which are most comparable as to procedure are by Burks (1928b) in California and by Leahy (1935) in Minnesota. Each investigated approximately 200 children placed in foster homes before 12 months of age. Each obtained intelligence tests of the foster parents, a cultural-economic assessment of the home environment, and a record of the foster child's IQ after he had reached school age (between 5 and 14 years). Moreover, in each investigation a "true child" control group was set up which would permit comparisons of parent-child relationship with and without the presence of a systematic hereditary factor.

It is often found that the selection of children available for adoption in official placement agencies is slightly superior in average intelligence; for Burks's 204 cases the mean IQ was 107.4, and for Leahy's 194 cases (all of whom were illegitimate) the mean IQ was 110.5. Figure 8 presents some of the more important results from these studies. The degree of resemblance to measures of the home environment, or to parents' intelligence, is clearly greater for true children than for foster children. From this an inference can be drawn that the correlations with home environment which have been found in the case of true children are due primarily to the common factor of the parents' intelligence rather than to the environment acting as a causative agent. That is to say, the intelligence of the parents finds expression both in the culture of their home and in the IQ's of their children. What, now, will happen when the hereditary factor is eliminated from parent-child correlations (through

drop to low values, ranging from .07 to .21. That they remain higher than zero can perhaps be ascribed in part to the

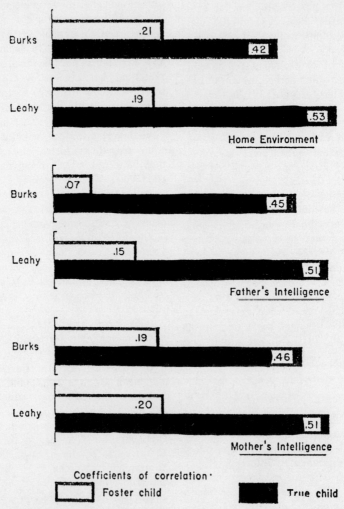

FIGURE 8. A comparison of foster child and true child correlations.

the use of foster children)? Should we not expect that this elimination will also directly affect the correlation of the child's IQ with measures of the (foster) home environment? These correlations do actually

tendency for adopted children to shift toward the level of the homes in which they are placed. However, an additional factor is present in that the placement of children is rarely experimentally random. In other words, when placement officers have knowledge of the cultural circumstances of the true parents, this is likely to influence their choice of foster homes. Even with elaborate precautions against selective placement, a positive relation has been shown to exist between the occupations of true and foster parents.

When children are placed at ages later than infancy, the aim of "fitting the child to the home" will result in an increased likelihood of selective placement. This appears to have been a factor in the study of Freeman, Holzinger, and Mitchell (1928) of 401 children in Illinois who were placed at an average age of 4 years, 2 months. When tested at around 11 years, the correlation with a measure of the foster home [1] was .48. This value, as high as would be expected in a "true child" sample, was apparently influenced somewhat by a choice of foster homes appropriate to the intelligence or to the family origins of the children. If this choice were made without including intelligence tests of the true parents, the subsequent correlation of children's IQ with foster parents' intelligence would be expected to be lower than for true parent-child relationships. This proved to be the case; for 255 mothers and 180 fathers who were tested when the children were 11 years of age, on the average, the correlation with the foster child's IQ was .28 for the mothers and .37 for the fathers. For a subgroup of 74 children another and more direct type of analysis is possible since tests were available both before and after the children had been in a foster home. The average age of the children at placement was 8 years; at the time of the retest, approximately 12 years. A significant average gain in IQ

[1] Based on ratings of the material environment, evidences of culture, education of the parents, occupation of the father, and social activity of the parents.

was shown for children placed in superior homes, and a less significant gain for those placed in poorer homes.

Similar results have been reported in a number of studies in which children were removed from bad home situations and placed in an orphanage or a boarding home (Lithauer and Klineberg, 1933; Wells and Arthur, 1939; Skeels, 1940; Speer, 1940a, 1940b). In such cases, apparent gains are suspect because of difficulties in obtaining a valid test at a time when a child's home is broken, or when emotional factors may be present from previous home conditions. Poverty, drunkenness, sex delinquency, inadequate food and housing, and many other disturbing factors are frequently cited as characteristic of the true homes and as giving rise to the need for placement elsewhere. It is difficult or impossible to appraise IQ gains in foster homes unless the initial tests are given under conditions in which test performance can genuinely register the child's ability. A further, and perhaps the chief, explanation of differences between the results of this study and those of Burks and Leahy can be sought in terms of random sampling differences.

An incidental outcome of the Freeman, Holzinger, and Mitchell study has been pointed out by Lorimer and Osborn (1934). For 156 children classified as members of good, average, and poor foster homes, mean IQ's were obtained of 111, 103, and 91. These differences could be attributed both to environmental influence and to selective placement. However, when the group was subdivided into legitimate and illegitimate children, the former were found to have a mean IQ of 95 and the latter of 106, with similar differences present in each grade of homes. The illegitimate children apparently represent a superior hereditary selection, and this superiority has by no means been obliterated by removal from their true parents.

Similar inferences can be drawn from a recent preliminary report by Stippich (1940) involving a comparison between 48 children whose mothers were feeble-minded, and 29 children of normal mothers; all had been placed in boarding homes before 12 months of age. On the basis of tests given after they were 3 years old, marked differences were noted between the two groups, although they were developing in apparently comparable environments. Twenty-one per cent of the experimental group (children of mentally deficient mothers) and none of the control group fell below 75 IQ. Here again, the ubiquitous problem of selective placement must be considered. Comparability of the two groups of foster homes appears to be more a matter of assertion than of proof; if there was any tendency to place the children of feeble-minded mothers in less adequate homes this might to some extent account for the results obtained.

Somewhat different results have been reported by Skeels (1941) for a sample of 87 children of mothers who were mentally retarded. After placement in adoptive homes the children attained a mental level "equaling or exceeding that of the population as a whole." For the present purpose, comparisons of small samples of children of feeble-minded and normal mothers are unsatisfactory unless there is adequate information about (1) the diagnosis of the mothers, (2) the conditions of placement, and (3) the mental status of the fathers. Cases should be ruled out in which the mothers' mental deficiency is of clearly secondary origin, as from injury or disease, and in which there is no other record of mental defect in the family. It is also important to know whether the children who have become available for adoption repre-

sent a genuinely unselected sample for the families considered. Results would be extremely difficult to interpret if the more retarded children of a defective mother are kept at home or sent to an institution, whereas the more normal offspring are accepted by foster homes. Finally, the mental status and family origins of the fathers cannot be neglected. In the case of illegitimate children of feeble-minded mothers, the ordinary principles of assortative mating may not be operative. It is obvious that "crucial" findings cannot be expected if a substantial proportion of the true fathers are of normal intelligence or derive from families of normal intelligence.[1]

The remaining principal study in this field, by Skodak (1939), dealt with 154 children who were placed before the age of six months in average or superior foster homes. Since selective placement was involved, the most effective comparison to be made is between children coming from true homes within a given occupational classification and those placed out in homes of varying classification. The conclusion is offered that the effect of superior home environments is clearly shown in the results, and also that in general the children exhibit higher test scores than would be ex-

[1] Foster child studies have not as yet utilized intelligence scores for true fathers. The first study making use of test scores for true mothers was carried out by Skeels (1936). His group, including 39 mothers, was a preliminary subgroup of that later used by Skodak. More recently, results have been reported from Stanford-Binet IQ's of 312 true mothers and adopted children, in a Toronto study by Snygg (1938). Parent-child correlations in these two investigations were .09 and .13, respectively; mean IQ's of the mothers were, respectively, 84 and 78, and of the children, 115 (?) and 95. These results are not in line with those based on our most carefully controlled and most fully reported foster child studies. Unfortunately, a further interpretation is difficult because sufficiently complete data have not been presented concerning methods of sampling and conditions of testing.

pected on the basis of their true homes.[1] In view of the fact that further reports are expected from these Iowa studies, with additional cases, it may be desirable to delay an evaluation until more evidence is in. One striking finding, however, somewhat contrary to what would be looked for on the basis of Skodak's main conclusions, is that after an average of several years in the foster home the children show correlations of .16 to .19 with education of the foster parents. These are comparable to coefficients reported by Leahy and Burks and are in part due to selective placement. With the education of the true parents, however, a more marked correlation was shown of .33 to .38,[2] in spite of the fact that there had been little or no contact with the true parents since earliest infancy.

One of the most important types of research to be conducted in the future will involve the placement of foster children on the basis of a planned experimental design, rather than the study of children whose location has been previously determined by uncontrolled and incompletely known factors. To appraise the results of such an investigation, it would be necessary to have intelligence tests of all the true and foster parents, a goal that has never yet been reached. The intelligence of the children should be observed cumulatively rather than stated, as at present, on the basis of one or two tests, and a cumulative inventory should also be maintained of relevant environmental factors in and outside the home. Previous studies, which are neces-

sarily inconclusive at many points, may be regarded as preparing the ground for more thorough and better-controlled investigations which still remain to be conducted.

So much has been written on the topic of environmental influence that it has not been possible within a single chapter to review all the significant reports and discussions, or even to refer to all the principal methods of approach. Little mention has been made, for example, of studies of feeble-minded or gifted children, of the mental growth of institutionalized children, or of mental growth or achievement gauged in other ways than by intelligence tests. Reference has been given, however, to numerous other sources in which further materials can be found. A topic as yet very incompletely studied involves the relationship between intelligence and personality and the effect of variations in emotional adjustment and personal integration upon the nature and the efficiency of mental functioning.[3]

Burks (1939) has pointed out that in this general field

... there is, in fact, less of a cleavage between pure research and application than is true of many scientific fields, since the most crucial data for the nature-nurture problem are obtained not through laboratory experiments, but through experiments which society itself has undertaken for social goals. This circumstance seems to lower the emotional thresholds of research workers, but paradoxically it places upon them an added responsibility to disengage themselves from emotional biases. If the results of scientific research are of the kind that find immediate application, errors are costly to society. On the other hand, sound data have immeasurable social value (p. 548).

In its social import the nature-nurture problem extends not merely into every

---

[1] A number of the assumptions and procedures in this study have been vigorously criticized by Burks (1939), McNemar (1940), and Goodenough (1940a), with replies from Skeels (1940), Stoddard and Wellman (1940), and Wellman, Skeels, and Skodak (1940).

[2] These coefficients represent a correction from original coefficients of .28 to .33. The correction was suggested by Goodenough (1940a), to take account of a difference in variability of the two groups of parents.

[3] Cf. discussions by L. S. Hollingworth (1940), Lorge (1940), and Lund (1940).

branch of education but also (because of the differential birth rate) into the field of population and social planning. It is evident that the approach to this problem has, during the past two decades, led to striking improvements in research method and to a clearer awareness of the complexity of the issues with which we must deal. When we seek a better understanding of human potentialities in intelligence, we are at the same time appraising the rôles which environmental factors can play in the functional development of our capacities for adaptation. It must be emphasized that this is an extremely varied task. Future research must address itself not to a single ultimate solution of the problem, but to an examination of its many aspects, in many specific situations.

Bibliography

ABERNETHY, E. M. 1936. Relationships between mental and physical growth. *Monogr. Soc. Res. Child Develpm.*, 1, No. 7. Pp. 80.

ADKINS, D. C. 1937. The effects of practice on intelligence test scores. *J. Educ. Psychol.*, 28, 222-231.

ANASTASI, A. 1937. *Differential psychology.* New York: Macmillan.

ANDERSON, F. N., and N. V. SCHEIDEMANN. 1933. A study of triplets. *Genet. Psychol. Monogr.*, 14, 93-176.

ANDERSON, J. E. 1940. The prediction of terminal intelligence from infant and preschool tests. *Yearb. Nat. Soc. Stud. Educ.*, 39(I), 385-403.

ANDERSON, L. D. 1939. The predictive value of infancy tests in relation to intelligence at five years. *Child Develpm.*, 10, 203-212.

———. 1940. A longitudinal study of the effects of nursery-school training on successive intelgence-test ratings. *Yearb. Nat. Soc. Stud. Educ.*, 39(II), 3-10.

ASHER, E. J. 1935. The inadequacy of current intelligence tests for testing Kentucky mountain children. *J. Genet. Psychol.*, 46, 480-486.

AYRES, L. P. 1909. The effect of physical defects on school progress. *Psychol. Clin.*, 3, 71-77.

BALDWIN, B. T., E. A. FILLMORE, and L. HADLEY. 1930. *Farm children: An investigation of rural child life in selected areas of Iowa.* New York: Appleton.

BANKER, H. J. 1928. Genealogical correlation of student ability. *J. Hered.*, 19, 503-508.

BARRETT, H. E., and H. L. KOCH. 1930. The effect of nursery-school training upon the mental test performance of a group of orphanage children. *J. Genet. Psychol.*, 37, 102-122.

BAYLEY, N. 1933. Mental growth during the first three years. A developmental study of 61 children by repeated tests. *Genet. Psychol. Monogr.*, 14, 1-92.

———. 1940a. Mental growth in young children. *Yearb. Nat. Soc. Stud. Educ.*, 39(II), 11-47.

———. 1940b. Factors influencing the growth of intelligence in young children. *Yearb. Nat. Soc. Stud. Educ.*, 39(II), 49-79.

BAYLEY, N., and H. E. JONES. 1937. Environmental correlates of mental and motor development: A cumulative study from infancy to six years. *Child Develpm.*, 8, 329-341.

BICKERSTETH, M. E. 1919. The application of mental tests to children of various ages. *Brit. J. Psychol.*, 9, 23-73.

BIRD, G. E. 1940. The effect of nursery-school attendance upon mental growth of children. *Yearb. Nat. Soc. Stud. Educ.*, 39(II), 81-84.

BLACK, I. S. 1939. The use of the Stanford-Binet (1937 revision) in a group of nursery school children. *Child Develpm.*, 10, 157-171.

BLATZ, W. E., N. CHANT, M. W. CHARLES *et al.* 1937. *Collected studies on the Dionne quintuplets.* Toronto: University of Toronto Press.

BRADWAY, K. P., and E. L. HOFFEDITZ. 1937. The basis for the personal constant. *J. Educ. Psychol.*, 28, 501-513.

BRUCE, M. 1940. Factors affecting intelligence test performance of whites and Negroes in the rural south. *Arch. Psychol., N. Y.*, No. 252. Pp. 100.

BURKS, B. S. 1928a. Statistical hazards in nature-nurture investigations. *Yearb. Nat. Soc. Stud. Educ.*, 27(I), 9-33.

———. 1928b. The relative influence of nature and nurture upon mental development: A comparative study of foster parent-foster child resemblance and true parent-true child resemblance. *Yearb. Nat. Soc. Stud. Educ.*, 27(I), 219-316.

———. 1928c. A summary of literature on the determiners of the intelligence quotient and the educational quotient. *Yearb. Nat. Soc. Stud. Educ.*, 27(II), 248-353.

———. 1938a. Review of twins: A study of heredity and environment. *J. Abnorm. Soc. Psychol.*, 33, 128-133.

———. 1938b. On the relative contributions of nature and nurture to average group differences in intelligence. *Proc. Nat. Acad. Sci. Wash.*, 24, 276-282.

———. 1939. Review of "Children in foster homes: A study of mental development," by

MARIE SKODAK. *J. Educ. Psychol.*, 30, 548–555.

BURT, C. 1921. *Mental and scholastic tests.* London : King.

BYRNS, R., and V. A. C. HENMON. 1935. Long range prediction of college achievement. *Sch. and Soc.*, 41, 877–880.

CARMICHAEL, L. 1940. The physiological correlates of intelligence. *Yearb. Nat. Soc. Stud. Educ.*, 39(I). 93–155.

CARTER, H. D. 1932. Family resemblances in verbal and numerical abilities. *Genet. Psychol. Monogr.*, 12, No. 1. Pp. 104.

———. 1934. Case studies of mature identical twins. *J. Genet. Psychol.*, 44, 154–174.

———. 1940. Ten years of research of twins : contributions to the nature-nurture problem. *Yearb. Nat. Soc. Stud. Educ.*, 39(I), 235–255.

CASEY, M. L., H. P. DAVIDSON, and D. I. HARTER. 1928. Three studies on the effect of training in similar and identical material upon Stanford-Binet test scores. *Yearb. Nat. Soc. Stud. Educ.*, 27(I), 431–439.

CATTELL, J. McK. 1927. *American men of science.* (4th ed.) Garrison, N. Y.: Science Press.

CATTELL, P. 1937. Stanford-Binet IQ variations. *Sch. and Soc.*, 45, 615–618.

CHAPMAN, J. C., and D. M. WIGGINS. 1925. Relation of family size to intelligence of offspring and socio-economic status of family. *Ped. Sem.*, 32, 414–421.

CLARK, C. D., and N. P. GIST. 1938. Intelligence as a factor in occupational choice. *Amer. Sociol. Rev.*, 3, 683–694.

CLARK, E. L. 1939. Significance of month of birth as judged by test scores and grades. *Psychol. Bull.*, 36, 629 (abstr.).

CONRAD, H. S. 1931. *Sibling resemblance and the inheritance of intelligence.* Ph.D. Dissertation, University of California.

CONRAD, H. S., and H. E. JONES. 1940. A second study of familial resemblance in intelligence : Environmental and genetic implications of parent-child and sibling correlations in the total sample. *Yearb. Nat. Soc. Stud. Educ.*, 39(II), 97–141.

DAHLBERG, G. 1926. *Twin births and twins from a hereditary point of view.* Stockholm : Bokförlags-A.-B. Tidens Tryckeri.

DAYTON, N. A. 1928–1929. The relationship between physical defects and intelligence. *J. Psycho-Asthenics*, 34, 112–139.

DEARBORN, W. F., and J. W. M. ROTHNEY. 1941. *Predicting the child's development.* Cambridge, Mass.: Sci-Art Publishers.

DUBNOFF, B. 1938. A comparative study of mental development in infancy. *J. Genet. Psychol.*, 53, 67–73.

EDWARDS, A. S., and L. JONES. 1938. An experimental and field study of north Georgia mountaineers. *J. Soc. Psychol.*, 9, 317–333.

ELDERTON, E. M. 1923. A summary of the present position with regard to the inheritance of intelligence. *Biometrika*, 14, 378–408.

ELLIS, H. 1926. *A study of British genius.* (New ed., rev.) Boston : Houghton Mifflin.

ENGLAND, N. J. 1936. The relation between health and intelligence in school children. *J. Hyg.*, 36, 74–94.

FINCH, F. H. 1933. A study of the relation of age interval to degree of resemblance of siblings in intelligence. *J. Genet. Psychol.*, 43, 389–404.

FISHER, R. A. 1918. The correlation between relatives on the supposition of Mendelian inheritance. *Trans. Roy. Soc. Edinburgh*, 52, 399–433.

———. 1930. *Statistical methods for research workers.* (3d ed.) London : Oliver and Boyd.

FORAN, T. G. 1926. The constancy of the intelligence quotient : A review. *Cath. Univ. Amer. Educ. Res. Bull.*, 1, No. 10. Pp. 40.

———. 1929. A supplementary review of the constancy of the intelligence quotient. *Cath. Univ. Amer. Educ. Res. Bull.*, 4, No. 9. Pp. 29.

FORLANO, G., and V. Z. EHRLICH. 1941. Month and season of birth in relation to intelligence, introversion-extroversion and inferiority feelings. *J. Educ. Psychol.*, 32, 1–12.

FRANDSEN, A., and F. P. BARLOW. 1940. Influence of the nursery school on mental growth. *Yearb. Nat. Soc. Stud. Educ.*, 39(II), 143–148.

FREEMAN, F. N. 1940. The meaning of intelligence. *Yearb. Nat. Soc. Stud. Educ.*, 39(I), 11–20.

FREEMAN, F. N., and C. D. FLORY. 1937. Growth in intellectual ability as measured by repeated tests. *Monogr. Soc. Res. Child Develpm.*, 2, No. 2. Pp. xi + 116.

FREEMAN, F. N., K. J. HOLZINGER, and B. C. MITCHELL. 1928. The influence of environment on the intelligence, school achievement, and conduct of foster children. *Yearb. Nat. Soc. Stud. Educ.*, 27(I), 103–217.

FRITZ, M. F. 1935. The effect of diet on intelligence and learning. *Psychol. Bull.*, 32, 355–363.

FURFEY, P. H., and J. MUEHLENBEIN. 1932. The validity of infant intelligence tests. *J. Genet. Psychol.*, 40, 219–223.

GATES, A. I. 1924. The nature and educational significance of physical status and of mental, physiological, social, and emotional maturity. *J. Educ. Psychol.*, 15, 329–358.

GEE, W., and J. J. CORSON. 1929. Rural depopulation in certain Tidewater and Piedmont areas of Virginia. *Univ. Va. Inst. Res. Soc. Sci. Monogr.*, No. 3.

GESELL, A. 1928. *Infancy and human growth.* New York : Macmillan.

———. 1931. The developmental psychology of twins. In C. Murchison (Ed.), *A handbook of child psychology*, pp. 158–203. Worcester: Clark University Press.

GESELL, A., B. M. CASTNER, H. THOMPSON, and C. S. AMATRUDA. 1939. *Biographies of child development. The mental growth careers of eighty-four infants and children.* New York: Hoeber.

GOODENOUGH, F. L. 1928a. A preliminary report on the effect of nursery school training upon the intelligence test scores of young children. *Yearb. Nat. Soc. Stud. Educ.*, 27(I), 361–369.

———. 1928b. *The Kuhlmann-Binet tests for children of preschool age: A critical study and evaluation.* (*Inst. Child Welfare Monogr. Scr.*, No. 2.) Minneapolis: University of Minnesota Press. Pp. 146.

———. 1940a. New evidence on environmental influence on intelligence. *Yearb. Nat. Soc. Stud. Educ.*, 39(I), 307–365.

———. 1940b. Some special problems of nature-nurture research. *Yearb. Nat. Soc. Stud. Educ.*, 39(I), 367–384.

———. 1940c. Intelligence and month of birth. *Psychol. Bull.*, 37, 442 (abstr.).

GOODENOUGH, F. L., and K. M. MAURER. 1940. The mental development of nursery-school children compared with that of non-nursery-school children. *Yearb. Nat. Soc. Stud. Educ.*, 39(II), 161–178.

GORDON, H. 1923. Mental and scholastic tests among retarded children: An enquiry into the effects of schooling on the various tests. *Educ. Pamphlets, Bd. Educ., London*, No. 44.

GORDON, K. 1918–1920. The influence of heredity on mental ability. *Rep. Children's Dept., State Bd. Control, Calif.*

———. 1919. Report on psychological tests of orphan children. *J. Delinq.*, 4, 46–55.

GREENE, K. B. 1928. The influence of specialized training on tests of general intelligence. *Yearb. Nat. Soc. Stud. Educ.*, 27(I), 421–428.

HALDANE, J. B. S. 1938. *Heredity and politics.* New York: Norton.

HARDY, M. C. 1936. Improvement in educational achievement accompanying a health education program. *J. Educ. Res.*, 30, 110–123.

HARDY, M. C., and C. H. HOEFER. 1936. *Healthy growth: A study of the influence of health education on growth and development of school children.* Chicago: University of Chicago Press.

HEINIS, H. 1926. A personal constant. *J. Educ. Psychol.*, 17, 163–186.

HELD, O. C. 1940. The influence of month of birth on the intelligence of college freshmen. *J. Genet. Psychol.*, 57, 211–217.

HILDRETH, G. H. 1925. The resemblance of siblings in intelligence and achievement. *Teach. Coll. Contr. Educ.*, No. 186.

———. 1926. Stanford-Binet retests of 441 school children. *Ped. Sem.*, 33, 356–386.

HILDRETH, G. H. 1928. The effect of school environment upon Stanford-Binet tests of young children. *Yearb. Nat. Soc. Stud. Educ.*, 27(I), 355–359.

HILGARD, J. R. 1933. The effect of early and delayed practice on memory and motor performances studied by the method of co-twin control. *Genet. Psychol. Monogr.*, 14, 493–567.

HINTON, R. T. 1936. The rôle of the basal metabolic rate in the intelligence of ninety grade school students. *J. Educ. Psychol.*, 27, 546–550.

———. 1939. A further study of the basal metabolic rate in the intelligence of children. *J. Educ. Psychol.*, 30, 309–314.

HIRSCH, N. D. M. 1930a. An experimental study upon three hundred school children over a six-year period. *Genet. Psychol. Monogr.*, 7, No. 6, 487–549.

———. 1930b. *Twins; heredity and environment.* Cambridge: Harvard University Press.

HOEFER, C., and M. C. HARDY. 1928. The influence of improvement in physical condition on intelligence and educational achievement. *Yearb. Nat. Soc. Stud. Educ.*, 27(I), 371–387.

HOGBEN, L. 1933. *Nature and nurture.* London: Allen and Unwin.

HOLLINGWORTH, L. S. 1940. Intelligence as an element in personality. *Yearb. Nat. Soc. Stud. Educ.*, 39(I), 271–275.

HOLLINGWORTH, L. S., and P. WITTY. 1940. Intelligence as related to race. *Yearb. Nat. Soc. Stud. Educ.*, 39(I), 257–269.

HOLZINGER, K. J., and F. N. FREEMAN. 1925. The interpretation of Burt's regression equation. *J. Educ. Psychol.*, 16, 577–582.

HONZIK, M. P. 1938. The constancy of mental test performance during the preschool period. *J. Genet. Psychol.*, 52, 285–302.

HONZIK, M. P., and H. E. JONES. 1937. Mental-physical relationships during the preschool period. *J. Exp. Educ.*, 6, 139–146.

HSIAO, H. H. 1931. The status of the first-born with special reference to intelligence. *Genet. Psychol. Monogr.*, 9, 1–118.

HUNTINGTON, E. 1938. *Season of birth; its relation to human abilities.* New York: Wiley.

JONES, D. C., and A. M. CARR-SAUNDERS. 1927. The relation between intelligence and social status among orphan children. *Brit. J. Psychol.*, 17, 343–364.

JONES, H. E. 1928. A first study of parent-child resemblance in intelligence. *Yearb. Nat. Soc. Stud. Educ.*, 27(I), 61–72.

———. 1929. Homogamy in intellectual abilities. *Amer. J. Sociol.*, 35, 369–382.

———. 1931. The pattern of abilities in juvenile and adult defectives. *Univ. Calif. Publ. Psychol.*, 5, 47–61.

———. 1933a. Order of birth, pp. 551–589. In C. MURCHISON (Ed.), *A handbook of child psy* chology. (2d ed., rev.) Worcester: Clark University Press.

JONES, H. E. 1933b. Relationships in physical and mental development. *Rev. Educ. Res.*, 3, 150–162; 177–181.

———. 1936. Relationships in physical and mental development. *Rev. Educ. Res.*, 6, 102–123; 146–152.

———. 1939. Relationships in physical and mental development. *Rev. Educ. Res.*, 9, 91–103; 134–137.

———. 1941. Seasonal variations in IQ. *J. Exp. Educ.*, 10, 91–99.

JONES, H. E., *et al.* 1939. Mental and physical development. *Rev. Educ. Res.*, 9, 1–141.

JONES, H. E., H. S. CONRAD, and M. B. BLANCHARD. 1932. Environmental handicap in mental-test performance. *Univ. Calif. Publ. Psychol.*, 5, No. 3, 63–99.

JONES, H. E., and H. H. HSIAO. 1933. Pregnancy order and early development. *Child Develpm.*, 4, 140–147.

JONES, H. E., and A. P. JORGENSEN. 1940. Mental growth as related to nursery-school attendance. *Yearb. Nat. Soc. Stud. Educ.*, 39 (II), 207–222.

JONES, H. E., and P. T. WILSON. 1932–1933. Reputation differences in like-sex twins. *J. Exp. Educ.*, 1, 86–91.

JORDAN, A. M. 1933. Parental occupations and children's intelligence scores. *J. Appl. Psychol.*, 17, 103–119.

KATZ, E. 1940. The relationship of IQ to height and weight from three to five years. *J. Genet. Psychol.*, 57, 65–82.

KAWIN, E. 1934. *Children of preschool age.* Chicago: University of Chicago Press.

KEENE, C. M., and C. P. STONE. 1937. Mental status as related to puberty praecox. *Psychol. Bull.*, 34, 123–133.

KEMPF, G. A., and S. D. COLLINS. 1929. A study of the relation between mental and physical status of children in two counties of Illinois. *U. S. Publ. Health Rep., Wash.*, 44, No. 29, 1743–1784.

KLINEBERG, O. 1935. *Negro intelligence and selective migration.* New York: Columbia University Press.

———. 1938. The intelligence of migrants. *Amer. Sociol. Rev.*, 3, 218–224.

KOCH, H. L. 1927. Some measurements of a pair of Siamese twins. *J. Comp. Psychol.*, 7, 313–333.

KOHNKY, E. 1913. Preliminary study of the effect of dental treatment upon the physical and mental efficiency of school children. *J. Educ. Psychol.*, 4, 571–578.

KRUGMAN, M. 1939. Some impressions of the Revised Stanford-Binet Scale. *J. Educ. Psychol.*, 30, 594–603.

LAMSON, E. E. 1940. A follow-up study of a group of nursery-school children. *Yearb. Nat. Soc. Stud. Educ.*, 39(II), 231–236.

LAUTERBACH, C. E. 1925. Studies in twin resemblance. *Genetics*, 10, 525–568.

LAWRENCE, E. M. 1931. An investigation into the relation between intelligence and inheritance. *Brit. J. Psychol. Monogr. Suppl.*, 16, 1–80.

LEAHY, A. M. 1935. Nature-nurture and intelligence. *Genet. Psychol. Monogr.*, 17, 236–308.

LEHTOVAARA, A. 1938. *Psychologische Zwillingsuntersuchungen.* Helsinki: Academiae Scientiarum Fennicae.

LEVIT, S. G. 1935. Twin investigations in the U.S.S.R. *Character and Pers.*, 3, 188–193.

LITHAUER, D. B., and O. KLINEBERG. 1933. A study of the variation in IQ of a group of dependent children in institution and foster home. *J. Genet. Psychol.*, 42, 236–242.

LODGE, T. 1938. Variation in Stanford-Binet IQ's of preschool children according to the months in which the examinations were given. *J. Psychol.*, 6, 385–395.

LOEVINGER, J. 1940. Intelligence as related to socioeconomic factors. *Yearb. Nat. Soc. Stud. Educ.*, 39(I), 159–210.

LORGE, I. 1940. Intelligence and personality as revealed in questionnaires and inventories. *Yearb. Nat. Soc. Stud. Educ.*, 39(I), 275–281.

LORIMER, F., and F. OSBORN. 1934. *Dynamics of population.* New York: Macmillan.

LOWE, G. M. 1923. Mental changes after removing tonsils and adenoids. *Psychol. Clin.*, 15, 92–100.

LUND, F. H. 1940. Intelligence and emotionality. *Yearb. Nat. Soc. Stud. Educ.*, 39(I), 282–285.

MACMEEKEN, A. M. 1939. *The intelligence of a representative group of Scottish children.* London: University of London Press.

MALLER, J. B. 1933. Vital indices and their relation to psychological and social factors: A study of 310 health areas in New York City with reference to birth rate, death rate, juvenile delinquency, school progress, and intelligence. *Human Biol.*, 5, 94–121.

MAULDIN, W. P. 1940. Selective migration from small towns. *Amer. Sociol. Rev.*, 5, 748–758.

MAYER, B. A. 1935. Negativistic reactions of preschool children on the new revision of the Stanford-Binet. *J. Genet. Psychol.*, 46, 311–334.

McNEMAR, Q. 1938. Special review: Newman, Freeman and Holzinger's *Twins: A study of heredity and environment. Psychol. Bull.*, 35, 237–249.

———. 1940. A critical examination of the University of Iowa studies of environmental influences upon the IQ. *Psychol. Bull.*, 37, 63–92.

MILLS, C. A. 1941. Mental and physical development as influenced by season of conception. *Human Biol.*, 13, 378–389.

NEFF, W. S. 1938. Socioeconomic status and intelligence: A critical survey. *Psychol. Bull.*, 35, 727–757.

NELSON, V. L., and T. W. RICHARDS. 1938. Studies in mental development: I. Performance on Gesell items at six months and its predictive value for performance on mental tests at two and three years. *J. Genet. Psychol.*, 52, 303–325.

———. 1939. Studies in mental development: III. Performance of twelve-months-old children on the Gesell Schedule, and its predictive value for mental status at two and three years. *J. Genet. Psychol.*, 54, 181–191.

NEMZEK, C. L. 1933. The constancy of the I.Q. *Psychol. Bull.*, 30, 143–168.

NEWMAN, H. H. 1940. *Multiple human births.* (Publ. Amer. Ass. Adv. Sci.) New York: Doubleday-Doran.

NEWMAN, H. H., F. N. FREEMAN, and K. J. HOLZINGER. 1937. *Twins: A study of heredity and environment.* Chicago: University of Chicago Press.

O'HANLON, G. S. A. 1940. An investigation into the relationship between fertility and intelligence. *Brit. J. Educ. Psychol.*, 10, 196–211.

OLSON, W. C., and B. O. HUGHES. 1940. Subsequent growth of children with and without nursery school experience. *Ycarb. Nat. Soc. Stud. Educ.*, 39(II), 237–244.

OUTHIT, M. C. 1933. A study of the resemblance of parents and children in general intelligence. *Arch. Psychol., N. Y.*, No. 149. Pp. 60.

PAGE, J. D. 1941. Twin, sibling, and chance IQ differences. *J. Educ. Psychol.*, 32, 73–76.

PATERSON, D. G. 1930. *Physique and intellect.* New York: Century.

PEARSON, K. 1903. On the inheritance of the mental and moral characters in man, and its comparison with the inheritance of physical characters. *J. Anthrop. Inst.*, 33, 179–237.

———. 1910. *Nature and nurture.* (Eugen. Lab. Lect. Series, 1910, 6.) London: Dulau.

———. 1918–1919. The inheritance of psychical characters. *Biometrika*, 12, 367–372.

PETERSON, J. 1923. Methods of investigating comparative abilities in races. *Ann. Amer. Acad. Sci.*, 140, 178–185.

PIETER, J. 1939. Intelligence quotient and environment. *Kwart. Psychol.*, 11, 265–322.

PINTNER, R. 1931. *Intelligence testing: Methods and results.* (2d ed.) New York: Holt.

PINTNER, R., and G. FORLANO. 1933. The influence of month of birth on intelligence quotients. *J. Educ. Psychol.*, 24, 561–584.

———. 1939. Season of birth and intelligence. *J. Genet. Psychol.*, 54, 353–358.

PINTNER, R., and J. B. MALLER. 1937. Month of birth and average intelligence among different ethnic groups. *J. Genet. Psychol.*, 50, 91–107.

POULL, L. E. 1938. The effect of improvement in nutrition on the mental capacity of young children. *Child Develpm.*, 9, 123–126.

REYMERT, M. L. 1940. Relationships between menarcheal age, behavior disorders, and intelligence. *Character and Pers.*, 8, 292–300.

RICHARDS, T. W., and V. L. NELSON. 1939. Abilities of infants during the first eighteen months. *J. Genet. Psychol.*, 55, 299–318.

RICHARDSON, H. M. 1939. Studies of mental resemblance between husbands and wives and between friends. *Psychol. Bull.*, 36, 104–120.

RICHARDSON, S. K. 1936. The correlation of intelligence quotients of siblings of the same chronological age levels. *J. Juv. Res.*, 20, 186–198.

RICHEY, A. 1934. The effects of diseased tonsils and adenoids on intelligence quotients of 204 children. *J. Juv. Res.*, 18, 1–4.

ROBERTS, J. A. F., R. M. NORMAN, and R. GRIFFITHS. 1938. Studies on a child population: IV. The form of the lower end of the frequency distribution and the fall of low intelligence quotients with advancing age. *Ann. Eugen., Cambridge*, 8, 319–336.

ROGERS, M. C. 1922. Adenoids and diseased tonsils; their effect on general intelligence. *Arch. Psychol., N. Y.*, No. 50.

ROSANOFF, A. J., L. M. HARDY, and I. R. PLESSET. 1937. The etiology of mental deficiency with special reference to its occurrence in twins. *Psychol. Monogr.*, 48, No. 4. Pp. 137.

SANDERS, B. S. 1934. *Environment and growth.* Baltimore: Warwick & York.

SANDERS, M. 1932. Similarities in triplets. *J. Hered.*, 23, 225–234.

SANDWICK, R. L. 1920. Correlation of physical health and mental efficiency. *J. Educ. Res.*, 1, 199–203.

SANFORD, G. A. 1940. Selective migration in a rural Alabama community. *Amer. Sociol. Rev.*, 5, 759–766.

SCHLESINGER, E. 1923. Die Kinder des kinderreichen Familien. *Arch. f. Kinderheilk*, 73, 50–68.

SCHWESINGER, G. C. 1933. *Heredity and environment.* New York; Macmillan.

SEVERSON, S. O. 1920–1921. The relation of the anatomical age to the chronological, pedagogical, and mental ages with special reference to sex differences. *J. Psycho-Asthenics*, 25, 150–170.

SEYMOUR, A. H., and J. E. F. WHITAKER. 1938. An experiment on nutrition. *Occup. Psychol.*, 12, 215–223.

SHERMAN, M., and T. R. HENRY. 1933. *Hollow folk.* New York: Crowell.

SHERMAN, M., and C. B. KEY. 1932. The intelligence of isolated mountain children. *Child Develpm.*, 3, 279–290.

SHIMBERG, M. E. 1929. An investigation into the validity of norms with special reference to urban and rural groups. *Arch. Psychol., N. Y.,* No. 104. Pp. 84.

SHOCK, N. W. 1939a. Physiological factors in mental development. *Rev. Educ. Res.,* 9, 103–110; 137–139.

——. 1939b. Some psychophysiological relations. *Psychol. Bull.,* 36, 447–476.

SHOCK, N. W., and H. E. JONES. 1940. The relationship between basal physiological functions and intelligence in adolescents. *J. Educ. Psychol.,* 31, 369–375.

——. 1941. Mental development and performance as related to physical and physiological factors. *Rev. Educ. Res.,* 11, 531–552.

SHUTTLEWORTH, F. K. 1935. The nature *versus* nurture problem: II. The contributions of nature and nurture to individual differences in intelligence. *J. Educ. Psychol.,* 26, 655–681.

SKEELS, H. M. 1936. Mental development of children in foster homes. *J. Genet. Psychol.,* 49, 91–106.

——. 1940. Some Iowa studies of the mental growth of children in relation to differentials of the environment: A summary. *Yearb. Nat. Soc. Stud. Educ.,* 39(II), 281–308.

——. 1941. Children with inferior social histories: Their mental development in foster homes. *Psychol. Bull.,* 38, 594 (abstr.).

SKEELS, H. M., and E. A. FILLMORE. 1937. Mental development of children from underprivileged homes. *J. Genet. Psychol.,* 50, 427–439.

SKODAK, M. 1939. Children in foster homes: A study of mental development. *Univ. Iowa Stud. Child Welfare,* 16, No. 1.

SMITH, A. J., and A. M. FIELD. 1926. A study of the effect of nutrition on mental growth. *J. Home Econ.,* 18, 686–690.

SNYGG, D. 1938. The relation between the intelligence of mothers and of their children living in foster homes. *J. Genet. Psychol.,* 52, 401–406.

SPEER, G. S. 1940a. The mental development of children of feeble-minded and normal mothers. *Yearb. Nat. Soc. Stud. Educ.,* 39(II), 309–314.

——. 1940b. The intelligence of foster children. *J. Genet. Psychol.,* 57, 49–56.

STARKWEATHER, E. K., and K. E. ROBERTS. 1940. IQ changes occurring during nursery-school attendance at the Merrill-Palmer school. *Yearb. Nat. Soc. Stud. Educ.,* 39(II), 315–335.

STIPPICH, M. E. 1940. The mental development of children of feeble-minded mothers: A preliminary report. *Yearb. Nat. Soc. Stud. Educ.,* 39(II), 337–350.

STOCKS, P. 1930–1931. A biometric investigation of twins and their brothers and sisters. *Ann. Eugen., Cambridge,* 4, 49–108.

STOCKS, P., and M. N. KARN. 1933. A biometric investigation of twins and their brothers and sisters. *Ann. Eugen., Cambridge,* 5, 1–55.

STODDARD, G. D., *et al.* 1933, 1936. Mental and physical development. *Rev. Educ. Res.,* 3, 81–181; 6, 1–152.

——. 1940. Intelligence: Its nature and nurture. Part I. Comparative and critical exposition. Part II. Original studies and experiments. *Yearb. Nat. Soc. Stud. Educ.,* 39(I), 39(II).

STODDARD, G. D., and B. L. WELLMAN. 1940. Environment and the IQ. *Yearb. Nat. Soc. Stud. Educ.,* 39(I), 405–442.

STOUT, H. G. 1937. Variations of normal children. *J. Exp. Educ.,* 6, 84–100.

STRAYER, L. C. 1930. Language and growth: The relative efficacy of early and deferred vocabulary training, studied by the method of co-twin control. *Genet. Psychol. Monogr.,* 8, 209–319.

STROUD, J. B. 1928. A study of the relation of intelligence-test score of public-school children to the economic status of their parents. *J. Genet. Psychol.,* 35, 105–110.

TERMAN, L. M., *et al.* 1925. *Genetic studies of genius:* Vol. 1. *The mental and physical traits of a thousand gifted children.* Stanford University, Calif.: Stanford University Press.

——. 1928. Nature and nurture: Part I. Their influence upon intelligence: Part II. Their influence upon achievement. *Yearb. Nat. Soc. Stud. Educ.,* 27(I), 27(II).

TERMAN, L. M., and M. A. MERRILL. 1937. *Measuring intelligence.* Boston: Houghton Mifflin.

THOMSON, G. H. 1921. The Northumberland mental tests. *Brit. J. Psychol.,* 12, 201–222.

THORNDIKE, E. L. 1905. *Measurement of twins.* New York: Science Press. (Also in *J. Phil., Psychol. and Sci. Meth.,* 2, 547–553.

THORNDIKE, E. L., *et al.* 1927. *The measurement of intelligence.* New York: Teachers College Press, Columbia University.

THORNDIKE, R. L. 1933. The effect of the interval between test and retest on the constancy of the IQ. *J. Educ. Psychol.,* 24, 543–549.

——. 1940. "Constancy" of the IQ. *Psychol. Bull.,* 37, 167–186.

TODD, T. W. 1938. Objective ratings of the constitution of the growing child: Based on examination of physical development and mental expansion. *Amer. J. Dis. Child.,* 55, 149–159.

VAN ALSTYNE, D. 1929. The environment of three-year-old children. Factors related to intelligence and vocabulary tests. *Teach. Coll. Contr. Educ.,* No. 366.

VOAS, W. H. 1940. Does attendance at the Winnetka nursery school tend to raise the IQ? *Yearb. Nat. Soc. Stud. Educ.,* 39(II), 363–376.

WALLIS, W. D. 1936. Observations on Leahy's *Nature-Nurture and Intelligence*. *J. Genet. Psychol.*, 49, 315–324.

WELLMAN, B. L. 1934. Growth in intelligence under differing school environments. *J. Exp. Educ.*, 3, 59–83.

WELLMAN, B. L., H. M. SKEELS, and M. SKODAK. 1940. Review of McNemar's critical examination of Iowa studies. *Psychol. Bull.*, 37, 93–111.

WELLS, J., and G. ARTHUR. 1939. Effect of foster-home placement on the intelligence ratings of children of feeble-minded parents. *Ment. Hyg., N. Y.*, 23, 277–285.

WEST, E. D. 1936. Stage of ossification as a measure of growth and its relation to intelligence-test score. *Harv. Teach. Rec.*, 6, 162–168.

WESTENBERGER, E. J. 1927. A study of the influence of physical defects upon intelligence. *Cath. Univ. Amer. Educ. Res. Bull.*, 2, No. 9.

WHEELER, L. R. 1932. The intelligence of east Tennessee mountain children. *J. Educ. Psychol.*, 23, 351–370.

WHIPPLE, G. M. 1928. Nature and nurture: Their influence upon intelligence and upon achievement. (Selected papers read at the Boston meeting of the Nat. Soc. Stud. Educ.) *J. Educ. Psychol.*, 19, 361–409.

WILLOUGHBY, R. R. 1927. Family similarities in mental-test abilities. *Genet. Psychol. Monogr.*, 2, 235–277.

WILLOUGHBY, R. R. 1928. Family similarities in mental-test abilities. *Yearb. Nat. Soc. Stud. Educ.*, 27(I), 55–59.

WILSON, P. T. 1934. A study of twins with special reference to heredity as a factor determining differences in environment. *Human Biol.*, 6, 324–354.

WILSON, P. T., and H. E. JONES. 1931. A study of like-sexed twins. I. The vital statistics and familial data of the sample. *Human Biol.*, 3, 107–132.

WINGFIELD, A. H. 1928. *Twins and orphans: The inheritance of intelligence.* London and Toronto: Dent.

WOODWORTH, R. S. 1941. *Heredity and environment: A critical survey of recently published material on twins and foster children.* New York: Social Science Research Council.

WOOLLEY, H. T. 1925. The validity of standards of mental measurement in young childhood. *Sch. and Soc.*, 21, 476–482.

WRIGHT, S. 1921. Correlation and causation. *J. Agric. Res.*, 20, 557–585.

———. 1931. Statistical methods in biology. *J. Amer. Statist. Ass.*, 26, 155–163.

ZUCK, T. T. 1936. The relation of physical development to mental expansion. *Proc. 3d Inst. Except. Child, Child Res. Clin. Woods Schs*, 6–15.

Classics In
Child Development

An Arno Press Collection

Baldwin, James Mark. **Thought and Things.** Four vols. in two.
1906-1915

Blatz, W[illiam] E[met], et al. **Collected Studies on the Dionne
Quintuplets.** 1937

Bühler, Charlotte. **The First Year of Life.** 1930

Bühler, Karl. **The Mental Development of the Child.** 1930

Claparède, Ed[ouard]. **Experimental Pedagogy and the
Psychology of the Child.** 1911

Factors Determining Intellectual Attainment. 1975

First Notes by Observant Parents. 1975

Freud, Anna. **Introduction to the Technic of Child Analysis.**
1928

Gesell, Arnold, et al. **Biographies of Child Development.** 1939

Goodenough, Florence L. **Measurement of Intelligence By
Drawings.** 1926

Griffiths, Ruth. **A Study of Imagination in Early Childhood
and Its Function in Mental Development.** 1918

Hall, G. Stanley and Some of His Pupils. **Aspects of Child Life
and Education.** 1907

Hartshorne, Hugh and Mark May. **Studies in the Nature of
Character. Vol. I: Studies in Deceit; Book One, General
Methods and Results.** 1928

Hogan, Louise E. **A Study of a Child.** 1898

Hollingworth, Leta S. **Children Above 180 IQ, Stanford Binet:** Origins and Development. 1942

Kluver, Heinrich. **An Experimental Study of the Eidetic Type.** 1926

Lamson, Mary Swift. **Life and Education of Laura Dewey Bridgman, the Deaf, Dumb and Blind Girl.** 1881

Lewis, M[orris] M[ichael]. **Infant Speech:** A Study of the Beginnings of Language. 1936

McGraw, Myrtle B. **Growth: A Study of Johnny and Jimmy.** 1935

Monographs on Infancy. 1975

O'Shea, M. V., editor. **The Child: His Nature and His Needs.** 1925

Perez, Bernard. **The First Three Years of Childhood.** 1888

Romanes, George John. **Mental Evolution in Man:** Origin of Human Faculty. 1889

Shinn, Milicent Washburn. **The Biography of a Baby.** 1900

Stern, William. **Psychology of Early Childhood Up to the Sixth Year of Age.** 1924

Studies of Play. 1975

Terman, Lewis M. **Genius and Stupidity:** A Study of Some of the Intellectual Processes of Seven "Bright" and Seven "Stupid" Boys. 1906

Terman, Lewis M. **The Measurement of Intelligence.** 1916

Thorndike, Edward Lee. **Notes on Child Study.** 1901

Wilson, Louis N., compiler. **Bibliography of Child Study.** 1898-1912

[Witte, Karl Heinrich Gottfried]. **The Education of Karl Witte,** Or the Training of the Child. 1914